The Definitive Guide to HTML5 Video

■ ■ ■

Silvia Pfeiffer

Apress®

The Definitive Guide to HTML5 Video

ISBN-13 (pbk): 978-1-4302-3090-8

ISBN-13 (electronic): 978-1-4302-3091-2

Printed and bound in the United States of America 9 8 7 6 5 4 3 2 1

President and Publisher: Paul Manning
Lead Editor: Frank Pohlmann
Technical Reviewer: Chris Pearce
Editorial Board: Steve Anglin, Mark Beckner, Ewan Buckingham, Gary Cornell, Jonathan Gennick, Jonathan Hassell, Michelle Lowman, Matthew Moodie, Duncan Parkes, Jeffrey Pepper, Frank Pohlmann, Douglas Pundick, Ben Renow-Clarke, Dominic Shakeshaft, Matt Wade, Tom Welsh
Coordinating Editor: Adam Heath
Copy Editor: Mark Watanabe
Compositor: MacPS, LLC
Indexer: Becky Hornyak
Artist: April Milne
Cover Designer: Anna Ishchenko

Distributed to the book trade worldwide by Springer Science+Business Media, LLC., 233 Spring Street, 6th Floor, New York, NY 10013. Phone 1-800-SPRINGER, fax (201) 348-4505, e-mail orders-ny@springer-sbm.com, or visit www.springeronline.com.

For information on translations, please e-mail rights@apress.com, or visit www.apress.com.

Apress and friends of ED books may be purchased in bulk for academic, corporate, or promotional use. eBook versions and licenses are also available for most titles. For more information, reference our Special Bulk Sales–eBook Licensing web page at www.apress.com/info/bulksales.

The source code for this book is available to readers at www.apress.com.

To Benjamin, who asked me yesterday if he was
allowed to read his mum's book
so he could do all those cool video demos.

And to John, who has made it all possible.

– Silvia

Contents at a Glance

Contents

About the Author

 **Silvia Pfeiffer**, PhD (nat sci), was born and bred in Germany, where she received a combined degree in Computer Science and Business Management, and later gained a PhD in Computer Science. Her research focused on audio-visual content analysis aiming to manage the expected onslaught of digital audio and video content on the Internet. This was in the last century during the first days of the Web, long before the idea of YouTube was even born.

After finishing her PhD in 1999, Silvia was invited to join the CSIRO, the Commonwealth Scientific and Industrial Research Organisation, in Australia. It was here, after a brief involvement with the standardization of MPEG-7, that Silvia had the idea of using audio-visual annotations for increasing the usability of media content on the Web.

Together with her colleagues they developed the idea of a "Continuous Media Web", a Web where all the information would be composed of audio and video content and you would browse through it just as you do with text pages by following hyperlinks. Added onto this would be full, timed transcripts of audio-visual resources, enabling search engines to index them and users to find information deep inside media files through existing and well known web search approaches.

Silvia and her colleagues connected with the Xiph organization and realized their ideas through extensions to Ogg, plug-ins for Firefox, and Apache server plug-ins. By implementing file support into a CSIRO research web search engine, they set up the first video search engine in 2001 that was able to retrieve video on the clip level through temporal URIs—something Google's video search added only many years later.

Silvia remained with the CSIRO until 2006, when, inspired by Web 2.0 developments and YouTube's success, she left to start a video search and metrics company, Vquence, with Chris Gilbey and John Ferlito.

Currently, Silvia is a freelancer in web media applications, media standards and media accessibility. She is the main organizer of the annually held Foundations of Open Media Software workshop (FOMS). She is an invited expert at the W3C for the HTML, Media Fragments, Media Annotations, and Timed Text Working Groups. She is contributing to HTML5 media technology through the WHATWG and W3C and does short-term contracting with Mozilla and Google for progressing standards in media accessibility. Silvia's blog is at http://blog.gingertech.net.

About the Technical Reviewer

■ **Chris Pearce** is a software engineer working at Mozilla on the HTML5 audio and video playback support for the open-source Firefox web browser. He is also the creator of the keyframe index used by the Ogg media container and contributes to the Ogg/Xiph community. Chris has also worked on Mozilla's text editor widget, and previously worked developing mobile software developer tools. Chris works out of Mozilla's Auckland office in New Zealand, and blogs about matters related to Internet video and Firefox development at http://pearce.org.nz.

Acknowledgments

First and foremost I'd like to thank the great people involved in developing HTML5 and the related standards and technologies both at WHATWG and W3C for making a long-time dream of mine come true by making audio and video content prime citizens on the Web. I believe that the next 10 years will see a new boom created through these technologies that will be bigger than the recent "Web2.0" boom and have a large audio-visual component that again will fundamentally change the way in which people and businesses communicate online.

I'd like to thank particularly the software developers in the diverse browsers that implemented the media elements and their functionality and who have given me feedback on media-related questions whenever I needed it. I'd like to single out Chris Pearce of Mozilla, who has done a huge job in technical proofreading of the complete book and Philip Jägenstedt from Opera for his valuable feedback on Opera-related matters.

I'd like to personally thank the Xiph and the FOMS participants with whom it continues to be an amazing journey to develop open media technology and push the boundaries of the Web for audio and video.

I'd like to thank Ian Hickson for his tireless work on HTML5 specifications and in-depth discussion on video related matters.

I'd like to thank all those bloggers who have published their extraordinary experiments with the audio and video elements and have inspired many of my examples. I'd like to single out in particular Paul Rouget of Mozilla, whose diverse demos in HTML5 technology really push the boundaries.

I'd like to thank Chris Heilmann for allowing me to reuse his accessible player design for the custom controls demo in the JavaScript chapter.

I'd like to thank the developers of the Audio API both at Mozilla and Google for all the help they provided me to understand the two existing proposals for an Audio API for the media elements.

I'd like to thank the developers at Ericsson Labs for their experiments with the device element and for allowing me to use screenshots of their demos in the device chapter.

I'd like to thank the experts in the media subgroup of the HTML5 Accessibility Task Force for their productive discussions, which have contributed to the media accessibility chapter in this book. I'd like to single out John Foliot and Janina Sajka, whose proofreading of that chapter helped me accurately represent accessibility user needs.

I'd like to thank the colleagues in the W3C Media Fragment URI working group with whom it was a pleasure to develop the specs that will eventually allow direct access to sections of audio and video as described in the accessibility chapter.

I'd like to thank David Bolter and Chris Blizzard of Mozilla, who have on more than one occasion enabled me to be part of meetings and conferences and continue the standards work.

I'd like to thank the team at Apress for keeping the pressure on such that this book was able to be finished within this year.

And finally I'd like to thank all my family for their support, but particularly Mum and Dad for their patience when I had to write a chapter during our holiday in Fiji, Ben for tolerating a somewhat distracted mum, and John for continuing to cheer me on.

Preface

It is ironic that I started writing this book on the exact day that the last of the big browsers announced that it was going to support HTML5 and, with it, HTML5 video. On March 16, 2010, Microsoft joined Firefox, Opera, Google Chrome, and WebKit/Safari with an announcement that Internet Explorer 9 will support HTML5 and the HTML5 video element. Only weeks before the book was finished, the IE9 beta was also released, so I was able to actually include IE9 behavior into the book, making it so much more valuable to you.

During the course of writing this book, many more announcements were made and many new features introduced in all the browsers. The book's examples were all tested with the latest browser versions available at the time of finishing this book. These are Firefox 4.0b8pre, Safari 5.0.2, Opera 11.00 alpha build 1029, Google Chrome 9.0.572.0, all on Mac OS X, and Internet Explorer 9 beta (9.0.7930.16406) on Windows 7.

Understandably, browsers are continuing to evolve and what doesn't work today may work tomorrow. As you start using HTML5 video—and, in particular, as you start developing your own web sites with it—I recommend you check out the actual current status of implementation of all relevant browsers for support of your desired feature.

The Challenge of a Definitive Guide

You may be wondering about what makes this book a "definitive guide to HTML5 video" rather than just an introduction or an overview. I am fully aware that this is a precocious title and may sound arrogant, given that the HTML5 media elements are new and a lot about them is still being specified, not to speak of the lack of implementations of several features in browsers.

When Apress and I talked about a book proposal on HTML5 media, I received a form to fill in with some details—a table of contents, a summary, a comparison to existing books in the space etc. That form already had the title "Definitive Guide to HTML5 Video" on it. I thought hard about changing this title. I considered alternatives such as "Introduction to HTML5 Media," "Everything about HTML5 Video," "HTML5 Media Elements," "Ultimate Guide to HTML5 Video," but I really couldn't come up with something that didn't sound more lame or more precocious.

So I decided to just go with the flow and use the title as an expectation to live up to: I had to write the most complete guide to HTML5 audio and video available at the time of publishing. I have indeed covered all aspects of the HTML5 media elements that I am aware exist or are being worked on. It is almost certain that this book will not be a "definitive guide" for very long beyond its publication date. Therefore, I have made sure to mention changes I know are happening and where you should check actual browser behavior before relying on certain features.

Even my best efforts cannot predict the future. So there is only the option of a second edition, which Apress and I will most certainly discuss when the time is ripe and if the book is successful enough. Leave comments, errata, bug reports, suggestions for improvements, and ideas for topics to add at http://apress.com/book/errata/1470 and they won't be forgotten.

In the meantime, I hope you enjoy reading this book and take away a lot of practical recipes for how to achieve your web design goals with HTML5 media.

Approaching This book

This book is written for anyone interested in using HTML5 media elements. It assumes an existing background in writing basic HTML, CSS, and JavaScript, but little or no experience with media.

If you are a beginner and just want to learn the basics of how to include video in your web pages, the **first three chapters** will be sufficient. You will learn how to create cross-browser markup in HTML to include audio and video into your web pages and how to encode your video so you can serve all playback devices. We will cover some of the open-source tools available to deal with the new HTML5 media elements. You will also learn how to style the display of your audio and video elements in CSS to make them stand out on your site.

The **next four chapters** are about integrating the media elements with other web technologies. You will learn how to replace the default controls of web browsers with your own. This is called "skinning" your media player. You will learn how to use the JavaScript API for media elements. You will also learn how to integrate media elements with other HTML5 constructs, such as SVG, Canvas, and Web Worker Threads.

In the **final four chapters**, we turn our eyes on more advanced HTML5 media functionality. Most of this functionality is experimental and not yet available uniformly across browsers. You will receive an introduction about the current status and backgrounds for proposed progress. You will learn how to read and manipulate audio data, how to make audio and video accessible in an internationalized way, including captions, subtitles, and audio descriptions. You will learn how to access real-time videos from devices and transfer them across the network. Finally, we will close with a summary and an outlook as to what else may lie ahead.

Notation

In the book, we often speak of HTML elements and HTML element attributes. An element name is written as <element>, an attribute name as @attribute, and an attribute value as "*value*". Where an attribute is mentioned for the first time, it will be marked as bold. Where we need to identify the type of value that an element can accept, we use [url].

Downloading the Code

The source code to the examples used in this book is available to readers at `www.apress.com` and at `www.html5videoguide.net`. At the latter I will also provide updates to the code examples and examples for new developments, so you can remain on top of the development curve.

Contacting the author

Do not hesitate to contact me at `silvia@html5videoguide.net` with any feedback you have.

I can also be reached on:

Twitter: `@silviapfeiffer`

My Blog: `http://blog.gingertech.net`

CHAPTER 1

■ ■ ■

Introduction

This chapter gives you a background on the creation of the HTML5 media elements. The history of their introduction explains some of the design decisions that were taken, in particular why there is not a single baseline codec. If you are only interested in learning the technical details of the media elements, you can skip this chapter.

The introduction of the media elements into HTML5 is an interesting story. Never before have the needs around audio and video in web pages been analyzed in so much depth and been discussed among this many stakeholders. Never before has it led to a uniform implementation in all major web browsers.

1.1 A Bit of History

While it seems to have taken an eternity for all the individuals involved in HTML and multimedia to achieve the current state of the specifications and the implementations in the web browsers, to the person on the street, it has been a rather surprising and fast innovation.

From the first mention of the possibility of a <video> element in HTML5 in about 2005, to the first trial implementation in February 2007, to the first browser rolling it out in a nightly build in November 2007, and to Microsoft's Internet Explorer joining the party late in a developer preview in March 2010, it has still been barely five years.

In contrast, other efforts to introduce media functionality natively into HTML without the use of plug-ins in the <embed> or <object> elements have been less successful. HTML+Time was proposed in 1998 by Microsoft and implemented into IE 5, IE 5.5 and IE6, but was never supported by any other browser vendor. SMIL (pronounced "smile"), the Synchronized Multimedia Integration Language, has been developed since 1997 to enable authoring of interactive audiovisual presentations, but was never natively supported in any browser other than the part that matched the HTML+Time specification.

This rapid development was possible only because of the dozens of years of experience with media plug-ins and other media frameworks on the Web, including QuickTime, Microsoft Windows Media, RealNetworks RealMedia, Xiph Ogg, ISO/MPEG specifications, and, more recently, Adobe Media and Microsoft Silverlight. The successes of YouTube and similar hosting sites have vastly shaped the user requirements. Many more technologies, standards, and content sites also had an influence, but it would take too long to list them all here.

All this combined experience led eventually to the first proposal to introduce a <video> element into HTML5. This is the first time that all involved stakeholders, in particular all browser vendors, actually committed to a native implementation of media support in their browsers.

Before the introduction of the <video> and <audio> elements, a web developer could include video and audio in web pages only through <object> and <embed> elements, which required browser plug-ins be installed on user machines. Initially, these plug-ins simply launched a media player that was installed on the user's system to play back video. Later, they were able to display inside web pages, although often users were taken into a pop-up. This was the case for all of the popular plug-ins, such as RealMedia, QuickTime, and Windows Media. With the release of Flash Player 6 in 2002, Macromedia introduced video support into its browser plug-in. It relied on the Sorenson Spark codec, which was also used by

QuickTime at that time. Most publishers already published their content in RealMedia, QuickTime and Windows Media format to cover as much of the market as possible, so uptake of Flash for video was fairly small at first.

However, Macromedia improved its tools and formats over the next few years with ActionScript. With Flash Player 8 in 2005, it introduced On2's VP6 advanced video codec, alpha transparency in video, a standalone encoder and advanced video importer, cue point support in FLV files, an advanced video playback component, and an interactive mobile device emulator. All of this made it a very compelling development environment for online media.

In the meantime, through its animation and interactive capabilities, Flash had become the major plug-in for providing rich Internet applications which led to a situation where many users had it installed on their system. It started becoming the solution to publishing video online without having to encode it in three different formats. It was therefore not surprising when Google Videos launched on January 25, 2005 using Macromedia Flash. YouTube launched only a few months later, in May 2005, also using Macromedia Flash.

On December 3, 2005, Macromedia was bought by Adobe and Flash was henceforth known as Adobe Flash. As Adobe continued to introduce and improve Flash and the authoring tools around it, video publishing sites around the world started following the Google and YouTube move and also published their videos in the Adobe Flash format. With the introduction of Flash Player 9, Update 3, Adobe launched support in August 2007 for the MPEG family of codecs into Flash, in particular the advanced H.264 codec, which began a gradual move away from the FLV format to the MP4 format.

In the meantime, discussion of introducing a <video> element into HTML, which had started in 2005, continued. By 2007, people had to use gigantic <embed> statements to make Adobe Flash work well in HTML. There was a need to simplify the use of video and fully integrated it into the web browser.

The first demonstration of <video> implemented in a browser was done by Opera. On February 28, 2007, Opera announced[1] to the WHATWG (Web Hypertext Applications Technology Working Group[2]) an experimental build of a <video> element, which Opera Chief Technology Officer Håkon Wium Lie described as a first step towards making "video a first-class citizen of the web."[3] The specification was inspired by the <img> element and was built similarly to an interface created earlier for an Audio() JavaScript API.

Initially, there was much discussion about the need for a separate <video> element—why wouldn't the <embed> element be sufficient, why not use SMIL, why not reanimate HTML+Time? Eventually it dawned on people that, unless media was as simple to use as <img> and as integrated into all layers of web applications, including the DOM, CSS, and JavaScript, <video> and <audio> would be hampered from making further progress on the web beyond what was possible with plug-ins. This, of course, includes the need for all browsers to support the specifications in an interoperable way. Thus, the need for standardization of the <video> element was born.

1.2 A Common Format?

An early and ongoing debate around the HTML5 media elements is that of a baseline encoding format, also called a "baseline codec". A baseline codec is a video and audio encoding format that is supported and implemented by all browser vendors and thus a web developer can rely on it to work in all browsers.

The question of a baseline codec actually goes beyond just the question of codecs. Codec data is only the compressed audio or video data by itself. It never stands on its own, but is delivered in a "container format", which encapsulates the encoded audio and video samples in a structure to allow

---

[1] See http://lists.whatwg.org/pipermail/whatwg-whatwg.org/2007-February/009702.html

[2] See http://www.whatwg.org/

[3] See http://people.opera.com/howcome/2007/video/

later decoding. You can think of it as analogous to packaging data packets for delivery over a computer network, where the protocol headers provide the encapsulation.

Many different encapsulation formats exist, including QuickTime's MOV, MPEG's MP4, Microsoft's WMV, Adobe's FLV, the Matroska MKV container (having been the basis for the WebM format), AVI and Xiph's Ogg container. These are just a small number of examples. Each of these containers can in theory support encapsulation of any codec data sequence (except for some container formats not mentioned here that cannot deal with variable bitrate codecs).

Also, many different audio and video codecs exist. Examples of audio codecs are: MPEG-1 Audio Level 3 (better known as MP3), MPEG-2 and MPEG-4 AAC (Advanced Audio Coding), uncompressed WAV, Vorbis, FLAC and Speex. Examples of video codecs are: MPEG-4 AVC/H.264, VC-1, MPEG-2, H.263, VP8, Dirac and Theora.

Even though in theory every codec can be encapsulated into every container, only certain codecs are typically found in certain containers. WebM, for example, has been defined to only contain VP8 and Vorbis. Ogg typically contains Theora, Vorbis, Speex, or FLAC, and there are defined mappings for VP8 and Dirac, though not many such files exist. MP4 typically contains MP3, AAC, and H.264.

For a specification like HTML5, it is important to have interoperability, so the definition of a baseline codec is important. The debate about a baseline codec actually started on the day that Opera released its experimental build and hasn't stopped since.

A few weeks after the initial proposal of the <video> element, Opera CTO Wium Lie stated in a talk given at Google:

"I believe very strongly, that we need to agree on some kind of baseline video format if [the video element] is going to succeed. [...] We want a freely implementable open standard to hold the content we put out. That's why we developed the PNG image format. [...] PNG [...] came late to the party. Therefore I think it's important that from the beginning we think about this."[4]

Wium Lie further stated requirements for the video element as follows:

"It's important that the video format we choose can be supported by a wide range of devices and that it's royalty-free (RF). RF is a well-establish[ed] principle for W3C standards. The Ogg Theora format is a promising candidate which has been chosen by Wikipedia."[5]

The World Wide Web Consortium (W3C) is the standards body that publishes HTML. It seeks to issue only recommendations that can be implemented on a royalty-free (RF) basis.[6]

The "Ogg Theora" format proposed as a candidate by Wium Lie is actually the video codec Theora and the audio codec Vorbis in an Ogg container developed by the Xiph.org Foundation as open source.[7] Theora is a derivative of a video codec developed earlier by On2 Technologies under the name VP3[8] and released as open source in September 2001.[9] With the release of the code, On2 also essentially provided a royalty-free license to their patents that relate to the VP3 source code and its derivatives. After VP3 was published and turned into Theora, Ogg Theora/Vorbis became the first unencumbered video codec format. Google, which acquired On2 in 2010, confirmed Theora's royalty-free nature.[10]

---

[4] See video of Håkon Wium Lie's Google talk,
http://video.google.com/videoplay?docid=5545573096553082541&ei=LV6hSazOJpbA2AKh4OyPDg&hl=un

[5] See Håkon Wium Lie's page on the need for a video element, http://people.opera.com/howcome/2007/video/

[6] See W3C RF requirements at http://www.w3.org/Consortium/Patent-Policy-20030520.html#sec-Licensing

[7] See Xiph.Org's Website on Theora, http://theora.org/

[8] See On2 Technologies' press release dated June 24, 2002,
http://web.archive.org/web/20071203061350/http://www.on2.com/index.php?id=486&news_id=313

[9] See On2 Technologies' press release dated September 7, 2001,
http://web.archive.org/web/20071207021659/, http://www.on2.com/index.php?id=486&news_id=364

[10] See Google blog post dated April 9, 2010,
http://google-opensource.blogspot.com/2010/04/interesting-times-for-video-on-web.html

Note that although the video codec format should correctly be called "Ogg Theora/Vorbis", in common terminology you will only read "Ogg Theora".

On the audio side of things, Ogg Vorbis is a promising candidate for a baseline format. Vorbis is an open-source audio codec developed and published by Xiph.Org since about 2000. Vorbis is also well regarded as having superior encoding quality compared with MP3 and on par with AAC. Vorbis was developed with a clear intention of only using techniques that were long out of patent protection. Vorbis has been in use by commercial applications for a decade now, including Microsoft software and many games.

An alternative choice for a royalty-free modern video codec that Wium Lie could have suggested is the BBC-developed Dirac codec.[11] It is based on a more modern compression technology, namely wavelets. While Dirac's compression quality is good, it doesn't, however, quite yet expose the same compression efficiency as Theora for typical web video requirements.[12]

For all these reasons, Ogg Theora and Ogg Vorbis were initially written into the HTML5 specification as baseline codecs for video and audio, respectively, at the beginning of 2007:[13]

"User agents should support Ogg Theora video and Ogg Vorbis audio, as well as the Ogg container format."

However, by December 2007, it was clear to the editor of the HTML5 draft, Ian Hickson, that not all browser vendors were going to implement Ogg Theora and Ogg Vorbis support. Apple in particular had released the first browser with HTML5 video support with Safari 3.1 and had chosen to support only H.264, criticizing Theora for inferior quality, for lack of support on mobile devices, and a perceived increased infringement threat of as-yet unknown patents (also called the "submarine patent" threat).[14]

Nokia[15] and Microsoft[16] confirmed their positions for a similar choice. H.264 has been approved as a standard jointly by the International Telecommunications Union (ITU) and the International Standards Organization (ISO/IEC), but its use requires payment of royalties, making it unacceptable as a royalty-free baseline codec for HTML5. The announcement of MPEG LA on August 26, 2010 that H.264 encoded Internet video that is free to end users will never be charged for royalties[17] is not sufficient, since all other royalties, in particular royalties for commercial use and for hardware products, remain in place.

In December 2007, Ian Hickson replaced the should-requirement for Ogg Theora with the following:[18,19]

"It would be helpful for interoperability if all browsers could support the same codecs. However, there are no known codecs that satisfy all the current players: we need a codec that is known to not require per-unit or per-distributor licensing, that is compatible with the open source development model, that is of sufficient quality as to be usable, and that is not an additional submarine patent risk for large companies. This is an ongoing issue and this section will be updated once more information is available."

---

[11] See Dirac Website, http://diracvideo.org/

[12] See Encoder comparison by Martin Fiedler dated February 25, 2010, http://keyj.s2000.ws/?p=356

[13] See Archive.org's June 2007 version of the HTML5 specification at
http://web.archive.org/web/20070629025435/http://www.w3.org/html/wg/html5/#video0

[14] See as an example this story in Apple Insider
http://www.appleinsider.com/articles/09/07/06/ogg_theora_h_264_and_the_html_5_browser_squabble.html

[15] See Nokia submission to a W3C workshop on video for the Web at http://www.w3.org/2007/08/video/positions/Nokia.pdf

[16] See W3C HTML Working Group Issue tracker, Issue #7 at http://www.w3.org/html/wg/tracker/issues/7

[17] See http://www.mpegla.com/Lists/MPEG%20LA%20News%20List/Attachments/231/n-10-08-26.pdf

[18] See Ian Hickson's email in December 2007 to the WHATWG at http://lists.whatwg.org/pipermail/whatwg-whatwg.org/2007-December/013135.html

[19] See Archive.org's Feb 2008 version of the HTML5 specification at
http://web.archive.org/web/20080225170401/www.whatwg.org/specs/web-apps/current-work/multipage/section-video.html#video0

H.264 has indeed several advantages over Theora. First, it provides a slightly better overall encoding quality.[20] Second, the de-facto standard for video publication on the Web had been set by YouTube, which used Adobe Flash with MP4 H.264/AAC support. Choosing the same codec as Adobe Flash will provide a simple migration path to the HTML5 video element since no additional transcoding would be necessary. Third, there are existing hardware implementations of H.264 for mobile devices, used in particular by Apple's iPod, iPhone, and iPad, which support this codec out of the box.

However, it is not inconceivable that the market will catch up over the next few years with software support and hardware implementations for Ogg Theora, increasingly enabling professional use of these codecs. In fact, in April 2010, Google funded a free, optimized implementation of Theora for the ARM processor, which runs Google's Android devices.[21] Theora is praised to be less complex and therefore requiring less dedicated hardware support than H.264, making it particularly useful on mobile devices.

This was the situation until May 19, 2010, when Google announced the launch of the WebM project, which proposes another opportunity to overcome the concerns Apple, Nokia and Microsoft have voiced with Theora. WebM is a new open-source and royalty-free video file format, which includes the VP8 video codec, a codec Google had acquired as part of it acquisition of On2 Technologies, finalized in February 2010.[22] The VP8 video codec, together with the Vorbis audio codec, is placed inside a container format derived from the Matroska[23] file format to make up the full video encoding format called **WebM**.

Google released WebM with an obvious intention of solving the stalemate around a baseline video codec in HTML5.[24] To that end, Google released WebM and VP8 under a BSD style open-source license, which allows anyone to make use of the code freely. They also grant a worldwide, non-exclusive, no-charge, royalty-free patent license to the users of the codec[25] to encourage adoption. They collaborated with Opera, Mozilla, and Adobe and many others[26] to achieve support for WebM, such as an implementation of WebM in the Opera, Google Chrome, and Firefox browsers, and also move forward with commercial encoding tools and hardware implementations. On October 15, 2010, Texas Instruments was the first hardware vendor to demonstrate VP8 on its new TI OMAP™ 4 processor.[27] VP8 is on par in video quality with H.264, so it has a big chance of achieving baseline codec status.

Microsoft's reaction to the release of WebM[28] was rather positive, saying that it would "support VP8 when the user has installed a VP8 codec on Windows". Apple basically refrained from making any official statement. Supposedly, Steve Jobs replied to the question "What did you make of the recent VP8 announcement?" in an e-mail with a pointer to a blog post[29] by an X.264 developer. The blog post hosts an initial, unfavorable analysis of VP8's quality and patent status. Note that X.264 is an open-source implementation of an H.264 decoder, the developer is not a patent attorney, and the analysis was done on a very early version of the open codebase.

As the situation stands, small technology providers or nonprofits are finding it hard to support a non-royalty-free codec. Mozilla and Opera have stated that they will not be able to support MP4 H.264/AAC since the required annual royalties are excessive, not just for themselves, but also for their

---

[20] See Encoder comparison by Martin Fiedler dated February 25, 2010, http://keyj.s2000.ws/?p=356

[21] See Google blog post dated April 9, 2010, http://google-opensource.blogspot.com/2010/04/interesting-times-for-video-on-web.html

[22] See http://www.google.com/intl/en/press/pressrel/ir_20090805.html

[23] See http://www.matroska.org/

[24] See http://webmproject.blogspot.com/2010/05/introducing-webm-open-web-media-project.html

[25] See http://www.webmproject.org/license/additional/

[26] See http://webmproject.blogspot.com/2010/05/introducing-webm-open-web-media-project.html

[27] See http://e2e.ti.com/videos/m/application_specific/240443.aspx

[28] See http://windowsteamblog.com/windows/b/bloggingwindows/archive/2010/05/19/another-follow-up-on-html5-video-in-ie9.aspx

[29] See http://x264dev.multimedia.cx/?p=377

downstream users and, more important, because the use of patent encumbered technology is against the ideals of an open Web.[30] They have both implemented and released exclusive support for Ogg Theora and WebM in their browsers. Apple's Safari still supports only MP4 H.264/AAC. Google Chrome supports all these three codecs. Table 1–1 has a summary of the current implementation situation.

Table 1–1. Introduction of HTML5 video support into main browsers

Browser	Nightly	Release	Formats
Safari	November 2007	March 2008 (Safari 3.1)	MP4 H.264/AAC
Firefox	July 2008	June 2009 (Firefox 3.5)	Ogg Theora, WebM
Chrome	September 2008	May 2009 (Chrome 3)	Ogg Theora, MP4 H.264/AAC, WebM
Opera	February 2007 / July 2008	January 2010 (Opera 10.50)	Ogg Theora, WebM
IE	March 2010 (IE9 dev build)	September 2010 (IE9 beta)	MP4 H.264/AAC

In the publisher domain, things look a little different because Google has managed to encourage several of the larger publishers to join in with WebM trials. Brightcove, Ooyala and YouTube all have trials running with WebM content. Generally, though, the larger publishers and the technology providers that can hand on the royalty payments to their customers are able to support MP4 H.264/AAC. The others can offer only Ogg Theora or WebM (see Table 1–2).

Table 1–2. HTML5 video support into some major video publishing sites (social and commercial)

Site / Vendor	Announcement	Format
Wikipedia	Basically since 2004, stronger push since 2009	Ogg Theora, WebM
Dailymotion	May 27, 2009	Ogg Theora, WebM
YouTube	January 20, 2010	MP4 H.264/AAC, WebM
Vimeo	January 21, 2010	MP4 H.264/AAC, WebM
Kaltura	March 18, 2010	Ogg Theora, WebM, MP4 H.264/AAC
Ooyala	March 25,2010	MP4 H.264/AAC, WebM
Brightcove	March 28, 2010	MP4 H.264/AAC, WebM

---

[30] See http://shaver.off.net/diary/2010/01/23/html5-video-and-codecs/

An interesting move is the announcement of VP8 support by Adobe.[31] When Adobe releases support for WebM, this will imply that video publishers that choose to publish their videos in the WebM format will be able to use the Adobe Flash player as a fallback solution in browsers that do not support the WebM format, which includes legacy browsers and HTML5 browsers with exclusive MP4 H.264/AAC support. This is a very clever move by Adobe and will allow smaller content publishers to stay away from H.264 royalties without losing a large number of their audience and without having to make the content available in multiple formats.

1.3 Summary

In this chapter we have looked back at the history of introducing audio and video on the Web and how that led to the introduction of <video> and <audio> elements into HTML5. We also described the discussions and status around finding a single video codec that every browser vendor could support as a baseline format.

As the situation currently stands, any video publisher that wants to create web pages with videos that are expected to universally work with any browser will be required to publish video in at least two formats: in MP4 H.264/AAC and in either Ogg Theora or WebM. Currently, Ogg Theora support and tools are still further developed than WebM tools, but WebM tools are improving rapidly. If you need to set up a site from scratch, your best choice is probably MP4 H.264/AAC and WebM.

---

[31] See http://blogs.adobe.com/flashplatform/2010/05/adobe_support_for_vp8.html

CHAPTER 2

■ ■ ■

Audio and Video Elements

This chapter introduces ‹audio› and ‹video› as new HTML elements, explains how to encode audio and video so you can use them in HTML5 media elements, how to publish them, and what the user interface looks like.

At this instance, we need to point out that ‹audio› and ‹video› are still rather new elements in the HTML specification and that the markup described in this chapter may have changed since the book has gone to press. The core functionality of ‹audio› and ‹video› should remain the same, so if you find that something does not quite work the way you expect, you should probably check the actual specification for any updates. You can find the specification at http://www.w3.org/TR/html5/spec.html or at http://www.whatwg.org/specs/web-apps/current-work/multipage/.

All of the examples in this chapter and in the following chapters are available to you at http://html5videoguide.net. You might find it helpful to open up your Web browser and follow along with the actual browser versions that you have installed.

2.1 Video and Audio Markup

In this section you will learn about all the attributes of ‹video› and ‹audio›, which browsers they work on, how the browsers interpret them differently, and possibly what bugs you will need to be aware of.

2.1.1 The Video Element

As explained in the previous chapter, there are currently three file formats that publishers have to consider if they want to cover all browsers that support HTML5 ‹video›, see Table 2–1.

Table 2–1. Video codecs natively supported by the major browsers

Browser	WebM	Ogg Theora	MPEG-4 H.264
Firefox	✔	✔	--
Safari	--	--	✔
Opera	✔	✔	--
Google Chrome	✔	✔	✔
IE	--	--	✔

As there is no fixed baseline codec (see history in Chapter 1), we will provide examples for all these formats.

As is common practice in software, we start with a "Hello World" example. Here are three simple examples that will embed video in HTML5:

Listing 2–1. Embedding Ogg video in HTML5

```
<video src="HelloWorld.ogv"></video>
```

Listing 2–2. Embedding WebM video in HTML5

```
<video src="HelloWorld.webm"></video>
```

Listing 2–3. Embedding MPEG-4 video in HTML5

```
<video src="HelloWorld.mp4"></video>
```

We've put all three Listings together on a single web page, added controls (that's the transport bar at the bottom; we'll get to this later) and fixed the width to 300px to make a straight comparison between all the five major browsers. Figure 2–1 shows the results.

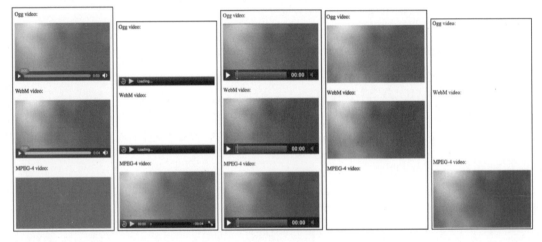

Figure 2–1. The <video> element in five browsers, from left to right: Firefox, Safari, Chrome, Opera, and IE

Firefox displays the Ogg and WebM video and shows an error for the MPEG-4 video. Opera reacts similarly, displaying nothing for the MPEG-4 video. Safari and IE both show nothing for the Ogg and WebM videos and display only the MPEG-4 video. Chrome displays all three formats.

You may already have noticed that there are some diverging implementations of the video elements; e.g. not all of them show an empty frame for a format they cannot decode and not all of them show the controls only on a mouse-over. We will come across more such differences in the course of this chapter. This is because the specification provides some leeway for interpretation. We expect that the browsers' behavior will become more aligned as the specification becomes clearer about what to display. We will analyze the features and differences in more detail below. This was just to give you a taste.

Fallback Content

You will have noticed that the `<video>` element has an opening and a closing tag. There are two reasons for this.

First, there are other elements introduced as children of the `<video>` element — in particular the `<source>` and the `<track>` elements. We will get to these.

Second, anything stated inside the `<video>` element that is not inside one of the specific child elements of the `<video>` element is regarded as "fallback content". It is "fallback" in so far as web browsers that do not support the HTML5 `<audio>` and `<video>` elements will ignore these elements, but still display their contents and thus is a means to be backwards compatible. Browsers that support the HTML5 `<video>` and `<audio>` elements will not display this content. Listing 2–4 shows an example.

Listing 2–4. Embedding MPEG-4 video in HTML5 with fallback content

```
<video src="HelloWorld.mp4">
   Your browser does not support the HTML5 video element.
</video>
```

When we include this in the combined example from above and run it in a legacy browser, we get the screenshot in Figure 2–2.

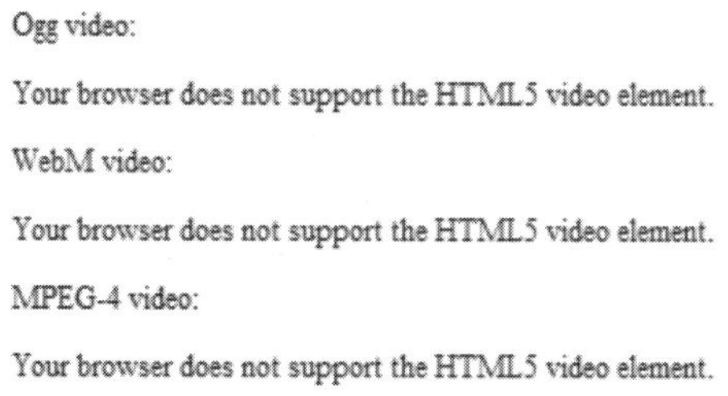

Ogg video:

Your browser does not support the HTML5 video element.

WebM video:

Your browser does not support the HTML5 video element.

MPEG-4 video:

Your browser does not support the HTML5 video element.

Figure 2–2. The <video> element in a legacy browser, here it's IE8

You can add any HTML markup inside the `<video>` element, including `<object>` and `<embed>` elements. Thus, for example, you can provide fallback using an Adobe Flash player alternative with mp4 or flv, or the Cortado Java applet for ogv. These video plug-ins will not support the JavaScript API of the HTML5 `<video>` element, but you can get JavaScript libraries that emulate some of the JavaScript API functionality and provide fallback for many different conditions. Example libraries are mwEmbed[1], Video for Everybody![2], Sublime Video[3], or VideoJS[4].

Note that in Listing 2–4, if you are using a modern HTML5 web browser that does not support the mp4 resource but supports Ogg or WebM, it still will not display the fallback content. You have to use JavaScript to catch the load error and take appropriate action. We will learn how to catch the load error in Chapter 4. This is really relevant only if you intend to use a single media format and want to catch errors for browsers that do not support that format. If you are happy to support more than one format,

---

[1] See http://www.kaltura.org/project/HTML5_Video_Media_JavaScript_Library

[2] See http://camendesign.com/code/video_for_everybody

[3] See http://sublimevideo.net/

[4] See http://videojs.com/

there is a different markup solution, where you do not use the @src attribute. Instead, you list all the available alternative resources for a single <video> element through the <source> element. We will introduce this later in Subsection 2.1.3.

Now, we'll go through all the content attributes of the <video> element to understand exactly what <video> has to offer.

@src

In its most basic form, the <video> element has only a @src attribute which is a link (or URL) to a video resource. The video resource is the file that contains the video data and is stored on a server.

To create a proper HTML5 document, we package the <video> element into HTML5 boilerplate code:

Listing 2–5. A HTML5 document with an MPEG-4 video

```
<!DOCTYPE html>
<html lang="en">
  <head>
    <title>Guide to HTML5 video: chapter 2: example </title>
  </head>
  <body>
    <h1>Chapter 2: example </h1>
      <video src="HelloWorld.mp4"></video>
  </body>
</html>
```

Figure 2–3 shows what the example looks like in Firefox (with "HelloWorld.webm" as the resource instead of "HelloWorld.mp4") and IE9 (as in Listing 2–5). In fact, all browsers look identical when using a supported resource in this use case.

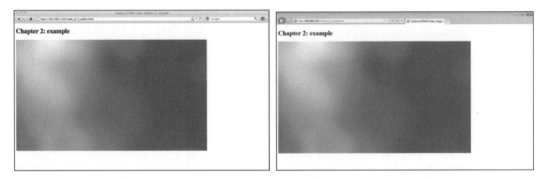

Figure 2–3. A <video> with only @src in Firefox (left) and IE9 (right)

You will notice that the videos look just like simple images. This is because there are no controls to start the video, nothing that shows it really is a video. Use of the video element in such a bare manner is sensible in two circumstances only: either the video is controlled through JavaScript (which we will look at in Chapter 4) or the video is explicitly set to automatically start play back immediately after loading. Without any further attributes, the default is to pause after initializing the <video> element, and thus we get the picture-like display.

@autoplay

To make the video autostart, you only need to add an attribute called @autoplay. Without being set to autoplay, a browser will download only enough bytes from the beginning of a video resource to be able to tell whether it is able to decode it and to decode the header, such that the decoding pipeline for the video and audio data is set up. That header data is also called "metadata", a term used in multiple different contexts with video, so be sure to understand what exactly it refers to from the context.

When the @autoplay attribute is provided, the video will automatically request more audio and video data after setting up the decode pipeline, buffer that data, and play back when sufficient data has been provided and decoded so that the browser thinks it can play the video through at the given buffering rate without rebuffering. Listings 2–6 shows an example use of the @autoplay attribute.

Listing 2–6. Ogg video with @autoplay

```
<video src="HelloWorld.ogv" autoplay></video>
```

The @autoplay attribute is a so-called boolean attribute, an attribute that doesn't take on any values, but its presence signifies that it is set to true. Its absence signifies that it is set to false. Thus, anything provided as an attribute value will be ignored; even if you set it to @autoplay="false", it still signifies that autoplay is activated.

Providing the @autoplay attribute will make the video start playing. If no user or script interaction happens, a video with an @autoplay attribute will play through from the beginning to the end of the video resource and stop at the end. If the download speed of the video data is not fast enough to provide a smooth playback or the browser's decoding speed is too slow, the video playback will stall and allow for the playback buffers to be filled before continuing playback. The browser will give the user some notice of the stalling — e.g. a spinner or a "Loading…" message.

Figure 2–4 shows the browsers at diverse stages of playback through the HelloWorld example: IE and Safari on the MPEG-4 file and Firefox, Opera, and Chrome on the WebM file. When the video is finished playing back, it stops on the last frame to await more video data in case it's a live stream.

Figure 2–4. Different autoplay states in five browsers, from left to right: Firefox, Safari, Chrome, Opera, and IE

@loop

To make the video automatically restart after finishing playback, there is an attribute called @loop. Obviously, the @loop attribute makes the video resource continue playing in an endless loop.

Listing 2–7. WebM video with @autoplay and @loop

```
<video src="HelloWorld.webm" autoplay loop></video>
```

The @loop attribute is also a boolean attribute, so you cannot specify a number of loops, just whether or not to loop. If you wanted to run it only for a specified number of loops, you will need to use the JavaScript API. We will learn the appropriate functions in Chapter 4. If specified in conjunction with

@autoplay, the video will start automatically and continue playing in a loop until some user or script interaction stops or pauses it.

All browsers except Firefox support this attribute.

@poster

In the screenshots in Figure 2–3 you can see the first frame of the video being displayed as the representative image for the video. The choice of frame to display is actually up to the browser. Most browsers will pick the first frame since its data typically comes right after the headers in the video resource and therefore are easy to download. But there is no guarantee. Also, if the first frame is black, it is not the best frame to present.

The user therefore has the ability to provide an explicit image as the poster. The poster is also a representative image for the video. Videos that haven't started playback are replaced by the poster, which is typically an image taken from somewhere further inside the video that provides an idea of what the video will be like. However, any picture is possible. Some web sites even choose an animated gif to display multiple representative images out of the video in a loop. This is also possible with the <video> element in HTML5.

The @poster attribute of the <video> element provides a link to an image resource that the browser can show while no video data is available. It is displayed as the video loads into the browser. The poster in use here is shown in Figure 2–5.

Figure 2–5. *The poster image in use in the following examples*

Listing 2–8 shows how it is used in a video element.

Listing 2–8. *Ogg video with @poster*

```
<video src="HelloWorld.ogv" poster="HelloWorld.png"></video>
```

Figure 2–6 shows what the Listing looks like in the different browsers with appropriate video resources.

Figure 2–6. *A <video> with @src and @poster in Firefox, Safari, Opera, Chrome, and IE (left to right)*

Note that there is a bug in the tested version of Opera with the display of the poster frame; that's why nothing is showing. The bug has been fixed since and will not appear in future releases. It is still possible to get the video to start playing — either through JavaScript or through activating the context menu. We will look at both these options at a later stage.

Firefox and Chrome will display the poster instead of the video and pause there, if given a @poster attribute and no @autoplay attribute.

Safari and IE's behavior is somewhat less useful. Safari will show the poster while it is setting up the decoding pipeline, but as soon as that is completed, it will display the first video frame. IE does the same thing, but in between the poster display and the display of the first frame it also displays a black frame.

It is expected that further work in the standards bodies will harmonize these diverging behaviors. Right now, it is up to the browsers and both behaviors are valid.

If @poster is specified in conjunction with @autoplay, a given @poster image will appear only briefly while the metadata of the video resource is loaded and before the video playback is started. It is therefore recommended not to use @poster in conjunction with @autoplay.

@width, @height

How do browsers decide in what dimensions to display the video?

You will have noticed in the above screenshots that the video is displayed with a given width and height as scaled by the video's aspect ratio (i.e. the ratio between width and height). In the example screenshots in Figure 2–3, the browsers display the videos in their native dimensions, i.e. the dimensions in which the video resource is encoded. The dimensions are calculated from the first picture of the video resource, which in the example cases are 960px by 540px.

In the example screenshots in Figure 2–2, the browsers were given a poster image so they used the dimensions of the poster image for initial display, which in these cases was 960px by 546px, i.e. 6px higher than the video. As the videos start playing back, the video viewport is scaled down to the video dimensions as retrieved from the first picture of the video resource.

If no poster image dimensions and video image dimensions are available — e.g. because of video load errors and lack of a @poster attribute — the video display area (also sometimes called "viewport") is displayed at 300px by 150px (minimum display) or at its intrinsic size.

As you can see, a lot of different scaling happens by default. This can actually create a performance bottleneck in the browsers and a disruptive display when the viewport suddenly changes size between a differently scaled poster image and the video. It is therefore recommended to control the scaling activities by explicitly setting the @width and @height attributes on the <video> element. For best performance, use the native dimensions of the video.

The poster image will be scaled to the dimensions given in @width and @height, and the video will be displayed in that viewport with a preserved aspect ratio, such that the video is centered and letter-boxed or pillar-boxed if the dimensions don't match. The @width and @height attributes are not intended to be used to stretch the video size, but merely to shorten and align it. The value of @width and @height are an unsigned long, which is interpreted as CSS pixels.

All browsers also tolerate it when the value of @width or @height is provided with "px" — e.g. as "300px" — even though that strictly speaking is invalid. All browsers except IE also tolerate values provided with "%" and then scale the video to that percentage in relation to the native video dimensions. This also is not valid. If you want to do such relative scaling, you should use CSS (see Chapter 3). Listing 2–9 shows an example with these dimensions.

Listing 2–9. WebM video with @width and @height to fix dimensions

```
<video src="HelloWorld.webm" poster="HelloWorld.png"
    width="320" height="180"></video>
<video src="HelloWorld.webm" poster="HelloWorld.png"
    width="25%" height="25%"></video>
```

Figure 2–7 shows what the example looks like in the browsers, each using the appropriate file format.

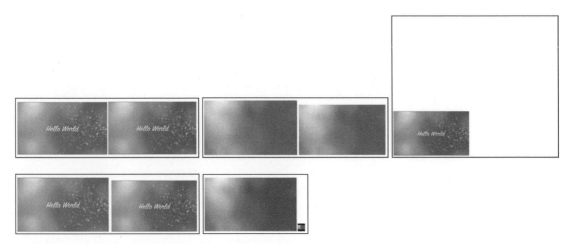

Figure 2–7. *A <video> with @width and @height in Firefox and Safari (top), Opera (right), Chrome, and IE (bottom)*

Note that Firefox scales both identically — i.e. it uses the video dimensions to also scale the poster — most likely to avoid the annoying scaling jump when the video starts playing. Both, Safari and Chrome scale the percentage according to the height of the poster. IE doesn't support percentage scaling, but instead interprets the percent value in CSS pixels. Opera has a bug introduced through use of the @poster attribute in that the percentage-scaled video refuses to display at all (the dimensions of the invisible video are 253px by 548px). However, the explicitly scaled video appears normally. Obviously, providing explicit @width and @height in pixels is a means to overcome the Opera poster bug.

So, what happens when you provide @width and @height attribute values that do not match the aspect ratio of the video resource? Listing 2–10 has an example.

Listing 2–10. *MPEG-4 video with @width and @height to fix dimensions with incorrect aspect ratio*

```
<video src="HelloWorld.mp4" poster="HelloWorld.png"
    width="320" height="90"></video>
<video src="HelloWorld.mp4" poster="HelloWorld.png"
    width="160" height="180"></video>
```

Figure 2–8 shows what the example looks like in the browsers, each using the appropriate file format. For better visibility, the video viewport has been surrounded by a one-pixel outline.

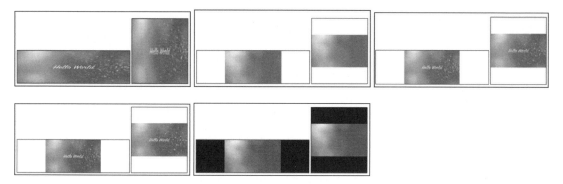

Figure 2–8. A <video> with @width and @height in Firefox, Safari, Opera (top), Chrome, and IE (bottom)

Letter-boxing or pillar-boxing is not intended to be performed using traditional black bars, but rather by making those sections of the playback area transparent areas where the background shows through, which is more natural on the Web. To turn the boxes into a different color, you need to explicitly set a specific background color using CSS (more on CSS in Chapter 3).

However, the browsers don't yet uniformly implement letter- and pillar-boxing. Firefox and IE do no boxing on the poster attribute, but instead scale it. Because IE doesn't dwell on the poster, it moves on to use black bars instead of transparent ones. Once you start playing in Firefox, the boxing on the video is performed correctly.

@controls

Next, we introduce one of the most useful attributes of the <video> element: the @controls attribute. If you simply want to embed a video and give it default controls for user interaction, this attribute is your friend.

The @controls attribute is a boolean attribute. If specified without @autoplay, the controls are displayed either always (as in Safari and Chrome), or when you mouse over and out of the video (as in Firefox), or only when you mouse over the video (as in Opera and IE).

Listing 2–11 has an example use of @controls with an Ogg video. Figure 2–9 shows what the example looks like in the browsers with a video width of 300px.

Listing 2–11. Ogg video with @controls attribute

```
<video src="HelloWorld.ogv" controls></video>
```

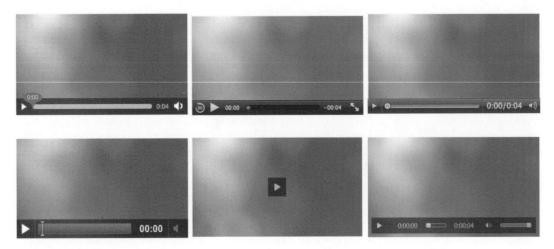

Figure 2–9. *A <video> with @controls in Firefox, Safari and Opera (top row), Chrome, IE with width 300px, and IE with width 400px (bottom row)*

Note that IE provides you with two different controls: one is a simple toggle button for play/pause and one is an overlay at the bottom of the video, similar to the other browsers. The simple button is very useful when the video becomes small and kicks in at less than 372px width for the given example.

@preload

The final attribute that we need to look at is the `@preload` attribute. It replaces an earlier attribute called `@autobuffer`, which was a boolean attribute and thus unable to distinguish between several different buffering requirements of users. This is why the `@preload` attribute was introduced, which allows web developers to give the browser more detailed information about what they expect as the user's buffering needs.

The `@preload` attribute is an attribute that you will not ordinarily want to use unless you have very specific needs. Thus, these paragraphs are only meant for advanced users.

As a web browser comes across a `<video>` element, it needs to decide what to do with the resource that it links to.

If the `<video>` is set to `@autoplay`, then the browser needs to start downloading the video resource, set up the video decoding pipeline, start decoding audio and video frames and start displaying the decoded audio and video in sync. Typically, the browser will start displaying audio and video even before the full resource has been downloaded, since a video resource is typically large and will take a long time to download. Thus, as the Web browser is displaying the decoded video, it can in parallel continue downloading the remainder of the video resource, decode those frames, buffer them for playback, and display them at the right display time. This approach is called "progressive download".

In contrast, if no `@autoplay` attribute is set on `<video>` and no `@poster` image is given, the browser will display only the first frame of the video resource. It has no need to immediately start a progressive download without even knowing whether the user will start the video playback. Thus, the browser only has to download the video properties and metadata required to set up the decoding pipeline, decode the first video image, and display it. It will then stop downloading the video resource in order not to use up users' bandwidth with data that they may not want to watch. The metadata section of a video resource typically consists of no more than several kilobytes.

A further bandwidth optimization is possible if the `<video>` element actually has a @poster attribute. In this case, the browser may not even bother to start downloading any video resource data and just display the @poster image. Note that in this situation, the browser is in an information-poor state: it has not been able to find out any metadata about the video resource. In particular, it has not been able to determine the duration of the video, or potentially even whether it is able to decode the resource. Therefore, most browsers on laptop or desktop devices will still download the setup and first frame of the video, while on mobile devices, browsers more typically avoid this extra bandwidth use.

Now, as a web developer, you may be in a better position than the web browser to decide what bandwidth use may be acceptable to your users. This decision is also an issue because a delayed download of video data will also cause a delay in playback. Maybe web developers do not want to make their users wait for the decoding pipeline to be set up.

Thus, the @preload attribute gives the web page author explicit means to control the download behavior of the Web browser on `<video>` elements.

The @preload attribute can take on the values *"none"*, *"metadata"*, or *"auto"*.

***Listing 2–12.** Ogg video with @preload of "none"*

```
<video src="HelloWorld.ogv" poster="HelloWorld.png"
    preload="none" controls></video>
```

You would choose *"none"* in a situation where you do not expect the user to actually play back the media resource and want to minimize bandwidth use. A typical example is a web page with many video elements — something like a video gallery — where every video element has a @poster image and the browser does not have to decode the first video frame to represent the video resource. On a video gallery, the probability that a user chooses to play back all videos is fairly small. Thus, it is good practice to set the @preload attribute to *"none"* in such a situation and avoid bandwidth wasting, but accept a delay when a video is actually selected for playback. You also accept that some metadata is not actually available for the video and cannot be displayed by the browser, e.g. the duration of the video.

***Listing 2–13.** MPEG-4 video with @preload of "metadata"*

```
<video src="HelloWorld.mp4" poster="HelloWorld.png"
    preload="metadata" controls></video>
```

You will choose *"metadata"* in a situation where you need the metadata and possibly the first video frame, but do not want the browser to start progressive download. This again can be in a video gallery situation. For example, you may want to choose *"none"* if you are delivering your web page to a mobile device or a low-bandwidth connection, but choose *"metadata"* on high-bandwidth connections. Also, you may want to choose *"metadata"* if you are returning to a page with a single video that a user has already visited previously, since you might not expect the user to view the video again, but you do want the metadata to be displayed. The default preload mode is "metadata".

***Listing 2–14.** WebM video with @preload of "auto"*

```
<video src="HelloWorld.webm" poster="HelloWorld.png"
    preload="auto" controls></video>
```

You will choose *"auto"* to encourage the browser to actually start downloading the entire resource, i.e. to do a progressive download even if the video resource is not set to @autoplay. The particular browser may not want to do this, e.g. if it is on a mobile device, but you as a web developer signal in this way to the browser that your server will not have an issue with it and would prefer it in this way so as to optimize the user experience with as little wait time as possible on playback.

Figure 2–10 shows the results of the different @preload values in Firefox, which also displays the loaded byte ranges. It shows, in particular, that for *"none"* no video data is downloaded at all.

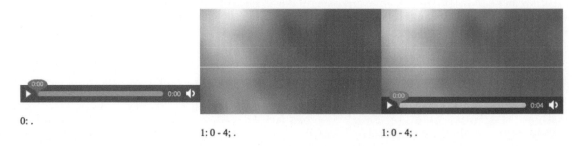

Figure 2–10. A *<video>* with @preload set to "none", "metadata", "auto" in Firefox

Note how we have put the same video resource with three different loading strategies into the example of Figure 2–10. That approach actually confuses several of the browsers and gets them to degrade in performance or die, so don't try to mix @preload strategies for the same resource on the same web page.

Support for @preload is implemented in Firefox and Safari, such that *"none"* loads nothing and *"metadata"* and *"auto"* set up the video element with its metadata and decoding pipeline, as well as the first video frame as poster frame. Chrome, Opera, and IE don't seem to support the attribute yet and ignore it.

As a recommendation, it is in general best not to interfere with the browser's default buffering behavior and to avoid using the @preload attribute.

2.1.2 The Audio Element

Before diving further into the functionality of the `<video>` element, we briefly introduce its brother, the `<audio>` element. `<audio>` shares a lot of markup and functionality with the `<video>` element, but it does not have @poster, @width, and @height attributes, since the native representation of an `<audio>` element is to not display visually.

At this point, we need to look at the supported audio codecs in HTML5. Table 2–2 displays the table of codecs supported by the main HTML5 media supporting web browsers.

Table 2–2. Audio codecs natively supported by the major browsers

Browser	WAV	Ogg Vorbis	MP3
Firefox	✔	✔	--
Safari	✔	--	✔
Opera	✔	✔	--
Google Chrome	✔	✔	✔
IE	--	--	✔

Note that again there isn't a single encoding format supported by all web browsers. It can be expected that IE may implement support for WAV, but as WAV is uncompressed, it is not a very efficient option and should be used only for short audio files. At minimum you will need to provide Ogg Vorbis and MP3 files to publish to all browsers.

@src

Here is a simple example that will embed an audio resource in HTML5:

Listing 2–15. WAV audio file

```
<audio src="HelloWorld.wav"></audio>
```

Listing 2–16. Ogg Vorbis audio file

```
<audio src="HelloWorld.ogg"></audio>
```

Listing 2–17. MP3 audio file

```
<audio src="HelloWorld.mp3"></audio>
```

Because this audio element has no controls, there will be no visual representation of the `<audio>` element. This is sensible only in two circumstances: either the `<audio>` is controlled through JavaScript (see Chapter 4), or the `<audio>` is set to start playback automatically, for which it requires an @autoplay attribute.

@autoplay

To make the audio autostart, you need to add an attribute called @autoplay.

Listing 2–18. WAV audio file with an @autoplay attribute

```
<audio src="HelloWorld.wav" autoplay></audio>
```

The `@autoplay` attribute is a boolean attribute, just as it is with the `<video>` element. Providing it will make the audio begin playing as soon as the browser has downloaded and decoded sufficient audio data. The audio file will play through once from start to end. It is recommended this feature be used sparingly, since it can be highly irritating for users.

The `@autoplay` attribute is supported by all browsers.

@loop

To make the audio automatically restart after finishing playback, you use the @loop attribute.

Listing 2–19. Ogg Vorbis audio file with a @loop attribute

```
<audio src="HelloWorld.ogg" autoplay loop></audio>
```

The `@loop` attribute, in conjunction with the `@autoplay` attribute, provides a means to set continuously playing "background" music or sound on your web page. This is not recommended; it is just mentioned here for completeness.

Note that if you accidentally create several such elements, they will all play at the same time and over the top of each other, but not synchronously. In fact, they may expose a massive drift against each other since each <audio> element only follows its own playback timeline. Synchronizing such elements currently is not easily possible. You can use only JavaScript to poll for the current playback time of each element and reset all elements to the same playback position at regular intervals. We will learn about the tools to do this in Chapter 4 with the JavaScript API.

The @loop attribute is supported by all browsers except Firefox, where it is scheduled for version 5.

@controls

If you are planning to display an audio resource on your web page for user interaction rather than for background entertainment, you will need to turn on @controls for your <audio> element.

Listing 2–20. MP3 audio file

```
<audio src="HelloWorld.mp3" controls></audio>
```

Figure 2–11 shows what the example looks like in the browsers.

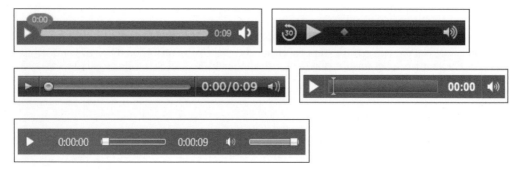

Figure 2–11. An <audio> element with @controls in Firefox, Safari (top row), Opera, Chrome (middle row), and IE (bottom)

You will notice that the controls of each browser use a different design. Their width and height are different and not all of them display the duration of the audio resource. Since the <audio> element has no intrinsic width and height, the controls may be rendered as the browser finds appropriate. This means that Safari uses a width of 200px; the others all use a width of 300px. The height ranges from 25px (Safari, Opera), to 28px (Firefox), to 32px (Google Chrome), and to 52px (IE). In Chapter 4 we show how you can run your own controls and thus make them consistent across browsers.

@preload

The @preload attribute for <audio> works like the one for <video>. You ordinarily should not have to deal with this attribute.

The @preload attribute accepts three different values: "*none*", "*metadata*", or "*auto*".

Listing 2–21. WAV audio file with preload set to "none"

```
<audio src="HelloWorld.wav" controls preload="none"></audio>
```

Web developers may choose "*none*" in a situation where they do not expect the user to actually play back the media resource and want to minimize bandwidth use. A browser would typically load the setup information of the audio resource, including metadata, such as the duration of the resource. Without the metadata, the duration of the resource cannot be displayed. Thus, choosing no preload only makes sense when dealing with a large number of audio resources. This is typically only useful for web pages that display many audio resources — an archive of podcasts, for example.

Listing 2–22. Ogg Vorbis audio file with preload set to "metadata"

```
<audio src="HelloWorld.ogg" controls preload="metadata"></audio>
```

Web developers may chose "*metadata*" in a situation where they do not expect the user to actually play back the media resource and want to minimize bandwidth use, but not at the cost of missing audio metadata information. This is typically the default behavior of the web browser unless the element is set to autoplay, but can be reinforced by the web developer through this attribute if supported by the browser.

 Listing 2–23. MP3 audio file with preload set to "auto"

```
<audio src="HelloWorld.mp3" controls preload="auto"></audio>
```

Web developers may chose "*auto*" in a situation where they expect an audio resource to actually be played back and want to encourage the browser to prebuffer the resource, i.e. to start progressively downloading the complete resource rather than just the setup information. This is typically the case where the <audio> element is the main element on the page, such as a podcast page. The aim of using @preload with "*auto*" value is to use bandwidth preemptively to create a better user experience with a quicker playback start.

Support for @preload is implemented in Firefox and Safari, such that "*none*" loads nothing and "*metadata*" and "*auto*" set up the audio element with its metadata and decoding pipeline. Chrome, Opera, and IE don't seem to support the attribute yet and ignore it.

2.1.3 The Source Element

As we have seen, both the <video> and the <audio> element do not have a universally supported baseline codec. Therefore, the HTML5 specification has created a means to allow specification of alternative source files through the <source> element. This allows a web developer to integrate all the required links to alternative media resources within the markup without having to test for browsers' support and use JavaScript to change the currently active resource.

@src

An example for a <video> element with multiple resources is given in Listing 2–24, an example for <audio> in Listing 2–25.

Listing 2–24. Embedding video in HTML5 with WebM Ogg and MPEG-4 formats

```
<video poster="HelloWorld.png" controls>
  <source src="HelloWorld.mp4">
  <source src="HelloWorld.webm">
  <source src="HelloWorld.ogv">
</video>
```

Listing 2–25. Embedding audio in HTML5 with WAV, Ogg Vorbis and MP3 formats

```
<audio controls>
  <source src="HelloWorld.mp3">
  <source src="HelloWorld.ogg">
  <source src="HelloWorld.wav">
</audio>
```

The `<source>` element is an empty element. It is not permitted to have any content and therefore doesn't have a `</source>` closing tag. If such a closing tag were used, it may in fact create another `<source>` element without any attributes, so don't use it. It is, however, possible to add a slash "/" at the end of the `<source>` element start tag as in `<source/>` — HTML user agents will parse this — but it is not an HTML5 requirement. If you were using XHTML5, though, you would need to close the empty element in this way.

The list of `<source>` elements specifies alternative media resources for the `<video>` or `<audio>` element, with the @src attribute providing the address of the media resource as a URL.

A browser steps through the `<source>` elements in the given order. It will try to load each media resource and the first one that succeeds will be the resource chosen for the media element. If none succeeds, the media element load fails, just as it fails when the direct @src attribute of `<audio>` or `<video>` cannot be resolved.

Note that right now, there is a bug in the iPad that will stop the `<video>` element from working when the MPEG-4 file is not the first one in the list of `<source>` elements. All browsers support `<source>` elements and the @src attribute.

@type

The `<source>` element has a @type attribute to specify the media type of the referenced media resource. This attribute is a hint from the web developer and makes it easier for the browser to determine whether it can play the referenced media resource. It can even make this decision without having to fetch any media data.

The @type attribute contains a MIME type with an optional codecs parameter.

Listing 2–26. Embedding video with Ogg Theora, WebM, and MPEG-4 formats and explicit @type

```
<video poster="HelloWorld.png" controls>
  <source src="HelloWorld.mp4"  type='video/mp4; codecs="avc1.42E01E, mp4a.40.2"'>
  <source src="HelloWorld.webm" type='video/webm; codecs="vp8, vorbis"'>
  <source src="HelloWorld.ogv"  type='video/ogg; codecs="theora, vorbis"'>
</video>
```

Note that you need to frame multiple parameters with double quotes and thus you have to put the @type value in single quotes or otherwise escape the double quotes around the @type attribute value.

You cannot use single quotes on the codecs parameter, since RFC 4281[5] specifies that they have a special meaning. RFC 4281 is the one that specifies the codecs parameter on a MIME type.

Listing 2–27. Embedding audio with WAV, Ogg Vorbis and MPEG-4 formats and explicit @type

```
<audio controls>
  <source src="HelloWorld.wav" type="audio/wav; codecs=1">
  <source src="HelloWorld.ogg" type="audio/ogg; codecs=vorbis">
  <source src="HelloWorld.mp3" type="audio/mpeg; codecs=mp3">
</audio>
```

The browsers will parse the @type attribute and use it as a hint to determine if they can play the file. MIME types do not always provide a full description of the media resource. For example, if "audio/ogg" is provided, it is unclear whether that would be an Ogg Vorbis, Ogg Flac, or Ogg Speex file. Or if "audio/mpeg" is given, it is unclear whether that would be an MPEG-1 or MPEG-2 audio file Layer 1, 2, or 3 (only Layer 3 is MP3). Also note that codecs=1 for audio/wav is PCM.

Thus, based on the value of the @type attribute, the browser will guess whether it may be able to play the media resource. It can make three decisions:

- It does not support the resource type.

- "Maybe": there is a chance that the resource type is supported.

- "Probably": the web browser is confident that it supports the resource type.

A confident decision for "probably" can generally be made only if a codecs parameter is present.

A decision for "maybe" is made by the browser based on information it has available as to which codecs it supports. This can be a fixed set of codecs as implemented directly in the browser, or it can be a list of codecs as retrieved from an underlying media framework such as GStreamer, DirectShow, or QuickTime.

You can use the code snippet in Listing 2–28 to test your browser for what MIME types it supports. Note that the canPlayType() function is from the JavaScript API, which we will look at in Chapter 4.

Listing 2–28. Code to test what video MIME types a web browser supports

```
<p>Video supports the following MIME types:
  <ul>
    <script type="text/javascript">
      var types = new Array();
      types[0] = "video/ogg";
      types[1] = 'video/ogg; codecs="theora, vorbis"';
      types[2] = "video/webm";
      types[3] = 'video/webm; codecs="vp8, vorbis"';
      types[4] = "video/mp4";
      types[5] = 'video/mp4; codecs="avc1.42E01E, mp4a.40.2"';
      // create a video element
      var video = document.createElement('video');
      // test types
      for (i=0; i<types.length; i++) {
        var support = video.canPlayType(types[i]);
        if (support == "") support="no";
```

---

[5] See http://www.ietf.org/rfc/rfc4281.txt

```
        document.write("<li><b>"+types[i]+"</b> : "+support+"</li>");
      }
    </script>
  </ul>
</p>
```

We can see the results for the MIME types in each browser in Figure 2–12.

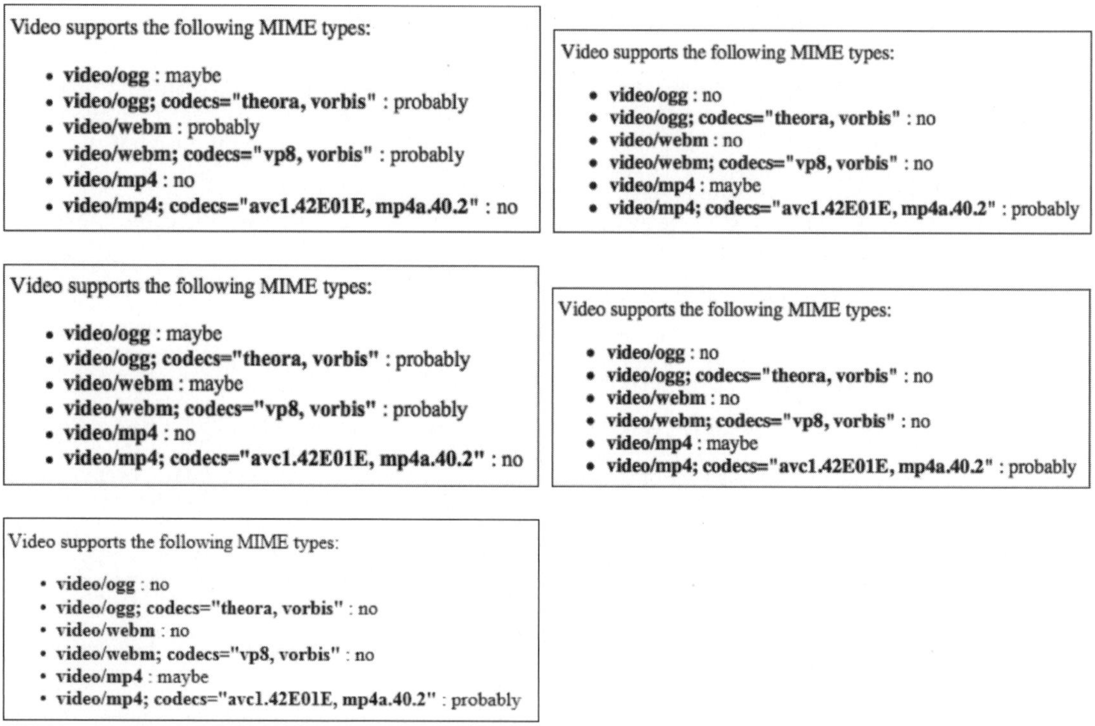

Video supports the following MIME types:

- **video/ogg** : maybe
- **video/ogg; codecs="theora, vorbis"** : probably
- **video/webm** : probably
- **video/webm; codecs="vp8, vorbis"** : probably
- **video/mp4** : no
- **video/mp4; codecs="avc1.42E01E, mp4a.40.2"** : no

Video supports the following MIME types:

- **video/ogg** : no
- **video/ogg; codecs="theora, vorbis"** : no
- **video/webm** : no
- **video/webm; codecs="vp8, vorbis"** : no
- **video/mp4** : maybe
- **video/mp4; codecs="avc1.42E01E, mp4a.40.2"** : probably

Video supports the following MIME types:

- **video/ogg** : maybe
- **video/ogg; codecs="theora, vorbis"** : probably
- **video/webm** : maybe
- **video/webm; codecs="vp8, vorbis"** : probably
- **video/mp4** : no
- **video/mp4; codecs="avc1.42E01E, mp4a.40.2"** : no

Video supports the following MIME types:

- **video/ogg** : no
- **video/ogg; codecs="theora, vorbis"** : no
- **video/webm** : no
- **video/webm; codecs="vp8, vorbis"** : no
- **video/mp4** : maybe
- **video/mp4; codecs="avc1.42E01E, mp4a.40.2"** : probably

Video supports the following MIME types:

- **video/ogg** : no
- **video/ogg; codecs="theora, vorbis"** : no
- **video/webm** : no
- **video/webm; codecs="vp8, vorbis"** : no
- **video/mp4** : maybe
- **video/mp4; codecs="avc1.42E01E, mp4a.40.2"** : probably

Figure 2–12. The video codec support in Firefox and Safari (top row), Opera and Chrome (middle row), and IE (bottom)

IE and Safari will return "maybe" when given a MIME type without codecs parameters and "probably" when given one with codecs parameters.

Let's do the same exercise for audio MIME types with the code snippet in Listing 2–33.

Listing 2–29. Code to test what audio MIME types a web browser supports

```
<p>Audio supports the following MIME types:
  <ul>
    <script type="text/javascript">
      var types = new Array();
      types[0] = "audio/ogg";
      types[1] = "audio/ogg; codecs=vorbis";
      types[2] = "audio/mpeg";
```

```
        types[3]  = "audio/mpeg; codecs=mp3";
        types[4]  = "audio/wav";
        types[5]  = "audio/wav; codecs=1";
        types[6]  = "audio/mp4";
        types[7]  = "audio/mp4; codecs=aac";
        types[8]  = "audio/x-m4b";
        types[9]  = "audio/x-m4b; codecs=aac";
        types[10] = "audio/x-m4p";
        types[11] = "audio/x-m4p; codecs=aac";
        types[12] = "audio/aac";
        types[13] = "audio/aac; codecs=aac";
        types[14] = "audio/x-aac";
        types[15] = "audio/x-aac; codecs=aac";

        // create a audio element
        var audio = document.createElement('audio');
        // test types
        for (i=0; i<types.length; i++) {
          var support = audio.canPlayType(types[i]);
          if (support == "") support="no";
          document.write("<li><b>"+types[i]+"</b> : "+support+"</li>");
        }
      </script>
    </ul>
  </p>
```

We can see the results for the MIME types in each browser in Figure 2–13. The screenshots cover even more codecs, since some browsers also support MPEG-4 AAC. Note that while Opera and Google Chrome claim they may be able to play MPEG-4 AAC, they actually don't. Firefox is realistic about this, and Safari is the only one that actually supports it.

Note that the "codecs" parameter is optional and even though it helps browsers be more confident about whether they will be able to decode a resource, ultimately that test comes only with trying to load the resource. It is therefore recommended to use only the MIME type without the codecs parameters.

There are even discussions to completely remove this attribute and have the browser determine through successive header downloads which resource it can decode. This is called "sniffing". The @type attribute was created to remove the need for sniffing and speed up the resource selection and loading.

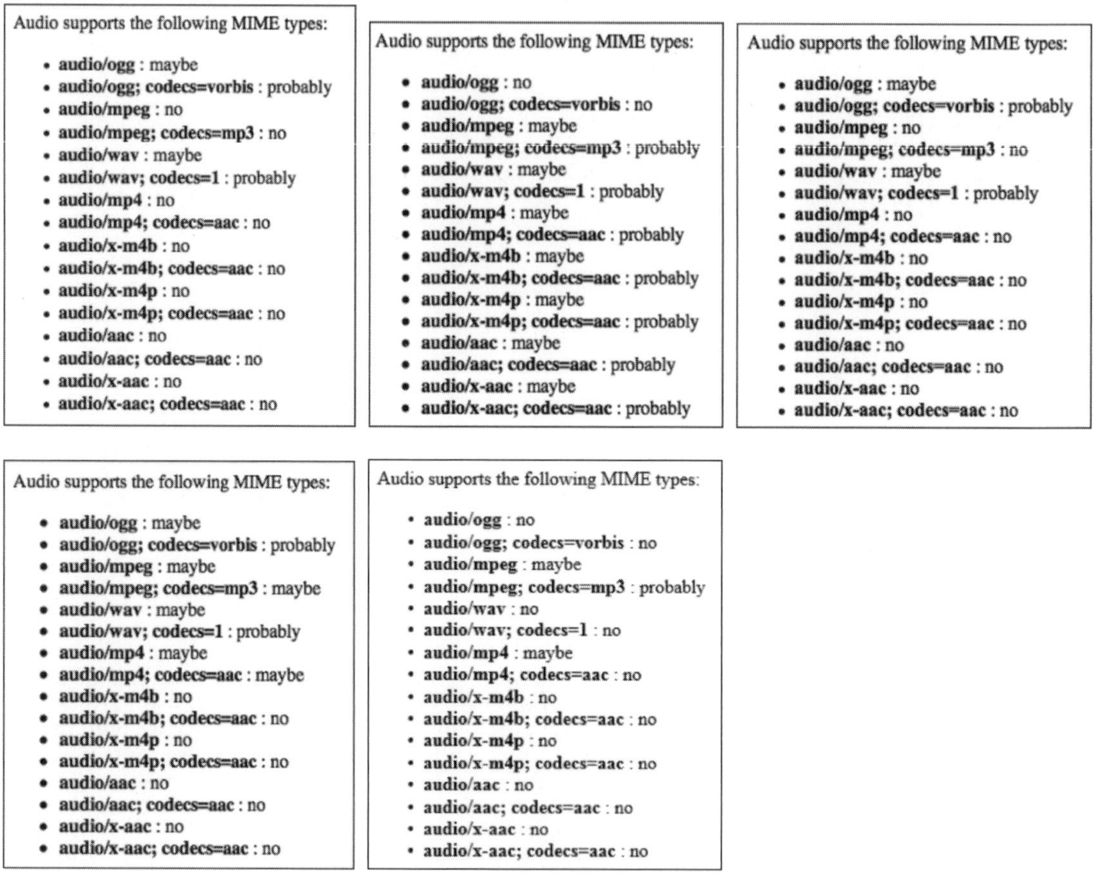

Audio supports the following MIME types:

- **audio/ogg** : maybe
- **audio/ogg; codecs=vorbis** : probably
- **audio/mpeg** : no
- **audio/mpeg; codecs=mp3** : no
- **audio/wav** : maybe
- **audio/wav; codecs=1** : probably
- **audio/mp4** : no
- **audio/mp4; codecs=aac** : no
- **audio/x-m4b** : no
- **audio/x-m4b; codecs=aac** : no
- **audio/x-m4p** : no
- **audio/x-m4p; codecs=aac** : no
- **audio/aac** : no
- **audio/aac; codecs=aac** : no
- **audio/x-aac** : no
- **audio/x-aac; codecs=aac** : no

Audio supports the following MIME types:

- **audio/ogg** : no
- **audio/ogg; codecs=vorbis** : no
- **audio/mpeg** : maybe
- **audio/mpeg; codecs=mp3** : probably
- **audio/wav** : maybe
- **audio/wav; codecs=1** : probably
- **audio/mp4** : maybe
- **audio/mp4; codecs=aac** : probably
- **audio/x-m4b** : maybe
- **audio/x-m4b; codecs=aac** : probably
- **audio/x-m4p** : maybe
- **audio/x-m4p; codecs=aac** : probably
- **audio/aac** : maybe
- **audio/aac; codecs=aac** : probably
- **audio/x-aac** : maybe
- **audio/x-aac; codecs=aac** : probably

Audio supports the following MIME types:

- **audio/ogg** : maybe
- **audio/ogg; codecs=vorbis** : probably
- **audio/mpeg** : no
- **audio/mpeg; codecs=mp3** : no
- **audio/wav** : maybe
- **audio/wav; codecs=1** : probably
- **audio/mp4** : no
- **audio/mp4; codecs=aac** : no
- **audio/x-m4b** : no
- **audio/x-m4b; codecs=aac** : no
- **audio/x-m4p** : no
- **audio/x-m4p; codecs=aac** : no
- **audio/aac** : no
- **audio/aac; codecs=aac** : no
- **audio/x-aac** : no
- **audio/x-aac; codecs=aac** : no

Audio supports the following MIME types:

- **audio/ogg** : maybe
- **audio/ogg; codecs=vorbis** : probably
- **audio/mpeg** : maybe
- **audio/mpeg; codecs=mp3** : maybe
- **audio/wav** : maybe
- **audio/wav; codecs=1** : probably
- **audio/mp4** : maybe
- **audio/mp4; codecs=aac** : maybe
- **audio/x-m4b** : no
- **audio/x-m4b; codecs=aac** : no
- **audio/x-m4p** : no
- **audio/x-m4p; codecs=aac** : no
- **audio/aac** : no
- **audio/aac; codecs=aac** : no
- **audio/x-aac** : no
- **audio/x-aac; codecs=aac** : no

Audio supports the following MIME types:

- audio/ogg : no
- audio/ogg; codecs=vorbis : no
- audio/mpeg : maybe
- audio/mpeg; codecs=mp3 : probably
- audio/wav : no
- audio/wav; codecs=1 : no
- audio/mp4 : maybe
- audio/mp4; codecs=aac : no
- audio/x-m4b : no
- audio/x-m4b; codecs=aac : no
- audio/x-m4p : no
- audio/x-m4p; codecs=aac : no
- audio/aac : no
- audio/aac; codecs=aac : no
- audio/x-aac : no
- audio/x-aac; codecs=aac : no

Figure 2–13. The audio codec support in Firefox, Safari, Opera (top row), Chrome, and IE (bottom row)

@media

The `<source>` element only exists to help the browser select the first acceptable media resource from a list. The @type attribute helps identify whether the browser supports that media format. The @media attribute further provides for associating so-called media queries[6] with a resource.

Media queries exist to specify that a specific resource is tailored for a specific (range of) output device(s). For example, a @media value of "*min-width: 400px*" specifies that the resource is targeted toward display areas of at least 400px width.

Many different media queries are possible. Here are just a few examples used on media elements.

___

[6] See http://www.w3.org/TR/css3-mediaqueries/

- @media="*handheld*" to indicate that the media resource is appropriate for handheld devices.

- @media="*all and (min-device-height:720px)*" to indicate that the media resource is appropriate for screens with 720 lines of pixels or bigger.

- @media="*screen and (min-device-width: 100px)*" to indicate that the media resource is appropriate for screens with 100 lines of pixels or higher.

While we are working with browsers on desktops and laptops, this attribute should not be of much interest. Only Opera and Safari have implemented support for it..

2.1.4 Markup Summary

Lastly, we list all the introduced elements and attributes for reference purposes. This should help to quickly find what you are looking for.

Table 2–3. Overview of all the media elements and their attributes

Element	Attribute	Values	Description
<video>	@src	[url]	Link to video resource.
	@autoplay		Autostart video playback after video loading.
	@loop		Restart video when reaching end.
	@poster	[url]	Link to representative image for video.
	@width, @height	[length] |[percentage]	Provide width and height dimensions for video.
	@preload	"none" | "metadata" | "auto"	Suggestion for how much of the video resource to load.
	@controls		Display default video controls.
<audio>	@src	[url]	Link to audio resource.
	@autoplay		Autostart audio playback after audio loading.
	@loop		Restart audio when reaching end.
	@preload	"none" | "metadata" | "auto"	Suggestion for how much of the audio resource to load.
	@controls		Display default audio controls.
<source>	@src	[url]	Link to media resource.
	@type	[MIME type]	MIME type of media resource.
	@media	[media query]	Media resource is tailored for such a device.

2.2 Encoding Media Resources

After reading the previous section, you will have a clear understanding of how to include audio and video resources into HTML But you may still be wondering how to actually create those audio and video resources. In this subsection, we will look briefly at how to encode the main formats web browsers support: Ogg Theora, WebM, and MPEG-4 H.264 for <video> and Ogg Vorbis and MP3 for <audio>. Feel free to skip this subsection if you have already mastered the encoding challenge.

We focus on using open-source software to perform the encoding, since this software is available to everyone, on every major platform and vendor-neutral. The use of online encoding services is particularly interesting since they will run the software for you with already optimized parameters, and the cost will scale with the amount of encoding you need to undertake.

2.2.1 Encoding MPEG-4 H.264 Video

Open-source tools for encoding MPEG-4 H.264 basically all use the x264[7] encoding library, which is published under the GNU GPL license. x264 is among the most feature-complete H.264 codecs and widely accepted as one of the fastest.[8] The best software for transcoding an existing video file to MPEG-4 H.264 is probably FFmpeg[9], which uses x264 for MPEG-4 H.264 encoding.

FFmpeg is a command line tool to convert multimedia files between formats. It has binaries for all major platforms. Even if you have an exotic platform, you pretty likely can make it work by compiling from source code. Alternative open-source encoding software with a GUI include Handbrake[10] and VLC[11]. We will not look at these encoding tools, but focus on FFmpeg instead. Should you use one of those GUI tools, it is still instructive to read about the profiles and presettings that FFmpeg uses for a better understanding of encoding options.

Let's assume you have a video file as a result of extracting video from a digital video camera. It could already be in MPEG-4 H.264 format, but let's assume it instead is in DV, QuickTime, VOB, AVI, MXF, or any other such format. FFmpeg understands almost all input formats (assuming you have the right decoding libraries installed). Running "ffmpeg –formats" will list all the supported codec formats. You should avoid transcoding if at all possible. Transcoding means you are decoding from one encoding format and reencoding in another. All transcoding creates new artifacts, even if you are transcoding for the same codec. Artifacts are visible or audible effects created in the audio or video data that are not present in the original material and introduced through the encoding process and which reduce the quality of the material.

MPEG-4 H.264 actually includes a number of encoding profiles with varying characteristics.[12] The sheer number of available profiles makes it difficult to understand when to use what, but the most used profiles are the following:

---

[7] See http://www.videolan.org/developers/x264.html

[8] See http://en.wikipedia.org/wiki/H.264#Software_encoder_feature_comparison

[9] See http://www.FFmpeg.org/

[10] See http://handbrake.fr/

[11] See http://www.videolan.org/vlc/

[12] See http://en.wikipedia.org/wiki/H.264/MPEG-4_AVC

- Baseline Profile: use this profile for iPod and iPhone.[13]

- Main Profile: this is mostly a historic profile used for SD digital TV broadcasts.

- High Profile: use this profile for Web, SD, and HD video publishing.

FFmpeg provides simple presets to encode in typical formats. You can find them in the `.ffpreset` files — e.g. *libx264-main.ffpreset*. The following presets may be useful[14]:

- baseline – a generic baseline profile.

- ipod320 – a baseline profile for 320×240 video.

- ipod640 – a baseline profile for 640×480 video.

- default – a generic main profile.

- normal – a generic high profile recommended for everyday use (and the default).

- hq – improved quality compared with the "normal" preset taking about twice as long to encode, but with improved motion estimation

- max – a further improved quality compared with the "hq" preset taking about 20 times as long to encode, but with further improved motion estimation

With the following command in Listing 2–30, you should be able to create an MPEG-4 H.264 video file with AAC audio from an input format supported by your installation of FFmpeg.

Listing 2–30. Encoding a video resource to the MPEG-4 H.264 format using presets

```
ffmpeg -i infile \
        -vcodec libx264 -vpre <preset> \
        -acodec libfaac \
        -threads 0 outfile.mp4
```

In Listing 2–30 we've put all the video codec related options on one line and all the audio codec related options on another. Setting the -threads parameter to 0 encourages FFmpeg to use as many threads as appropriate. Choose your preferred preset and replace it for <preset>. Further, if you want to control the bitrate, you can set it for the video with -vb <bitrate> and for the audio with -ab <bitrate>. A typical encoding call is provided in Listing 2–31.

Listing 2–31. Typical encoding using the normal profile

```
ffmpeg -i HelloWorld.dv \
        -vcodec libx264 -vpre normal -vb 3000k \
        -acodec libfaac -ab 192k \
        -threads 0 HelloWorld.mp4
```

You can do a lot to further improve video quality. One particularly effective approach is to perform a two-pass encoding. For this, you run FFmpeg twice. The first time, you need to include only the video, no audio, and use the -fastfirstpass preset, as well as a -pass 1 parameter. Also, you need to write the

---

[13] More information at http://rob.opendot.cl/index.php/useful-stuff/ipod-video-guide/

[14] See http://juliensimon.blogspot.com/2009/01/howto-ffmpeg-x264-presets.html

output somewhere to a temporary file, since you are interested only in creating the log files that the second pass requires. Then, in the second pass, you include a `-pass 2` parameter and the audio.

Listing 2–32. Two-pass encoding example using the normal profile

```
ffmpeg -i Helloworld.dv -pass 1 \
       -vcodec libx264 -vpre fastfirstpass \
       -an -threads 0 tempfile.mp4
ffmpeg -i HelloWorld.dv -pass 2 \
       -vcodec libx264 -vpre normal -vb 3000k \
       -acodec libfaac -ab 192k \
       -threads 0 HelloWorld.mp4
```

2.2.2 Encoding Ogg Theora

Open-source tools for encoding Ogg Theora basically use the libtheora[15] encoding library, which is published under a BSD style license by Xiph.org. There are several encoders written on top of libtheora, of which the most broadly used are `ffmpeg2theora`[16] and `FFmpeg`[17].

The main difference between `ffmpeg2theora` and `FFmpeg` is that `ffmpeg2theora` is fixed to use the Xiph libraries for encoding, while `FFmpeg` has a choice of codec libraries, including its own Vorbis implementation and its own packaging. `ffmpeg2theora` has far fewer options to worry about. The files created by these two tools differ. Recently, their performance has been comparable. If you want to use `FFmpeg` for encoding Ogg Theora, make sure to use the `-acodec libvorbis` and not `-acodec vorbis`; otherwise your files may be suboptimal.

Because `ffmpeg2theora` is optimized toward creating Ogg Theora files and has therefore more specific options and functionality for Ogg Theora, we use it here.

You can use VLC[18] or Miro Video Converter[19] as a GUI-based encoding software for Ogg Theora. If you like to do your encoding in Windows video editing software, you should install the Ogg DSF DirectShow Filters[20], which will enable support for all Windows software that makes use of the DirectShow framework with Ogg Theora/Vorbis. If you are an Apple Mac user, you should install XiphQT[21], which are QuickTime components for the encoding and playback of Ogg Theora/Vorbis through the QuickTime framework. It will enable iMovie to encode Ogg Theora/Vorbis, and Safari and the QuickTime Player to decode Ogg Theora/Vorbis.

We should further point out that Firefox has a plug-in called FireFogg[22], which allows encoding of Ogg Theora/Vorbis directly in your Firefox browser, essentially turning it into a transcoding application. It also uses `ffmpeg2theora` for encoding.

With the following command in Listing 2–33, you should be able to create an Ogg Theora video file with Vorbis audio. It will simply retain the width, height, and framerate of your input video and the

---

[15] See http://www.theora.org/downloads/

[16] See http://v2v.cc/~j/ffmpeg2theora/

[17] See http://www.FFmpeg.org/

[18] See http://www.videolan.org/vlc/

[19] See http://www.mirovideoconverter.com/

[20] See http://www.xiph.org/dshow/

[21] See http://xiph.org/quicktime/

[22] See http://firefogg.org/

samplingrate and number of channels of your input audio in a new Ogg Theora/Vorbis encoded resource.

Listing 2–33. Encoding a video resource to the Ogg Theora/Vorbis format

```
ffmpeg2theora -o outfile.ogv infile
```

Seeing as you may want to encode all your files with the same kind of quality, you're probably interested in using a standard preset. You can find out which presets exist by calling ffmpeg2theora -p info. The following presets may be on your system:

- **preview** : Video: 320x240 if fps ~ 30, 384x288 otherwise
  Quality 6
  Audio: Max 2 channels - Quality 1

- **pro**: Video: 720x480 if fps ~ 30, 720x576 otherwise
  Quality 8
  Audio: Max 2 channels - Quality 3

- **videobin**: Video: 512x288 for 16:9 material, 448x336 for 4:3 material
  Bitrate 600kbs
  Audio: Max 2 channels - Quality 3

- **padma**: Video: 640x360 for 16:9 material, 640x480 for 4:3 material
  Quality 6
  Audio: Max 2 channels - Quality 3

- **padma-stream:** Video: 128x72 for 16:9 material, 128x96 for 4:3 material
  Audio: mono quality -1

Listing 2–34 shows use of the preset "pro" with some additional restrictions.

Listing 2–34. Adapting the bitrate for audio and video for ffmpeg2theora

```
ffmpeg2theora -o HelloWorld.ogv -p pro \
              --videobitrate 3000 \
              --audiobitrate 192 \
              infile
```

You will notice that there are different quality settings in these presets. ffmpeg2theora has 10 for both, audio and video, with 10 being maximum and 0 being minimum quality. Default for video is 6 and for audio 1. Listing 2–34 shows use of the profile pro with some additional restrictions.

Just like MPEG H.264, Ogg Theora also offers the possibility of two-pass encoding to improve the quality of the video image. Listing 2–35 shows how to run ffmpeg2theora with two-pass.

Listing 2–35. Using two-pass encoding for Ogg Theora

```
ffmpeg2theora -o HelloWorld.ogv -p pro \
        --two-pass infile
```

ffmpeg2theora also has many more options, in particular subtitles, metadata, an index to improve seekability on the Ogg Theora file, and even options to improve the video quality with some built-in filters. Note that inclusion of an index is activated by default since ffmpeg2theora version 0.27. The index will vastly improve seeking performance in browsers.

Find out about all the options by calling ffmpeg2theora -h.

2.2.3 Encoding WebM

Open-source tools for encoding WebM basically use the libvpx[23] encoding library, which is published under a BSD style license by Google.[24] There are several encoders written on top of libvpx, which includes DirectShow filters, a VP8 SDK, GStreamer plug-ins, and patches for FFmpeg.[25]

You can use VLC[26] or Miro Video Converter[27] as GUI-based encoding software for WebM. Also, the Ogg DSF DirectShow Filters now have integrated WebM support[28]. For Apple Mac users, there is no QuickTime component that supports WebM, but one is planned.

The Firefox plug-in FireFogg[29] also allows encoding of WebM directly in your Firefox browser, essentially turning it into a transcoding application. It uses FFmpeg for encoding.

With the command in Listing 2–40, you should be able to create a WebM file with VP8 video and Vorbis audio. It will simply retain the width, height, and framerate of your input video and the samplingrate and number of channels of your input audio in a new WebM-encoded resource.

Listing 2–36. Encoding a video resource to the WebM format

```
ffmpeg -i infile outfile.webm
```

Seeing as you might want to encode all your files into the same kind of quality, you're probably interested in using a standard preset. You can find them in the `.ffpreset` files, e.g. `libvpx-1080p.ffpreset`. The following presets may be useful:

- **1080p** :   Video: 1920x1080
- **1080p50/60:**   Video: 1920x1080, higher bitrate
- **720p:**   Video: 720x480
- **720p:**   Video: 720x480, higher bitrate
- **360p50/60:**   Video: 360x240

Listing 2–37 shows use of the profile "720p" with some additional restrictions.

Listing 2–37. Adapting the bitrate for audio and video for FFmpeg

```
ffmpeg -o HelloWorld.webm -p 720p \
       --videobitrate 3000 \
       --audiobitrate 192 \
       infile
```

---

[23] See http://www.webmproject.org/code/#libvpx_the_vp8_codec_sdk

[24] See http://review.webmproject.org/gitweb?p=libvpx.git;a=blob_plain;f=LICENSE;hb=HEAD

[25] See http://www.webmproject.org/tools/

[26] See http://www.videolan.org/vlc/

[27] See http://www.mirovideoconverter.com/

[28] See http://www.xiph.org/dshow/

[29] See http://firefogg.org/

2.2.4 Encoding MP3 and Ogg Vorbis

Encoding audio is far easier than encoding video. Thus, we will explain here briefly how to encode to MP3 or Ogg Vorbis.

Several programs are available for encoding an audio recording to MP3, including lame or FFmpeg (which incidentally uses the same encoding library as lame: libmp3lame). Most audio-editing software is able to encode mp3.

In Listing 2–38 we use FFmpeg for our encoding example, since it is the most commonly used audio/video encoder.

Listing 2–38. Encoding audio to MP3 using FFmpeg

```
ffmpeg -i audio -acodec libmp3lame -aq 0 audio.mp3
```

The aq parameter in Listing 2–38 signifies the audio quality and goes from 0 to 255 with 0 being the best quality. There are further parameters available to change, among others, bitrate, number of channels, volume, and sampling rate.

For encoding an audio recording to Ogg Vorbis, there are again a large number of programs available, such as oggenc or FFmpeg.

In Listing 2–39 we use FFmpeg for our encoding example, since it is the most commonly used audio/video encoder.

Listing 2–39. Encoding audio to Ogg Vorbis using FFmpeg

```
ffmpeg -i audio -f ogg -acodec libvorbis -ab 192k audio.ogg
```

The ab parameter in Listing 2–43 signifies the target audio bitrate. There are further parameters available to change, among others, the number of channels, volume, and sampling rate.

You can also use oggenc to encode to Ogg Vorbis, which is slightly easier to use and has some specific Ogg Vorbis functionality. Listing 2–40 shows a simple example with a target bitrate of 192k.

Listing 2–40. Encoding audio to Ogg Vorbis using oggenc

```
oggenc audio -b 192 -o audio.ogg
```

The oggenc command also offers multiple extra parameters, such as the inclusion of skeleton - which will create an index to improve seeking functionality on the file - a quality parameter -q that goes from -1 to 10, with 10 being the best quality, parameters to change channels, volume and sampling rate, and a means to include name-value pairs of metadata.

2.3 Publishing

In Section 2.1 we introduced how to write web pages with HTML5 video elements. In Section 2.2 we learned how to encode the media files so they are supported by HTML5 video capable browsers. Now we close the circle by looking at how to actually publish the videos and their web pages. After this, we have all the tools to make HTML5 web pages with video and audio available.

2.3.1 Web Server and HTTP Progressive Download

For publishing web pages, one will ordinarily use a web server, of course. A web server is a piece of software that can speak HTTP, the HyperText Transfer Protocol, and deliver web content through computer networks. Several open-source Web servers exist, the most popular being Apache[30].

Serving HTML5 video over HTTP is the standard way in which the HTML5 video element currently is being supported by web browsers. When making a choice between which server software to choose, make sure it supports HTTP 1.1 Byte Range requests. Most common web servers will support it, but occasionally you can still find one that doesn't or doesn't work properly.

Support of HTTP Byte Range requests is important because it is the standard way in which browsers receive HTML5 media resources from web servers. When using progressive download, the browser first retrieves the initial byte ranges of a media resource, which tells it what kind of media resource it is and gives it enough information to set up the audio and video decoding pipelines. This enables it to play back audio and video content.

Audio and video data in a media resource are typically provided in a multiplexed manner, i.e. a bit of video, then the related bit of audio, then the next bit of video etc. Thus, if the browser asks for a byte range on the resource, it will retrieve both, the audio and video data that belongs to the same time range together. It can thus progressively download byte ranges and at the same time decode and start playing back the audio-visual content already received.

The best result is achieved when the network is fast enough to feed the decoding pipeline quicker than the decoder and graphics engine can play back the video in real time. This will give a smooth playback impression to users without making them wait until the whole video is downloaded.

Progressive download and parallel playback by themselves pose a big restriction on users: they cannot seek to any offset unless the download has reached those bytes. Key to the usability of progressive download is therefore the ability to seek into not-yet downloaded sections by asking the web server to stop downloading and start providing those future data chunks. This is implemented in browsers using the HTTP 1.1 Byte Range request mechanism.

In practice the setup/connection time for each HTTP byte range request means that browsers try to make as few byte range requests as possible. After setting up the metadata, the browser will typically make only one request for the entire media resource and will start playing it back as the data arrives. For a very long file, when download is very far ahead of the current playback position and the user stopped watching the video, downloading may be interrupted by the browser. A condition that allows the browser to pause download is that the web server supports byte range requests so the browser may resume downloading when the playback position is again getting closer to the buffered position. This will save bandwidth use particularly on videos that are longer than a few minutes.

All the received data will be cached in the browser. When the user seeks and the seek time is not yet buffered, the browser will stop the download and request a byte range that starts at the given time offset the user seeked to.

This is technical background to something the user will never really notice. When setting up your web server to host HTML5 audio and video, you don't have to do anything special. For Firefox and Opera, which perform limited content sniffing, you need to make sure that the media resources are served with the correct MIME type. For an Apache web server this means adding the following media types to your mime.types setup file:

audio/ogg	ogg oga
audio/webm	webm
video/ogg	ogv
video/webm	webm

---

[30] See http://httpd.apache.org/

To publish HTML audio and video, you only need to copy the files into a directory structure on your web server and make sure that the resource location and hyperlinks are all correct and work. Listing 2–41 shows an example layout of a directory structure on a web server (/var/www is the typical root directory of a web site hosted with Apache on a Linux server).

Listing 2–41. An example web server directory structure for video and audio publishing

```
/var/www/ - the Web server root directory, exposed e.g. as http://www.example.net/

/var/www/page.html - the Web page with a video element

/var/www/video/video.webm and
/var/www/video/video.mp4 - the video in two formats

/var/www/thumbs/video.png - the video's thumbnail

/var/www/audio/audio.ogg and
/var/www/audio/audio.mp3 - the compressed audio in two formats
```

With Listing 2–41, the web page at http://www.example.net/page.html would include a video <source> with video/video.webm and video/video.mp4.

2.3.2 Streaming Using RTP/RTSP

Another traditional means of delivering audio and video over the Internet is streaming. Streaming is a means where byte ranges exchanged between the streaming server and the streaming client are volatile, i.e. they are not stored or cached on the client.

The original reason for development of streaming services was live video transmission, such as a live lecture. In this situation, streaming clients can join and leave a live stream at any time. Seeking is not possible on live streams.

More recently, streaming servers are also used for on-demand delivery of video files. RTSP, the Real-Time Streaming Protocol, supports a Range header for seeking in this situation. The expectation with such a delivery method is that it will be more difficult for a user to copy the content — in particular if an additional encryption method is used over the network such that grabbing packets off the network card won't help. In reality, it is impossible to fully protect against copying, since ultimately a screen recorder can be used to grab a decoded video.

Streaming is mentioned here because there seems to be a need for browsers to also support the Real-Time Streaming Protocol RTSP[31]: almost all web browsers have a user request for RTSP support: WebKit/Safari[32], Google Chrome[33], Opera[34], and Firefox[35].

It is unclear as yet whether browsers will develop support for RTSP. Both needs — live streaming and encrypted transmission — can also be satisfied with progressive download from a web server using HTTP or HTTPS. Encrypted transmission and anti-piracy measures may require some additional

---

[31] See http://www.ietf.org/rfc/rfc2326.txt

[32] See https://bugs.webkit.org/show_bug.cgi?id=26416

[33] See http://code.google.com/p/chromium/issues/detail?id=25573

[34] See http://my.opera.com/community/forums/topic.dml?id=455521

[35] See https://bugzilla.mozilla.org/show_bug.cgi?id=506834

functionality installed both at the server and at the client, but you can certainly do some authentication when you have control over the server and provide the adequate JavaScript on your Web page, or time-limit the validity of your video URLs.

There are many issues with RTSP that may stop browser vendors from implementing support for it.

One, of course, is the need to implement support for an additional protocol in the browser — a protocol that doesn't come easily to the Web. This is particularly an issue since available RTSP server software isn't always compliant with the standarized RTSP features. Available open-source RTSP servers are VLC, Flumotion, and Apple's QuickTime Streaming Server. Clients that can consume such streams are VLC and MPlayer.

One of the main disadvantages of RTSP is that it requires a special streaming server to deliver the streams — a web server won't do. This special streaming server also connects on special network ports, namely port 554 or 8554. The problem with such ports is that a firewall — unless configured to explicitly open these ports — will block traffic from them, making it impossible to create a universal video transmission infrastructure around RTSP. RTSP administrators have found ways around firewalls, which mostly consist of tunneling through the HTTP port 80, but that is only a poor fix to the situation.

RTSP is flexible with its underlying network protocol. When RTSP is run over the connection-free RTP/UDP (Real-Time Protocol/User Datagram Protocol) combination and the network gets congested, RTSP will lose data and the stream will be distorted or broken. This is similar to a drop-out of a phone connection. This behavior is expected in live interactive video transmissions, where synchronization to the real-world time is required, but it is not desirable for on-demand delivery. For this reason, RTSP can also be run over TCP. Then, the difference to delivering a video over HTTP, which also uses TCP, is minimal.

In summary, RTSP has been created for video communications analogous to voice-over-IP applications. It is not the best protocol for on-demand streaming, where HTTP with byte range requests achieves the same result. Extra functionality that RTSP supports is also increasingly available with HTTP progressive download approaches. Only the live communication case is one that may require a RTP/RTSP implementation over UDP to work with the required low latency.

Note that Adobe's proprietary RTMP protocol is very similar to RTSP and, in fact, shares most of the problems of RTSP. It is supported by Adobe's proprietary Flash Media Server or through the open-source Red5 server software. Adobe just recently opened the specifications for RTMP[36].

2.3.3 Extending HTTP Streaming

RTSP-like streaming approaches that require special server and client software have increasingly failed in an HTTP dominated world. For example, YouTube is entirely provided through HTTP progressive download and does not use RTMP. In this situation, vendors have embraced HTTP progressive download and developed their own feature extensions to improve HTTP-based streaming.

The aim here is to continue using normal web servers without any software extensions and to push the complexity of streaming into the client software. This avoids all the issues of creating new protocols, fighting firewalls, and installing new software on servers. It enables software vendors to put all the functionality into the user's software. This is great because they can roll out new functionality through user software updates and without having to update server software. In a world where most users are always online and software increasingly auto-updates over the Internet, this is a much easier approach to upgrading than the server- and protocol-centric approaches of the past.

One particular feature has caused the major vendors to actually create a new set of technologies: **adaptive HTTP streaming**. Adaptive HTTP streaming is a process that adjusts the quality of a video delivered over HTTP, based on changing network and user software conditions to ensure the best possible viewer experience. This is particularly targeted at varying bandwidth availabilities and aims at

---

[36] See http://www.adobe.com/devnet/rtmp/

removing the buffering interruptions users on low-bandwidth networks can experience when watching video over HTTP progressive download.

The different technologies in the market are:

- Apple HTTP Live Streaming.[37]

- Microsoft Smooth Streaming.[38]

- Adobe HTTP Dynamic Streaming.[39]

More recently, the MPEG group is working on a standard approach to adaptive HTTP streaming in the DASH[40] (Dynamic Adaptive Streaming for HTTP) specification. Independently of that, there are also designs being discussed for open codecs in general at the WHATWG.[41] So development of a generic open solution can be expected over the next year or so. For now, the three vendor solutions above are the main technologies in the market.

Apple supports HTTP Live Streaming in Safari and QuickTime on the desktop, iPhone, iPod, and iPad. Apple's approach is openly specified in an IETF RFC.[42] Microsoft Silverlight actually understands both, Microsoft Smooth Streaming and Apple HTTP Live Streaming. Adobe launched HTTP Dynamic Streaming with FlashPlayer 10.1 and is supporting it through Adobe Flash Media Server.

All of these basically work in the same way: several versions of the media resource encoded at different bitrates and possibly different resolutions are made available on the web server. The client software is informed about these resources and their features through a manifest file. The client will continuously analyze the situation in the media player from a bandwidth and CPU perspective and will select from the manifest file which next partial resource bit to request during its progressive download.

Listing 2–42 shows an example of how you can use Apple's live streaming approach with an m3u8 manifest file in Safari. It is the only browser that currently has native support for adaptive HTTP streaming.

Listing 2–42. An HTML5 video element with an Apple HTTP live streaming manifest file

```
<video src="HelloWorld.m3u8" />
</video>
```

In Listing 2–43 we show how to encode the files for Listing 2–42.[43] You need to use a modern build of FFmpeg and a segmenter that will split the created MPEG file into multiple transport stream segments. You can use, for example, the open source software called *"segmenter"* from Carson McDonald.[44]

---

[37] See
http://developer.apple.com/iphone/library/documentation/NetworkingInternet/Conceptual/StreamingMediaGuide/Introduction/Introduction.html

[38] See http://www.iis.net/download/SmoothStreaming

[39] See http://www.adobe.com/devnet/flashmediaserver/articles/dynstream_on_demand.html

[40] See http://multimediacommunication.blogspot.com/2010/08/mpeg-news-report-from-93rd-meeting.html

[41] See http://wiki.whatwg.org/wiki/Adaptive_Streaming

[42] See http://tools.ietf.org/html/draft-pantos-http-live-streaming-04

[43] See http://stackoverflow.com/questions/1093667/http-live-streaming-ffmpeg-ffserver-and-iphone-os-3

[44] See http://www.ioncannon.net/programming/452/iphone-http-streaming-with-ffmpeg-and-an-open-source-segmenter/comment-page-1/

Listing 2–43. Encoding multiple versions of the resource for Apple HTTP live streaming

```
ffmpeg -i input \
        -acodec libmp3lame -ac 1 \
        -vcodec libx264 -s 320x240 \
        -level 30 -f mpegts - | \
segmenter - 10 fileSequence HelloWorld.m3u8 \
    http://example.com/path/medium/
```

In Listing 2–44 we then show the content of the manifest file used in Listing 2–42 and three different bandwidth-scaled versions with their MPEG transport stream fragments. These m3u8 files will sit on the server together with the transport stream files in the right directories.

Listing 2–44. The respective m3u8 files for Listing 2–42

```
HelloWorld.m3u8:
    #EXTM3U
    #EXT-X-STREAM-INF:PROGRAM-ID=1, BANDWIDTH=860000
    high/HelloWorld.m3u8
    #EXT-X-STREAM-INF:PROGRAM-ID=1, BANDWIDTH=512000
    medium/HelloWorld.m3u8
    #EXT-X-STREAM-INF:PROGRAM-ID=1, BANDWIDTH=160000
    low/HelloWorld.m3u8

high/HelloWorld.m3u8; medium/HelloWorld.m3u8; low/HelloWorld.m3u8:
    #EXTM3U
    #EXT-X-TARGETDURATION:10
    #EXT-X-MEDIA-SEQUENCE:0
    #EXTINF:10,
    fileSequence0.ts
    #EXTINF:10,
    fileSequence1.ts
    #EXTINF:10,
    fileSequence2.ts
    #EXTINF:10,
    fileSequence3.ts
    #EXTINF:1,
    fileSequence4.ts
    #EXT-X-ENDLIST
```

Apple's and Adobe's approach include an encryption method, but are otherwise feature-identical to Microsoft's approach. Apple uses extended m3u playlist files[45], Microsoft creates SMIL-based manifest files[46], and Adobe creates its own extension to the Flash Media Manifest file F4M[47].

It will be interesting to see a solution that all browsers are able to adopt and that works uniformly across the different media formats.

---

[45] See
http://developer.apple.com/mac/library/documentation/NetworkingInternet/Conceptual/StreamingMediaGuide/HTTPStreamingAr chitecture/HTTPStreamingArchitecture.html

[46] See http://msdn.microsoft.com/en-us/library/ee230810(VS.90).aspx

[47] See http://opensource.adobe.com/wiki/display/osmf/Flash+Media+Manifest+File+Format+Specification

2.4 Default User Interface

In this section we take a quick look at the user interfaces that browsers have implemented for audio and video elements. These are still highly in flux, as YouTube launches a new player interface roughly every six months, it can likely be expected that web browsers will make improvements and add features to their audio and video players for a while to come.

The default user interface for HTML5 audio and video elements is separated into two different types: the visible controls and the controls hidden in the context menu, usually reached through a right-click on the element.

2.4.1 Visible controls

We have already come across the visible controls of the main browsers. Here, we look at them in more detail to see what is exposed by all of them and what special functionalities individual browsers may provide. Controls are mostly identical between audio and video elements.

Firefox's controls:

Figure 2–14 shows Firefox's controls with an exposed volume slider.

Figure 2–14. *The controls on the video and audio elements in Firefox*

Firefox's controls provide the following functionality:

- play/pause toggle.

- timeline with direct jump to time offset (seeking).

- timeline displays playback position and buffer progress.

- playback time display.

- volume slider.

- volume on/off button.

Firefox has made these controls accessible and easily usable through keyboard control. Firefox's controls provide the following keyboard access:

- tab: tab onto and off video element.

- space bar: toggles between play and pause.

- left/right arrow: winds video forward/back by 15 seconds.

- CTRL+left/right arrow: winds video forward/back by 1/10 of the media duration.

- HOME+left/right arrow: jumps to beginning/end of video.

- up/down arrow: when focused on the volume button, increases/decreases volume.

Safari's controls:

Figure 2–15 shows Safari's video controls.

Figure 2–15. The controls on the video elements in Safari

Safari's controls provide the following functionality:

- 30 second jump back button.
- play/pause toggle.
- timeline with direct jump to time offset (seeking).
- timeline displays playback position and buffer progress.
- playback count-down time display.
- fullscreen button.

If you flip back to Figure 2–9, you will see that the audio controls of Safari differ slightly. Instead of the full-screen button at the end of the video controls, there is a volume on/off button. The full-screen display of Safari is given in Figure 2–16. The controls have the same functionality as the normal video controls, except they also contain a volume slider and a mute toggle button.

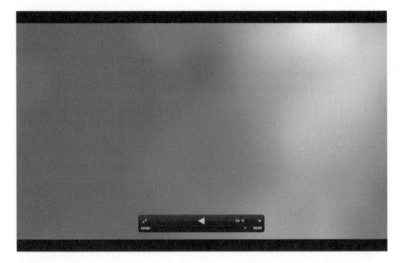

Figure 2–16. The full-screen display of the HelloWorld video in Safari

Safari doesn't yet seem to provide keyboard controls for the media elements.

Google Chrome's controls:

Figure 2–17 shows Google Chrome's controls.

Figure 2–17. *The controls on the video and audio elements in Google Chrome*

Google Chrome's controls provide the following functionality:

- play/pause toggle.

- timeline with direct jump to time offset (seeking).

- timeline displays playback position and buffer progress.

- playback time display.

- volume slider.

- volume on/off button.

You may have noticed that the volume button is grayed out in Figure 2–15. That's because the video element has no audio track. It seems to be the only browser that pays attention to this.

Google Chrome doesn't yet seem to provide keyboard controls for the media elements.

Opera's controls:

Figure 2–18 shows Operas controls with an exposed volume slider.

Figure 2–18. *The controls on the video and audio elements in Opera*

Opera's controls provide the following functionality:

- play/pause toggle.

- timeline with direct jump to time offset (seeking).

- timeline displays playback position and buffer progress.

- playback time and duration display.

- volume slider.

- volume on/off button.

Opera also makes these controls accessible and easily usable through keyboard control. Opera's controls provide the following keyboard access:

43

- tab: tab from play button to transport bar to volume control.

- space bar: toggles between play and pause.

- up/down arrow: when focused on the volume button, increases/decreases volume.

IE's controls:

Figure 2–19 shows IE9's controls.

Figure 2–19. *The controls on the video and audio elements in IE*

IE's controls provide the following functionality:

- play/pause toggle.

- timeline with direct jump to time offset (seeking).

- timeline displays playback position and buffer progress.

- playback time and duration display.

- volume slider.

- volume on/off button.

IE also makes some of these controls accessible and usable through keyboard control. IE's controls provide the following keyboard access:

- tab: tab onto and away from the video.

- space bar: toggles between play and pause.

- up/down arrow: increases/decreases volume.

- left/right arrow: winds video to the beginning/end.

When the displayed video size is rather small — in our example, the video was scaled to 372px by 209px — IE changes controls to a single pause/play toggle button, see Figure 2–20.

Figure 2–20. *The IE controls on a small video element in IE*

Note that the IE controls are semi-transparent. Firefox's controls are also semi-transparent. All the other browsers have solid colored controls.

2.4.2 Context Menus

Context menus provide users with short cuts to common operations. Context menus are visible when the user right-clicks on the video or audio element. Most functionality is the same for audio and video, except for full screen where supported.

Firefox's context menu:

Firefox's context menu functionality:

- toggle play/pause
- toggle mute/unmute
- toggle show/hide controls
- go full screen (for video only)
- view video (similar to view image)
- copy video location
- save video locally under a name
- send video via email

Figure 2–21. The context menu on the video element in Firefox

The full-screen display of Firefox can be activated only through the context menu. Figure 2–22 shows what it looks like.

Figure 2–22. Full-screen video in Firefox

Safari's context menu:

Safari's context menu functionality:

- no media-specific content menu yet

Figure 2–23. The context menu on the video element in Safari

Google Chrome's context menu:

Google Chrome's context menu functionality:

- toggle play/pause

- toggle mute/unmute (when sound is available)

- toggle looping on/off

- toggle show/hide controls

- save video locally under a name

- copy video location

- open video in new tab

Figure 2–24. The context menu on the video element in Google Chrome

Opera's context menu:

Opera's context menu functionality:

- toggle play/pause

- toggle mute/unmute

- toggle show/hide controls

- copy video location

- save video locally under a name

Figure 2–25. The context menu on the video element in Opera

IE's context menu:

IE's context menu functionality:

- save video locally under a name
- copy video location

Figure 2–26. The context menu on the video element in IE

2.4.3 Controls Summary

At the end of this subsection, for reference purposes, we list all the default controls functionalities. This should help to quickly identify any missing functionality you may rely on.

Table 2–4. Overview of all the default controls in Web browsers

Function	Firefox			Safari			Chrome			Opera			IE		
	Controls	Keyboard	Context Menu	Controls	Keyboard	Context Menu	Controls	Keyboard	Context Menu	Controls	Keyboard	Context Menu	Controls	Keyboard	Context Menu
play/pause toggle	✓	✓	✓	✓			✓		✓	✓	✓	✓	✓	✓	
timeline with direct jump to time offset (seeking)	✓			✓			✓			✓			✓		
timeline displays playback position and buffer progress	✓			✓			✓			✓			✓		
playback time display	✓			✓			✓			✓			✓		
volume slider	✓	✓					✓			✓	✓		✓	✓	
volume on/off	✓		✓	✓			✓		✓	✓		✓	✓		
loop									✓						
15 sec forward/rewind		✓													
1/10 duration forward/rewind		✓													

Function	Firefox			Safari			Chrome			Opera			IE		
	Controls	Keyboard	Context Menu	Controls	Keyboard	Context Menu	Controls	Keyboard	Context Menu	Controls	Keyboard	Context Menu	Controls	Keyboard	Context Menu
jump to beginning/end		✓									✓			✓	
30 sec rewind				✓											
show/hide controls			✓						✓			✓			✓
go full screen			✓										✓		
View video			✓						✓						
copy video location			✓						✓			✓			✓
Save video as			✓						✓			✓			✓
send video			✓												

2.5 Summary

In this chapter we introduced HTML5 as well as `<video>` and `<audio>` elements together with all their attributes. You should now be able to use audio and video in your HTML5 web pages. We have identified where browsers show the same behavior and where they differ, so you can take appropriate counter-measures.

We have further given you a brief view of some of the open-source tools available to encode the required video and audio formats, and to publish them to a web server. We have explained the different networking protocols in use for HTML5 media, in particular HTTP and adaptive HTTP streaming.

We finished the chapter with an overview of the user interface of `<audio>` and `<video>` and the functionalities that browsers are still working on, such as full-screen and accessibility features.

CHAPTER 3

■ ■ ■

CSS3 Styling

Styling in HTML is performed using cascading style sheets (CSS). Modern web sites have moved on from using inline styling in HTML pages to using CSS. They appreciate the separation that the W3C has introduced between the text content and its presentation, including layout, colors, and fonts. This separation enables multiple pages to share formatting, and reduces complexity and repetition in the structural content. It can also help improve accessibility by allowing a choice in styling—in particular for rendering on different devices.

We assume that you have a basic understanding of CSS. You should in particular understand that a style sheet consists of a sequence of **rules**, which specify the element(s) to which they apply through a **selector** and the styling through a block of **styling property declarations**. Selectors can identify:

- A single element.

- All elements of a specific **class.**

- Those that match a certain attribute.

- Those that are placed in a specific position within the HTML document object model (DOM), the parse tree of a HTML document.

You should also understand **pseudo-classes**, which are a conditional application of styles to an element, usually based on specific user actions or situational states, such as mousing over an element or having visited a link before. Finally, you should understand **pseudo-elements,** which are used to add special effects to situationally defined elements. These, in turn, are parts of real elements, such as the first line in a block of text.

CSS is receiving a makeover of similar proportions to HTML. The new version is called CSS level 3, or CSS3, and provides many new and improved features, including improved layout, more flexible shapes, extended media queries, and improved directions on how to render text with speech synthesis. Many of these features are also relevant to video and can make it easier for web developers to create animations and special effects around video without having to use Adobe Flash. We will look at some specific examples here.

All the usual CSS styling properties for visual elements can be applied to HTML5 video and audio elements, though they are mostly useful only for video. None of the styling and positioning features used in this chapter are specific to audio and video only; they apply equally to images and other objects. However, the choices made in this chapter present typical ways of using audio and video, or demonstrate novel ideas such as 3D cubes with videos on the faces. These ideas are meant to inspire you to come up with your own particular presentation means for audio and video.

Note that in this chapter and the rest of the book we will use CSS inline and in <style> elements. This is for illustration purposes only. It is recommended to use external style sheets in your own applications.

3.1 CSS Box Model and Video

For every visual element, CSS defines a box model consisting of the properties that define the box in which the element is laid out. These properties include:

- *height* and *width* – the actual width and height of the content box.

- *padding* – the space around the content box (takes on background of content box).

- *border* – the border around content and padding (takes on background of content box).

- *margin* – a transparent space around the border box.

CSS3 adds to these the following new relevant properties:

- *border-radius* – to have rounded corners.

- *border-image* and *border-corner-image* – to use images for borders.

- *border-shadow* – to specify a drop-shadow on the box outside the border.

- *box-sizing* – to specify what a width/height specification applies to – only the content (*content*-box) or the box, including padding and border (*border-box*).

Using *box-sizing: border-box* makes it easier to place elements with their padding and border next to each other on a percentage scaled width, since padding and border are already calculated into the element's extent.

Listing 3–1 shows an example document with a styled video element that has a border, a drop shadow, and a border-box specification.

Listing 3–1. A HTML5 example document with a styled video element

```
<!DOCTYPE html>
<html lang="en">
  <head>
    <style type="text/css">
    video {
      width:      50%;
      padding:  15px;
      margin:     0px;
      border:     5px solid black;
      border-radius:      15px;
      box-shadow:         10px 10px 5px gray;
      box-sizing:         border-box;
    }
    </style>
  </head>
  <body>
    <video controls>
      <source src="HelloWorld.mp4" type="video/mp4">
      <source src="HelloWorld.webm" type="video/webm">
      <source src="HelloWorld.ogv" type="video/ogg">
    </video>
  </body>
</html>
```

Note that the *border-radius, box-shadow,* and *box-sizing* CSS3 properties[1] used to require a -moz and -webkit prefix in Firefox and WebKit-based browsers (i.e. Safari and Chrome). Now, all browsers seem to have implemented support for the actual property names under discussion at the W3C.

Figure 3–1 shows what the example looks like in Firefox, Safari, Opera, Chrome and IE.

Figure 3–1. *A <video> with basic styling in Firefox, Safari (top row), Opera, Chrome (middle row) and IE (bottom)*

---

[1] See http://www.w3.org/TR/2002/WD-css3–border-20021107/

3.2 CSS Positioning and Video

A CSS box is normally rendered as an inline element, which places it visually in the normal flow of the presented elements.

There are several means to change how the box is placed in the flow of presented elements. The following properties influence an element's box type and thus its display position:

- *display* – whether to display it or not.

- *float* – whether to float it or not.

- *position* – explicitly position it.

There are four positioning modes in CSS: *normal, relative, float,* and *absolute.* And there are three basic box types: *inline, block,* and *none.*

3.2.1 Inline Box Type

Audio and video elements are by default of type *inline* and follow the *normal* positioning mode. *Normal* positioning mode can be turned on by setting the *display* property to *static.* In *normal* positioning mode, *block* boxes flow vertically starting at the top of their containing block with each placed directly below the preceding one. *Inline* boxes flow horizontally from left to right also within the boundaries of their containing block.

Listing 3–2 shows an example of a video element inside other *inline* content in a <div> block box.

Listing 3–2. An example document with video inside surrounding inline content

```
<!DOCTYPE html>
<html lang="en">
  <head>
    <style type="text/css">
    video {
      width:      50%;
      border:     5px solid black;
    }
    </style>
  </head>
  <body>
    <div>A sentence before the video element.
      <video controls>
        <source src="HelloWorld.mp4"  type="video/mp4">
        <source src="HelloWorld.webm" type="video/webm">
        <source src="HelloWorld.ogv"  type="video/ogg">
      </video>
      A sentence after the video element.
    </div>
  </body>
</html>
```

Figure 3–2 shows what the example looks like in Firefox, Safari, Opera, Chrome, and IE.

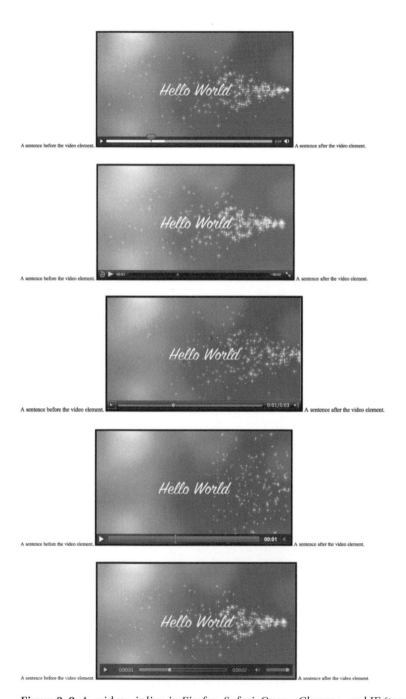

Figure 3–2. A <video> inline in Firefox, Safari, Opera, Chrome, and IE (top to bottom)

3.2.2 None Box Type

If an audio or video element is turned invisible through setting the *visibility* property to *hidden*, its box will still take up the space in the *normal* presentation flow. See Figure 3–3. Only by turning the box type to *none* through setting the *display* property to *none* will the space that its box takes up be freed.

Listing 3–3. An example style for a hidden video element.

```
<style type="text/css">
  video {
    width:     50%;
    visibility: hidden;
  }
</style>
<div>A sentence before the video element.
<video controls>
  <source src="HelloWorld.mp4"  type="video/mp4">
  <source src="HelloWorld.webm" type="video/webm">
  <source src="HelloWorld.ogv"  type="video/ogg">
</video>
A sentence after the video element.</div>
```

Figure 3–3 shows as an example the display in Firefox and Safari.

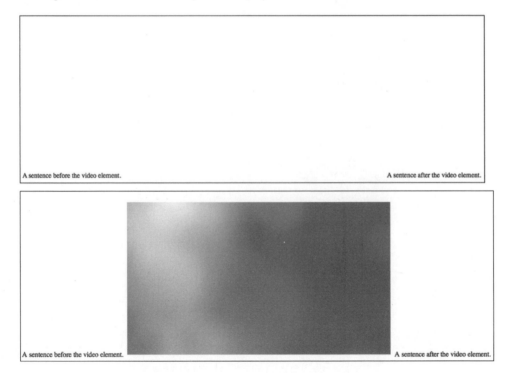

Figure 3–3. A <video> inline in Firefox (top) and Safari (bottom) with visibility set to hidden

Firefox, Opera, and IE show the same behavior with displaying an empty video frame. Safari and Chrome, however, display the first frame of the video. This is a bug and being worked on.

3.2.3 Block Box Type

Setting audio or video to a *block* type box is possible and sets a media element in its own paragraph apart from surrounding *inline* elements. See Figure 3–4.

Listing 3–4. An example style for an inline video element.

```
<style type="text/css">
video {
  width:     50%;
  border:    5px solid black;
  display: block;
}
</style>
<div>A sentence before the video element.
  <video controls>
    <source src="HelloWorld.mp4"  type="video/mp4">
    <source src="HelloWorld.webm" type="video/webm">
    <source src="HelloWorld.ogv"  type="video/ogg">
  </video>
  A sentence after the video element.
</div>
```

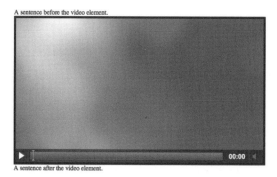

Figure 3–4. A <video> in Chrome with display set to block in surrounding inline text

All browsers support this functionality and produce the same result. Figure 3–4 shows Chrome as an example.

3.2.4 Relative Positioning Mode

The *relative* positioning mode is activated by setting the *position* property to *relative*. It allows you to change the position of a box relative to where it would be displayed in *normal* positioning mode. You can, for example, move the box up, down, left, or right by using the *top, bottom, left,* or *right* properties to offset the position from those edges. Such relative positioning may cause the box to overlap other boxes. Which box stays in the foreground is specified through the *z-index* property, which defines the stacking order. Such relative positioning allows stacking of video elements on top of each other or of other elements.

Listing 3–5. An example document with relative positioned video elements

```
<style type="text/css">
  video {
    width:     250px;
    position: relative;
  }
  video#vid2 {
    left: 40px; top: 10px;
  }
</style>
<video controls>
  <source src="video1.mp4"   type="video/mp4">
  <source src="video1.webm"  type="video/webm">
  <source src="video1.ogv"   type="video/ogg">
</video>
<video id="vid2" controls>
  <source src="HelloWorld.mp4"  type="video/mp4">
  <source src="HelloWorld.webm" type="video/webm">
  <source src="HelloWorld.ogv"  type="video/ogg">
</video>
<video controls>
  <source src="video2.mp4"   type="video/mp4">
  <source src="video2.webm"  type="video/webm">
  <source src="video2.ogv"   type="video/ogg">
</video>
```

Figure 3–5 shows what the example looks like in the browsers.

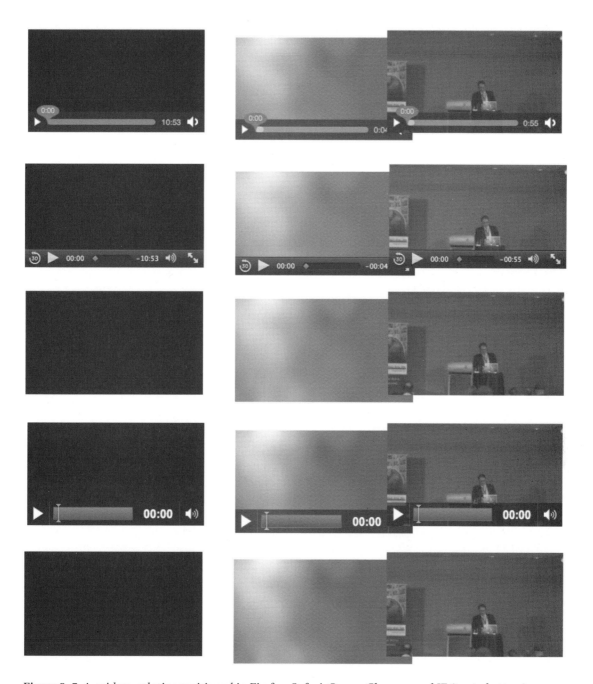

Figure 3–5. A <video> relative positioned in Firefox, Safari, Opera, Chrome, and IE (top to bottom)

Note that the appearance of controls in the browsers is not uniform. Opera and IE display them only when you mouse over the video, and they immediately disappear when you leave the video frame. Safari and Chrome display them in pause state, and they disappear during playback only when leaving the video frame. Firefox has them up when you load the video, but they disappear when you mouse in and out.

3.2.5 Float Positioning Mode

The *float* positioning mode is activated by setting the *float* property to *left* or *right*. If an element's parent is floating, a value of *inherit* will also activate *float* mode for an element, and a value of *none* will turn *float* mode off. A floating element is positioned vertically where it would be in *normal* positioning mode. But horizontally, it is positioned as far to the *left* or *right* of its containing block as possible. It will avoid other floating elements that have previously been positioned within the same block. It will also force neighboring *inline* content to flow around its edges and it can overlap block-level boxes neighboring it in the *normal* text flow (the latter can be avoided by using the *clear* property on the boxes). This allows placing a video element into a larger text flow. See Listing 3–6 and Figure 3–6 with an example in Opera.

Listing 3–6. An example document with a floating video element

```
<!DOCTYPE html>
<html lang="en">
  <head>
    <style type="text/css">
    video {
      width:      50%;
      border:     5px solid black;
      float:      right;
    }
    </style>
  </head>
  <body>
    <video controls>
      <source src="HelloWorld.mp4"  type="video/mp4">
      <source src="HelloWorld.webm" type="video/webm">
      <source src="HelloWorld.ogv"  type="video/ogg">
    </video>
    <p>A first paragraph after the video element. [etc.]</p>
    <p>A second paragraph after the video element. [etc.]</p>
  </body>
</html>
```

Lorem ipsum dolor sit amet, consectetur adipisicing elit, sed do eiusmod tempor incididunt ut labore et dolore magna aliqua. Ut enim ad minim veniam, quis nostrud exercitation ullamco laboris nisi ut aliquip ex ea commodo consequat. Duis aute irure dolor in reprehenderit in voluptate velit esse cillum dolore eu fugiat nulla pariatur. Excepteur sint occaecat cupidatat non proident, sunt in culpa qui officia deserunt mollit anim id est laborum.

Sed ut perspiciatis unde omnis iste natus error sit voluptatem accusantium doloremque laudantium, totam rem aperiam, eaque ipsa quae ab illo inventore veritatis et quasi architecto beatae vitae dicta sunt explicabo. Nemo enim ipsam voluptatem quia voluptas sit aspernatur aut odit aut fugit, sed quia consequuntur magni dolores eos qui ratione voluptatem sequi nesciunt. Neque porro quisquam est, qui dolorem ipsum quia dolor sit amet, consectetur, adipisci velit, sed quia non numquam eius modi tempora incidunt ut labore et dolore magnam aliquam quaerat voluptatem. Ut enim ad minima veniam, quis nostrum exercitationem ullam corporis suscipit laboriosam, nisi ut aliquid ex ea commodi consequatur? Quis autem vel eum iure reprehenderit qui in ea voluptate velit esse quam nihil molestiae consequatur, vel illum qui dolorem eum fugiat quo voluptas nulla pariatur?

At vero eos et accusamus et iusto odio dignissimos ducimus qui blanditiis praesentium voluptatum deleniti atque corrupti quos dolores et quas molestias excepturi sint occaecati cupiditate non provident, similique sunt in culpa qui officia deserunt mollitia animi, id est laborum et dolorum fuga. Et harum quidem rerum facilis est et expedita distinctio. Nam libero tempore, cum soluta nobis est eligendi optio cumque nihil impedit quo minus id quod maxime placeat facere possimus, omnis voluptas assumenda est, omnis dolor repellendus. Temporibus autem quibusdam et aut officiis debitis aut rerum necessitatibus saepe eveniet ut et voluptates repudiandae sint et molestiae non recusandae. Itaque earum rerum hic tenetur a sapiente delectus, ut aut reiciendis voluptatibus maiores alias consequatur aut perferendis doloribus asperiores repellat

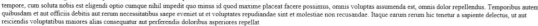

Figure 3–6. A <video> in IE floating over two paragraphs

Figure 3–6 shows the result of the example in IE. All browsers behave in the same way.

3.2.6 Absolute Positioning Mode

The *absolute* positioning mode is activated by setting the *position* property to *absolute* or *fixed*. Such boxes are placed outside the normal flow order and are positioned using the *left, top, right,* or *bottom* properties to offset the position from its containing block. An absolutely positioned element's containing block is its nearest ancestor that has a position of *absolute, relative,* or *fixed,* or ultimately the browser window.

When using the *fixed* property, the element is absolutely positioned in reference to the browser window and fixed there for scrolling purposes. Overlapping elements again may be stacked with the *z-index* property.

Absolute positioning allows positioning elements, including audio and video elements, at any desired location. See Listing 3–7 for an example, with Figure 3–7 providing a screenshot from Safari.

Listing 3–7. An example document with absolutely positioned video elements

```
<style type="text/css">
video {
  width:     250px; height:    140px;
  position: absolute;
}
video#vid1 { left: 340px; top: 220px; }
video#vid2 { left: 440px; top: 110px; }
video#vid3 { left: 120px; top: 160px; }
</style>
<video id="vid1" controls>
  <source src="video1.mp4"  type="video/mp4">
  <source src="video1.webm" type="video/webm">
  <source src="video1.ogv"  type="video/ogg">
</video>
<video id="vid2" controls>
  <source src="HelloWorld.mp4" type="video/mp4">
```

```
    <source src="HelloWorld.webm" type="video/webm">
    <source src="HelloWorld.ogv"  type="video/ogg">
</video>
<video id="vid3" controls>
  <source src="video2.mp4"   type="video/mp4">
  <source src="video2.webm"  type="video/webm">
  <source src="video2.ogv"   type="video/ogg">
</video>
```

Figure 3–7 shows the example in Safari. All browsers behave the same.

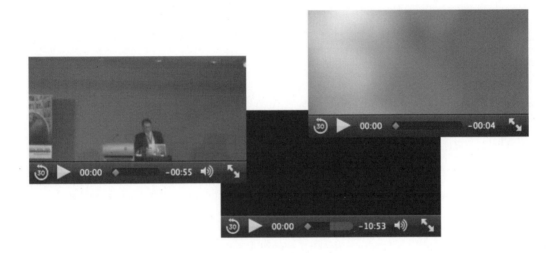

Figure 3–7. *Three absolutely positioned <video> elements in Safari.*

3.2.7 Video Scaling and Alignment Within Box

In addition to the common box and positioning properties, video has a few further quirks to deal with (similar to img). When a video is displayed within a box, but the box does not have the same aspect ratio as the video, by default letter- or pillar-boxing happens, as explained in Chapter 2.1.1. This also means that the video is placed in the center of the box. What if you need different functionality?

You can use the following properties:

- *object-position*[2]– defines the alignment of the video within the box.

- *object-fit*[3]– specifies how the contents of the video should be scaled relative to the box.

---

[2] See http://dev.w3.org/csswg/css3–images/#object-position

[3] See http://dev.w3.org/csswg/css3–images/#object-fit

Object-position is provided as a tuple of horizontal position and vertical position. As horizontal position you can use a percentage, a pixel length, or the values "left," "center," or "right." As vertical position you can use a percentage, a pixel length, or the values "top," "center," or "bottom." The default is "50% 50%." Percentage and pixel values are counted from the top left corner.

Object-fit can take on one of the values "fill," "contain," or "cover." The value "fill" will stretch the video to fill the box; "contain" will just scale the width and height down to fit into the box with borders—it's the default value. The value "cover" will scale the width and height such that at least one size fits and the other is chopped off for being too big. The complete box will be covered.

Listing 3–8 shows an example and Figure 3–8 the rendering in Opera, since Opera is the only browser that currently supports these elements. Note that Opera requires the "-o-" prefix for the property to work.

Listing 3–8. *An example document with object-scaled video*

```
<style type="text/css">
video {
  -o-object-position: left bottom;
  border:  1px solid black;
}
</style>
<video width="320" height="90">
  <source src="HelloWorld.mp4">
  <source src="HelloWorld.webm">
  <source src="HelloWorld.ogv">
</video>
<video width="160" height="180">
  <source src="HelloWorld.mp4">
  <source src="HelloWorld.webm">
  <source src="HelloWorld.ogv">
</video><br/>
<video width="320" height="90" style="-o-object-fit: fill;">
  <source src="HelloWorld.mp4">
  <source src="HelloWorld.webm">
  <source src="HelloWorld.ogv">
</video>
<video width="320" height="90" style="-o-object-fit: contain;">
  <source src="HelloWorld.mp4">
  <source src="HelloWorld.webm">
  <source src="HelloWorld.ogv">
</video>
<video width="320" height="90" style="-o-object-fit: cover;">
  <source src="HelloWorld.mp4">
  <source src="HelloWorld.webm">
  <source src="HelloWorld.ogv">
</video>
```

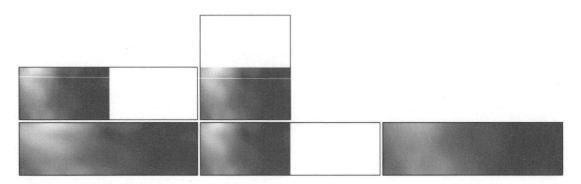

Figure 3–8. A <video> in Opera with object-position and object-fit properties

The top two elements show the video positioned inside its box with "*object-position: left bottom;.*"
The bottom row shows three elements with the different *object-fit* properties. The left-most shows "fit"; i.e. the video is scaled to fit the provided dimensions. This example scales horizontally. The middle shows "contain," the default display size. The right-most shows "cover"; i.e. the video is not scaled, but just positioned at the bottom left aligned, and only as much as fits into the given size viewport will be displayed. The video will get scaled up to cover the space if necessary.

3.3 CSS Basic Properties

A number of basic CSS functionalities are relevant to the HTML5 media elements. Here, we will take a look at:

- *background-color* – the background color behind an element.

- *opacity* – a means to make an element transparent.

- *gradient* – these are browser-created images that smoothly transition from one color to another, including the use of transparency.

- *marquee* – scrolling content.

Note that WebKit has some further, very nifty new properties, such as masks, gradients, and reflections not yet introduced into the CSS specification. We will not look at them here, but you may want to check them out if you have special needs.

The CSS *color* property is not very useful for media elements, since the foreground of a video is the video itself. However, the *background-color* property is used if the video has *padding*, since the padding space is regarded as part of the element and for filling the letter-boxing space. We will use *background-color* in an upcoming example.

A few things are surprisingly not possible with video elements, considering that video can be used for almost anything where images can be used.

First, video cannot generally be used as a background. There is a special *-moz-element* attribute for Firefox to support it, but it is not (yet) part of the CSS3 specification. Thus, the only means to overcome this is to place a large video at the bottom of the z stacking order in HTML. This means, though, that the video is not regarded as a background, but rather as an actual element on the page and cannot be part of stacking multiple backgrounds—to create background video with a gradient, for example.

Second, the creation of reflections is not possible in plain CSS. WebKit-based browsers have the *-webkit-box-reflect* property for this and Firefox has the *-moz-element* to achieve it[4], but these haven't found their way into CSS3 yet. You can create reflections in CSS only by duplicating the element and applying some transforms, but this will not work for videos, since the two video elements will not play in sync. We will therefore return to video reflections in the Canvas chapter.

3.3.1 Opacity

The property *opacity* has been around for a while, but was only standardized across browsers with CSS3[5]. *Opacity* is defined as a value between 0.0 and 1.0 where 0.0 means the element is fully transparent and 1.0 the element is fully opaque.

Listing 3–9 shows an example use of opacity where the video is placed on top of an image with 70% opacity.

Listing 3–9. An opacity example using video.

```
<style type="text/css">
video {
   width:      25%;
   position:   absolute;
   top:        100px;
   left:       30px;
   opacity:    0.70;
}
</style>
<img src="Sunrise.jpg"></img>
<video autoplay>
    <source src="HelloWorld.mp4"  type="video/mp4">
    <source src="HelloWorld.webm" type="video/webm">
    <source src="HelloWorld.ogv"  type="video/ogg">
</video>
```

Figure 3–9 shows what it looks like in Firefox. Note that the image is a CC BY 2.0 licensed image from Flickr.[6]

---

[4] See http://hacks.mozilla.org/2010/08/mozelement/

[5] See http://www.w3.org/TR/css3–color/#transparency

[6] See http://www.flickr.com/photos/snapped_up/941451312/

Figure 3–9. A transparent <video> element on top of an image in Firefox

All browsers support this functionality.

3.3.2 Gradient

Gradients are images created by morphing from one color to another over a given space from one given position to another. Because gradients are actually regarded as browser-generated images, they can be used where images are normally used in CSS, in particular for backgrounds. CSS3 specifies[7] two functions to create gradient images: *linear-gradient()* and *radial-gradient()*. Linear gradients apply the color change from one side of the image to the opposite, while radial gradients evolve from a point on the image out in a circle or ellipse. Changes between multiple colors can be introduced through stop-positions, which define what color should be reached at a given middle point.

We want to apply a gradient over a video. For this, we have to create a div with a gradient that goes from transparent to the background color of the video and overlay that div onto the video element. Listing 3–10 shows how it's done.

Listing 3–10. An example document with a gradient on a video element

```
<style type="text/css">
div#gradient {
  position: relative;
  width:    400px;
  height:   225px;
  bottom:   229px;
```

---

[7] See http://dev.w3.org/csswg/css3–images/#gradients

```
      background-image: linear-gradient(top,
                          rgba(255,255,255,0),
                          white);
      background-image: -moz-linear-gradient(top,
                            rgba(255,255,255,0),
                            white);
      background-image: -webkit-gradient(linear,
                          center top,
                          center bottom,
                          from(rgba(255,255,255,0)),
                          to(white));
    }
    video {
      width:  400px;
      height: 225px;
    }
    </style>
    <video autoplay>
      <source src="HelloWorld.mp4"  type="video/mp4">
      <source src="HelloWorld.webm" type="video/webm">
      <source src="HelloWorld.ogv"  type="video/ogg">
    </video>
    <div id="gradient"></div>
```

Note that this feature is not yet implemented in Opera and IE. Firefox and WebKit-based browsers require the browser-specific prefix but also use diverging parameters. Figure 3–10 shows how it is rendered in Safari – it looks the same in Chrome and Firefox.

Figure 3–10. A gradient on top of a <video> element in Safari

A side effect of this feature is that the video is actually hidden underneath the div, and, thus, controls are no longer accessible. You can set the *pointer-event* CSS property on the div to *none* to avoid this. The example uses *autoplay* to play back the video. If we rendered the controls instead, they would display faded. An option to reintroduce non-faded controls for the video in such a situation is to create your own controls using JavaScript. This is something we will learn in the next chapter.

3.3.3 Marquee

Most HTML browsers have supported a non-standard <marquee> element for many years. The element causes content to scroll up, down, left or right automatically at a given speed. The element, while implemented by all major browsers, has never become part of the HTML4 specification. It is also not part of HTML5.

In CSS3, a *marquee* property has been introduced[8] and is actually defined in the context of an overflowing element; i.e. an element that does not fit into its visible display area. When *marquee* is chosen as an *overflow-style*, the content is animated and moves automatically back and forth.

The following properties are relevant to *marquee:*

- *overflow-style* – can be one of *auto, marquee-line* , or *marquee-block*. For *auto*, the browser chooses the overflow style, which is typically scrollbars. *Marquee-line* chooses marquee for the horizontal overflow mechanism, and *marquee-block* for the vertical overflow mechanism.

- *marquee-style* – describes what marquee style to use as *scroll, slide,* or *alternate*. For *scroll*, the element starts just outside the display area on one side, appears and moves through until it disappears on the other end. For *slide*, the element starts just outside the display area on one side and slides in until everything that can slide in is visible. For *alternate*, the element slides in from either side alternately creating a bounce effect.

- *marquee-play-count* – specifies how many times the element is supposed to move.

- *marquee-direction* – determines the initial direction in which the element moves as a choice between *forward* and *reverse*, where forward is based on normal reading order.

- *marquee-speed* – determines the speed of the content scroll between *slow, normal,* and *fast.*

Listing 3–11 shows an example use of overflow where a sequence of three videos is placed in a div box, and the videos are on autoplay and scroll in from the right.

Listing 3–11. An example document with a video marquee

```
<style type="text/css">
video {
  height: 100px;
}
div#marquee{
  position: relative;
  width:    543px;
  height:   104px;
  padding:  4px 0px 0px 4px;
  left:     300px;
  border:   5px solid black;
  overflow: hidden;
  overflow-style: marquee-line;
  overflow-x: -webkit-marquee;
```

---

[8] See http://www.w3.org/TR/css3–marquee/

```
      marquee-speed: normal;
      -webkit-marquee-speed: normal;
      marquee-direction: reverse;
      -webkit-marquee-direction: backwards;
      marquee-style: slide;
      -webkit-marquee-style: slide;
      marquee-play-count: 1;
      -webkit-marquee-repetition: 1;
    }
  </style>
  <div id="marquee">
    <video autoplay>
      <source src="HelloWorld.mp4"  type="video/mp4">
      <source src="HelloWorld.webm" type="video/webm">
      <source src="HelloWorld.ogv"  type="video/ogg">
    </video>
    <video autoplay>
      <source src="Video1.mp4"  type="video/mp4">
      <source src="Video1.webm" type="video/webm">
      <source src="Video1.ogv"  type="video/ogg">
    </video>
    <video autoplay>
      <source src="Video2.mp4"  type="video/mp4">
      <source src="Video2.webm" type="video/webm">
      <source src="Video2.ogv"  type="video/ogg">
    </video>
  </div>
```

Note that the actual CSS3 specified marquee functionality hasn't been implemented in any browser yet. However, WebKit-based browsers (i.e. Chrome and Safari) have similar properties to the ones defined in the W3C specification, which are being used here as alternatives. These browsers provide even further functionality around marquee; however, none of that functionality has entered the CSS3 specification yet and is therefore not used in the example.

Figure 3–11 shows a sequence of three screenshots that demonstrate what happens in Chrome. This also works in Safari. The videos are moving into the div from the right until they hit the left most boundary and stop there.

Figure 3–11. *A sequence of three screenshots demonstrating the marquee CSS property in Chrome*

While experimenting with this feature, it has become apparent that there are still many issues in using it for practical purposes. Ideally one would like videos to stop moving as one hovers over – which is possible by adding the marquee-style of *none* to the :hover pseudo-class of the div. However, upon leaving the div, the scrolling jumps back to the beginning rather than continue where it stopped.

Also, it would be nice to start scrolling with videos already showing rather than having to start from blank. Further, it would be nice to have all videos muted except for the one being hovered over. Some of this can be achieved with CSS animations (see a later section in this chapter), but mostly we require a reimplementation of marquee in JavaScript to achieve the full needs of a typical video scroller.

3.4 CSS Transitions and Transforms

So far we have dealt only with rectangular regions for media elements that are simply placed somewhere in the browser window. For richer interfaces it is often a requirement to include some animation or effects to make the display more appealing to the user.

CSS3 introduces several features for this:

- **transitions** that allows movement of elements between different states.

- **2D transforms,** which allow applications of two-dimensional transformations to an element, such as rotating, scaling or skewing.

- **3D transforms**, which provide the ability to make the element appear as though it has three dimensions.

3.4.1 Transitions

Normally, when changing the value of a CSS property of an element, that value is applied immediately. With CSS transitions,[9] it is possible to animate that transition from one CSS state of a property to another.

The following properties are available:

- *transition-property* – identifies the CSS property for which to apply the transition,

- *transition-duration* – specifies over what time the transition should be applied,

- *transition-delay* – specifies if there should be a startup delay for applying the transition,

- *transition-timing-function* – defines the transition velocity; i.e. whether to speed it up/slow it down, etc.

- *transition* – combines all the properties in one statement.

There is a long list of properties that transitions can be applied to.[10] It includes borders, backgrounds, colors, element extents and positioning, opacity and visibility, stacking order in z-index, font weight, and size, shadows, and alignment.

The transition can be invoked through JavaScript, which explicitly changes the value of a property. But also CSS pseudo-classes can cause a change in state for elements, such as the :*hover, :focus*, and :*active* pseudo-classes. Finally, when a CSS element is animated through the CSS3 *animation* property, transitions can also be applied.

In Listing 3–12 we have an example of a transition applied on a video as we mouse over it.

---

[9] See http://www.w3.org/TR/css3–transitions/

[10] See http://www.w3.org/TR/css3–transitions/#animatable-properties

Listing 3–12. An example document with a video element that transitions on mouse-over

```
<style type="text/css">
video {
  height:    200px;
  padding:   10px;
  left:      50px;
  top:       50px;
  background-color: white;
}
video:hover {
  height:   250px;
  padding:  15px;
  left:     25px;
  top:      25px;
  background-color: black;
}
video, video:hover {
  position:  relative;
  border:    5px solid black;
  -moz-transition-property: all;
  -moz-transition-duration: 0.5s;
  -moz-transition-timing-function: linear;
  -webkit-transition-property: all;
  -webkit-transition-duration: 0.5s;
  -webkit-transition-timing-function: linear;
  -o-transition-property: all;
  -o-transition-duration: 0.5s;
  -o-transition-timing-function: linear;
}
</style>
<video controls>
  <source src="HelloWorld.mp4"  type="video/mp4">
  <source src="HelloWorld.webm" type="video/webm">
  <source src="HelloWorld.ogv"  type="video/ogg">
</video>
```

In Listing 3–12 we change the height, padding, left, top, and background color for the video element as we mouse over. The effect is that the video looks like it's coming towards us. We can do this even while the video plays back. Notice that as we increase the video size, we also increase the padding and the left/top positioning so it looks realistic. The background color shows in the padding area of the video and goes from white through diverse shades of gray to black. As we mouse out of the video area, everything returns to the previous state. Figure 3–12 tries to show the transition through a sequence of screenshots.

Note that again the actual CSS3 transition properties are not used by the browsers yet, but only browser-specific versions. As the CSS3 specification matures it can be expected that all browsers drop the browser-specific prefix on the properties.

Figure 3–12 *A transition on a <video> element in Chrome given through three successive screenshots*

All browsers except for IE support CSS transitions.

3.4.2 2D Transforms

The *transform* CSS property allows you to modify the coordinate space of the CSS visual formatting model. The following transform functions are available:

- *matrix* – describes a linear transformation matrix on the box,

- *rotate, rotateX, rotateY* – describes how the box should be rotated,

- *scale, scaleX, scaleY* – describes how the x and y dimensions of the box should be scaled,

- *skew, skewX, skewY* – describes how the element should be skewed around the x and y axis by an angle,

- *translate, translateX, translateY* – is equivalent to relative positioning on the x and y axis.

A simple rotation example is given in Listing 3–13 and Figure 3–13 shows the result in Firefox.

Listing 3–13. *An example document with a rotated video element*

```
<style type="text/css">
video {
  height:     200px;
  position:   absolute;
  left:        60px;
  top:        200px;
  border:     5px solid black;
  transform:         rotate(-30deg);
  -webkit-transform: rotate(-30deg);
  -o-transform:      rotate(-30deg);
  -moz-transform:    rotate(-30deg);
}
</style>
<video controls>
  <source src="HelloWorld.mp4"  type="video/mp4">
  <source src="HelloWorld.webm" type="video/webm">
  <source src="HelloWorld.ogv"  type="video/ogg">
</video>
```

Figure 3–13. A rotated <video> element in Firefox.

Note how the *transform* property is not yet uniformly adopted by all browsers, but instead it is required to use special prefixes for every browser platform. Once this feature of CSS3 stabilizes in the specification, it is expected that all browsers adopt it. Also note that IE doesn't support CSS3 *transforms* yet.

The most powerful 2D transform function is the *matrix*. It is possible to achieve all the other effects by using a linear transformation matrix. If you are a bit rusty on your math, you might want to check out the examples at the Wikipedia article on linear transforms.[11]

It is also possible to combine transforms by listing several of them in the *transform* property. You could for example define "*transform: scale(2) rotate(45deg) translate(80px);.*" Also, there is a lot more to learn about transforms in CSS, e.g. the *transform-origin* property, which defines around which point in the box the transform is to be executed. However, this is not a book about CSS, but we hope this has given you a sufficient introduction to get started.

3.4.3 3D Transforms

As an extension to the 2D transforms described in the previous section, CSS3 also standardizes a set of 3D transform functions.[12] They are used in the same way as the 2D transform functions as a value to the *transform* property.

The following additional 3D transform functions are specified:

- *translate3d, translateZ* – allows you to move the element in the z-dimension; a positive z moves it toward the viewer.

- *scale3d, scaleZ* – allows you to scale the element in the z dimension.

- *rotate3d* – allows rotation around a vector in the 3D space.

- *perspective* – allows introducing a 3D perspective into a transformation for a single element.

- *matrix3d* – a linear transformation matrix in 3D with 4x4 values in column-major order.

---

[11] See http://en.wikipedia.org/wiki/Linear_transformation#Examples_of_linear_transformation_matrices

[12] See http://www.w3.org/TR/css3–3d-transforms/

To allow placement of elements in the 3D space, the *transform-origin* property has been extended to allow three values, with the third one specifying a z offset for the transform origin.

As hierarchies of different objects in the 3D space are built, the perspectives between the different elements should be preserved and the picture not flattened. To this end, there is a *transform-style* property that allows you to choose between *flat* presentation and *preserve-3d*. The *preserve-3d* value states that the element to which it is assigned does not flatten its children into it, but instead has them live in a shared 3D space with the element.

In addition, for 3D effects, there is also the *perspective* property. The *perspective* and *perspective-origin* properties determines how elements change size as they move away from the z=0 plane on their z-offset. The default origin for the perspective effect is the center of the element's box model, but can be changed with the *perspective-origin* property.

Finally, there is the *backface-visibility* property, which allows you to prevent the back of content in 3D from shining through.

Listing 3–14 provides an example use of 3D properties. A cube is created in 3D with a video on each side.[13] The 3D space is created by setting a perspective and a perspective origin in a div. Within that div, a 300x300 pixel area is created by using width, height and a preserve-3d transform. In contrast to using 2D transforms with *skew* and *scale* for creating 3D presentations, this ascertains that aspect ratios are retained. Each side of the cube is then positioned within the 300x300 space by rotation around the x or y axis and positioning away from the center along the z axis. The videos live on these sides. Note how you can see the backface of the videos through the cube. This can be turned off by setting *backface-visibility* to *hidden*.

Listing 3–14. An example document with a rotated video element

```
<style type="text/css">
div#room {
  -webkit-perspective: 600;
  -webkit-perspective-origin: 20% 70%;
}
div#cube {
  margin: 0 auto;
  height: 300px; width: 300px;
  -webkit-transform-style: preserve-3d;
}
div.side {
  position: absolute;
  height: 280px; width:  280px;
  padding: 10px;
  border: 1px solid black;
  background-color: rgba(50, 50, 50, 0.6);
}
div#one  {
  -webkit-transform: rotateX(90deg) translateZ(150px);
}
div#two  {
  -webkit-transform: translateZ(150px);
}
div#three  {
  -webkit-transform: rotateY(90deg) translateZ(150px);
}
```

---

[13] Motivated by http://www.fofronline.com/2009-07/animated-css3–cube-interface-using-3d-transforms/

```
div#four  {
  -webkit-transform: rotateY(180deg) translateZ(150px);
}
div#five  {
  -webkit-transform: rotateY(-90deg) translateZ(150px);
}
div#six {
  -webkit-transform: rotateX(-90deg) rotate(180deg)
                     translateZ(150px) ;
}
video {
  position: absolute;
  top:      25%;
  width:    280px;
  opacity: 0.7;
}
</style>
<div id="room">
  <div id="cube">
    <div class="side" id="one">
      <video controls src="HelloWorld.mp4"></video>
    </div>
    <div class="side" id="two">
      <video controls src="video1.mp4"></video>
    </div>
    <div class="side" id="three">
      <video controls src="video2.mp4"></video>
    </div>
    <div class="side" id="four">
      <video controls src="video3.mp4"></video>
    </div>
    <div class="side" id="five">
      <video controls src="video4.mp4"></video>
    </div>
    <div class="side" id="six">
      <video controls src="video5.mp4"></video>
    </div>
  </div>
</div>
```

Note that the 3D CSS3 features are available only in Safari and Chrome. Thus, we have reduced the example to only webkit prefix properties – otherwise it would have been even longer. Figure 3–14 shows what it looks like in Safari.

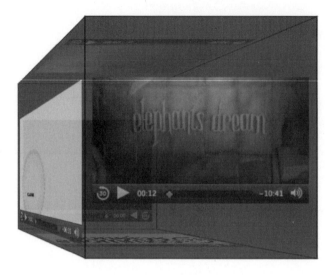

Figure 3–14. A <video> cube created with 3D CSS in Safari

Right now, the cube only sits there in 3D. Combining it with the transformation possibilities described earlier would enable us to make it interactive. For example, when hovering over certain areas of the cube, one could turn the cube in space. This exercise is left to the reader.

3.4.4 Putting a Video Gallery Together

To conclude this section, we will create an example that uses several features introduced in the section in a creatively styled video gallery.

The example has six videos, each of which is put in a div styled to look somewhat like a smartphone with silver rounded borders, and a black background. These "phones" are thrown in a pile, placed at different positions through absolute top and left offsets. Upon mousing over a "phone," a transition is performed to a larger version of the "phone" in the foreground with a larger version of the video and horizontally aligned. This produces somewhat of a zoom effect. In all browsers, the transition is performed smoothly and resembles an action of picking up that "phone." As you mouse out of the "phone," it drops back into place in the pile.

You can try to create the code for this example yourself. It uses only features that we have previously discussed. The core parts of the code are displayed in Listing 3–15. Don't forget to add the browser-specific versions of the CSS3 properties where necessary. The resulting display will be something like what is shown in Figure 3–15. It works in all browsers except IE, where the "phones" are all horizontally laid out. The screenshot is from Opera.

Listing 3–15. A HTML5 <video> gallery created with CSS exclusively

```
CSS code extract:
    <style type="text/css">
    div.container {
      position: absolute;
      width:    320px; height:    165px;
      padding:  10px 35px 10px 35px;
```

```
    margin:      0px;
    background-color: black;
    border:      4px solid silver;
    border-radius: 15px;
    box-shadow: 5px 5px 2px gray;
    box-sizing: border-box;
}
div.container:hover {
    width:  520px; height: 268px;
    padding:  16px 57px 16px 57px;
    z-index: 10;
}
div.container, div.container:hover  {
    transition-property: all;
    transition-duration: 0.5s;
    transition-timing-function: linear;
}
video {
    width:   100%;
    height:  100%;
    border: 1px solid #202020;
}
div#one:hover, div#two:hover, div#three:hover,
div#four:hover, div#five:hover, div#six:hover {
    transform:    rotate(0deg);
}
div#one {
    left: 123px;
    top:  228px;
    transform:          rotate(43deg);
}
// introduce your own versions for div #two to #six
</style>

HTML code extract:
<body>
    <div class="container" id="one">
    <video controls>
      <source src="HelloWorld.mp4" type="video/mp4">
      <source src="HelloWorld.webm" type="video/webm">
      <source src="HelloWorld.ogv" type="video/ogg">
    </video>
    </div>
// introduce the other videos and divs analogously
    </body>
```

Figure 3–15. *An HTML5 <video> gallery in Opera*

3.5 CSS Animations

CSS3 introduces animations,[14] which allow you to change CSS property values over time without requiring JavaScript. This feature is still very new and supported only by Safari.

The proposal to introduce animations into CSS was discussed in controversy—after all, JavaScript already allows achieving the effects that CSS animations provide. However, the key design principle for the Web is to use HTML for content, CSS for display, and JavaScript for interaction. In the past, JavaScript had to make up for many missing features in HTML and CSS – the new HTML5 and CSS3 are closing some of these gaps, so animations fit the architecture and will make it easier to achieve well styled content.

Animations are actually an extension to CSS transitions. In transitions, the start and end state are known, and the transition is executed by moving the object from the start to the end state over a given timing function. In animations, a sequence of intermediate states is added to a transition, which enables finer control of the transitions. These intermediate states are called *keyframes* and are defined in a special *@keyframes* selector. The *@keyframes* selector contains a sequence of rules for the different stages of a transition from 0% to 100% and defines the intermediate states of the transition. In this way, an *@keyframes* definition specifies the type of animation to be executed. It is given a name, so it can be referenced by animation properties.

---

[14] See http://www.w3.org/TR/css3–animations/

The following animation properties are introduced:

- *animation-name* – makes the link to the *@keyframes* definition name that defines the type of the animation to be used for an element.

- *animation-duration* – defines the total duration of the animation.

- *animation-timing-function* – declares the timing function to be used between the different keyframe states. It is possible to apply a timing function to every state change inside the @keyframes state rules. It has the same functionality and values as the transition-timing-function property.

- *animation-delay* – allows specifying that an animation is to start with a delay after the property has been applied.

- *animation-iteration-count* – defines how many times the animation is executed.

- *animation-direction* – defines whether the animation should play in reverse in alternate cycles, e.g. if an element is to bounce back and forth between two points.

- *animation-play-state* – allows you to set the animation in *paused*/*running* state.

- *animation* – combines the above seven properties into a single line specification.

If you need a state change to be executed repeatedly and not just upon change of a particular property, you will need to use animations rather than transitions.

Let's go back to Listing 3–14 of the 3D cube. This cube isn't very useful yet, since it is impossible to reach any of the hidden sides of the cube. We will therefore add an animation that will make the cube spin in the 3D space. Also, we will add an animation pause on mouse-over, such that it is possible to play back the visible video. Listing 3–16 shows the key parts of the code.

Listing 3–16. Extending the video cube with animations – CSS code extract

```
@-webkit-keyframes '3dturn' {
  0% {
    -webkit-transform: rotateX(0deg) rotateY(0deg);
  }
  20% {
    -webkit-transform: rotateX(0deg) rotateY(90deg);
  }
  40% {
    -webkit-transform: rotateX(90deg) rotateY(180deg);
  }
  60% {
    -webkit-transform: rotateX(0deg) rotateY(180deg);
  }
  80% {
    -webkit-transform: rotateX(0deg) rotateY(270deg);
  }
  100% {
    -webkit-transform: rotateX(-90deg) rotateY(360deg);
  }
}
div#cube {
  margin: 0 auto;
  height: 300px; width: 300px;
```

```
    -webkit-transform-style: preserve-3d;
    -webkit-transform: rotateX(0deg) rotateY(0deg);
    -webkit-animation-name: '3dturn';
    -webkit-animation-duration: 6s;
    -webkit-animation-iteration-count: 4;
    -webkit-animation-direction: alternate;
    -webkit-animation-play-state: running;
}
div#cube:hover {
    -webkit-animation-play-state: paused;
}
```

Because WebKit-based browsers are currently the only ones supporting the *animation* properties, the code extract shows only the relevant WebKit-style properties. Note that the cube turns from side to side in such a way that each one of the six faces will be shown once and in the correct orientation. This *3dturn* animation is attached to the *cube* div of the code and paused on *:hover*. It plays for six seconds going through four iterations; i.e. two full circles. The use of *animation-play-state* has an interesting side effect: as you hover over the cube, the animation is restarted.

Figure 3–16 has a screenshot of the turning cube in Safari.

Figure 3–16. *A spinning video cube fully created in CSS with animations in Safari*

3.6 Summary

This section has given you a set of examples to use CSS3 properties with media elements. While we focused on the <video> element, it is possible to apply most of the properties also to the <audio> element, as long as it is visible with controls.

There are many more examples that you can implement yourself. Try to implement a video scroller with CSS animations only, for example. (Hint: you will need two floating divs with videos that can follow each other inside a scroll animation div.)

At the end of this section we list all the CSS3 functionalities we discussed in this chapter, and we provide an overview of which browser supports which feature for reference purposes. This should help you to quickly identify any missing functionality you may rely on.

Function	Firefox	Safari	Chrome	Opera	IE
Box Model:	✓	✓	✓	✓	✓
border-radius	✓	✓	✓	✓	✓
box-shadow	✓	✓	✓	✓	✓
box-sizing	✓	✓	✓	✓	✓
CSS Positioning:					
display	✓	✓	✓	✓	✓
float	✓	✓	✓	✓	✓
position	✓	✓	✓	✓	✓
visibility	✓	✓	✓	✓	✓
object-fit	☒	☒	☒	✓	☒
object-position	☒	☒	☒	✓	☒
CSS Basic Properties:					
background-color	✓	✓	✓	✓	✓
opacity	✓	✓	✓	✓	✓
gradient	-moz-	-webkit-	-webkit-	✓	✓
marquee	☒	-webkit-	-webkit-	☒	☒
CSS Transitions & Transforms:					
transition	-moz-	-webkit-	-webkit-	-o-	☒
transform	-moz-	-webkit-	-webkit-	-o-	☒
3d transform	☒	-webkit-	-webkit-	☒	☒
perspective	☒	-webkit-	-webkit-	☒	☒
backface-visibility	☒	-webkit-	-webkit-	☒	☒
animation	☒	-webkit-	-webkit-	☒	☒

`http://www.cssplay.co.uk/menu/css3-marquee.html`

CHAPTER 4

■■■

JavaScript API

JavaScript is the scripting language used in web browsers for client-side programming tasks. As used in browsers, it is a dialect of the standardized ECMAScript[1] programming language. JavaScript programs can execute all kinds of simple to complex tasks for web pages, ranging from the manipulation of a simple user interface feature to the execution of a complex image analysis program. JavaScript overcomes the limitations of HTML and CSS by providing full flexibility to change anything in the Document Object Model (DOM) programmatically.

Because JavaScript support can be turned off in a web browser, it was important to explain what HTML and CSS provide without further scripting. Adding JavaScript to the mix, however, turns these web technologies into a powerful platform for the development of applications, and we will see what the media elements can contribute.

In the years before the development of HTML5 and CSS3, JavaScript was used to bring many new features to the Web. Where many people shared common requirements, JavaScript libraries[2] and frameworks, such as jQuery, YUI, Dojo or MooTools, were created that many Web developers now use to simplify their development of web content. The experience with these libraries in turn motivated the introduction of several new features of HTML5.

Because JavaScript executes in the web browser, it uses only the resources of the user's machine, rather than having to interact with the web server to make changes to the web page. This is particularly useful for dealing with any kind of user input and makes web pages much more responsive to users since no exchanges over a network will slow down the page's response. The use of JavaScript, therefore, is most appropriate when there isn't a need to save entered user information on the server. For example, a game can be written such that its logic executes in JavaScript in the browser and only the high score of the user requires an interaction with the web server. This assumes, of course, that all the required assets for the game—images, audio, etc.—have been retrieved.

JavaScript interfaces with HTML through the DOM (Document Object Model). The DOM is a hierarchical object structure that contains all the elements of a web page as objects with their attribute values and access functions. It represents the hierarchical structure of the HTML document and allows JavaScript to gain access to the HTML objects. WebIDL, the Web interface definition language,[3] has been created to allow for the specification of the interfaces that the objects expose to JavaScript and that browsers implement. WebIDL is particularly purpose-built to:

- Provide convenience structures that are used often in HTML, such as collections of DOM nodes, token lists, or lists of name-value pairs.

---

[1] See http://www.ecma-international.org/publications/standards/Ecma-262.htm

[2] See http://en.wikipedia.org/wiki/List_of_JavaScript_libraries for a list of JavaScript libraries

[3] See http://www.w3.org/TR/WebIDL/

- Expose the content attributes of the HTML element and enable the getting and setting of their values.

- Explain what JavaScript types the HTML element attributes map to and how.

- Explain the transformations that have to be made to attribute values upon reading them and before handing them to JavaScript; e.g. the resolution of a URL from a relative to an absolute URL.

- List the states that an element may go through and the events that may be executed on them.

- Relate to the browsing context of the HTML document.

It is important to understand the difference between the attributes of elements as they have been introduced in Chapter 2 and attributes that are exposed for an element in the DOM. The former are called **content attributes**, while the latter are **IDL attributes**.[4] To simplify explanation of the JavaScript API of the media elements, we will look at the IDL attributes created from content attributes and IDL-only attributes separately. This will provide a better understanding of which attributes come through to JavaScript from HTML and which are created to allow script control and manipulation.

For the purposes of this chapter, we assume that you have a basic understanding of JavaScript and can follow the WebIDL specifications. Reading WebIDL is really simple and compares to reading class definitions in object-oriented programming languages. We will explain the newly introduced interfaces that the HTML5 media elements provide to JavaScript in WebIDL and give some examples on what can be achieved with JavaScript by using these interfaces.

4.1 Content Attributes

We have already become acquainted with the content attributes of the HTML5 media elements in Chapter 2. All of these map straight into the IDL interface of the media elements, see Listing 4–1.

Listing 4–1. WebIDL attributes of audio, video and source elements coming from content attributes

```
interface HTMLMediaElement : HTMLElement {
  attribute DOMString src;
  attribute DOMString preload;
  attribute boolean autoplay;
  attribute boolean loop;
  attribute boolean controls;
};

interface HTMLAudioElement : HTMLMediaElement {};

interface HTMLVideoElement : HTMLMediaElement {
  attribute unsigned long width;
  attribute unsigned long height;
  attribute DOMString poster;
};

interface HTMLSourceElement : HTMLElement {
```

---

[4] See http://www.whatwg.org/specs/web-apps/current-work/multipage/infrastructure.html#terminology

```
  attribute DOMString src;
  attribute DOMString type;
  attribute DOMString media;
};
```

All these attributes can be read (also called "get") and set in JavaScript. Since we have already explained all these attributes in detail in Chapter 2, we will not repeat this here. You can see the JavaScript types that the content attributes map to in Listing 4–1.

For an example of how to set and get the values of the content attributes in JavaScript, see Listing 4–2.

Listing 4–2. Example media content attribute getting and setting in JavaScript

```
<video controls autoplay>
  <source src="HelloWorld.mp4" type="video/mp4">
  <source src="HelloWorld.ogv" type="video/ogg">
</video>
<script type="text/javascript">
  videos = document.getElementsByTagName("video");
  video = videos[0];
  video.controls = false;
  video.width = '400';
  alert(video.autoplay);
</script>
```

Note how we display the value of the autoplay content attribute through a "getter" API function and change the values of the width and controls attributes through a "setter," which make the video shrink and the controls disappear.

Attributes that do not have a value in the HTML source code will be treated as though they have an empty string as value. This is of particular interest for the src attribute, since it is associated with the video element. However, the media's source URL may actually be specified in a <source> element, as in the above example. In this case, getting the value of the video's src content attribute will return an empty string. This is where the additional IDL attributes become important.

4.2 IDL Attributes

IDL attributes—also called DOM attributes—reflect the state that a media element is in. The additional IDL attributes that we look at in this subsection are mostly read-only attributes. Only a few can be set that allow changing the playback of the media element. These are of particular importance to a web developer.

Listing 4–3 shows a list of these IDL attributes for audio and video elements (the <source> element has no IDL attributes, but only contributes back to the HTMLMediaElement). The state constants have been omitted from this list and will be described as we go through the IDL attributes. There are quite a few IDL attributes, so we will look at them in subsections of three groups: those conveying general state, those conveying playback-related state, and those conveying error states.

Listing 4–3. WebIDL IDL attributes of audio and video

```
interface HTMLMediaElement : HTMLElement {
  // error state
  readonly attribute MediaError error;

  // network state
```

```
    readonly attribute DOMString currentSrc;
    readonly attribute unsigned short networkState;
    readonly attribute TimeRanges buffered;

    // ready state
    readonly attribute unsigned short readyState;
    readonly attribute boolean seeking;

    // playback state
            attribute double currentTime;
    readonly attribute double initialTime;
    readonly attribute double duration;
    readonly attribute Date startOffsetTime;
    readonly attribute boolean paused;
            attribute double defaultPlaybackRate;
            attribute double playbackRate;
    readonly attribute TimeRanges played;
    readonly attribute TimeRanges seekable;
    readonly attribute boolean ended;

    // controls
            attribute double volume;
            attribute boolean muted;
};

interface HTMLAudioElement : HTMLMediaElement {};

interface HTMLVideoElement : HTMLMediaElement {
  readonly attribute unsigned long videoWidth;
  readonly attribute unsigned long videoHeight;
};
```

4.2.1 General Features of Media Resources

The following IDL attributes, which represent general features of a media resource, are explained in this section:

- currentSrc
- startTime
- duration
- volume
- muted
- videoWidth
- videoHeight

@currentSrc

The resource location of the media element can be specified through content attributes either directly on the <audio> or <video> element, or on the selected <source> element. The resulting resource location is stored in the @currentSrc IDL attribute and can be read by JavaScript. To dynamically change the resource location of the media element, you can always set the @src content attribute of the media element using JavaScript and call the load() method to reload the element's media resource.

The actual process of selecting a media resource is somewhat complicated and involves queuing tasks, firing events, setting network states, ready states, and potentially error states. This resource selection algorithm is invoked as the media element is loaded and asynchronously executes thereafter. It will also initiate the resource fetch algorithm, which actually downloads the media data and decodes it.

We will look at the different aspects of the resource selection algorithm through the different IDL attributes as we discuss them. Here we focus on how the media resource location is identified and @currentSrc is set.

@currentSrc is initially an empty string. You cannot rely on it to be available to JavaScript before the resource selection algorithm has started fetching media data, which is signified through firing a progress event. This, however, will not work when you are dealing with a buffered video resource, since in this case, no progress event is fired. Thus, the event that will indicate a media resource is now usable is the loadedmetadata event. You need to listen for the loadedmetadata event being fired before accessing @currentSrc.

In JavaScript, there are three means for setting up an event listener. The first two follow the traditional model,[5] the third is the W3C's modern and recommended model.[6]

The first event listener method uses an event attribute created by adding the prefix "on" to the event name. For example:

```
<video onprogress="execute()" src="video.ogv"></video>
```

The second is to use the event IDL attribute in JavaScript. For example:

```
video.onprogress = execute;
```

The third[7] follows the W3C's DOM Events model by registering events explicitly:

```
video.addEventListener("progress", execute(), false);
```

Listing 4–4 shows as an example for how to retrieve the @currentSrc attribute during page load time, after a progress event and after a loadedmetadata event. Figure 4–1 shows the results in the browsers.

Listing 4–4. Getting the currentSrc value for a media element

```
<video controls autoplay width="400">
  <source src="HelloWorld.mp4"  type="video/mp4">
  <source src="HelloWorld.webm" type="video/webm">
  <source src="HelloWorld.ogv"  type="video/ogg">
</video>
<p>CurrentSrc on start:       <span id="first"></span>.</p>
<p>CurrentSrc after progress: <span id="progress"></span>.</p>
<p>CurrentSrc after loadedmetadata:
                              <span id="loadedmetadata"></span>.</p>
```

[5] See http://www.quirksmode.org/js/events_tradmod.html

[6] See http://www.quirksmode.org/js/events_advanced.html

[7] See http://www.w3.org/TR/2000/REC-DOM-Level-2-Events-20001113/events.html

```
<script type="text/javascript">
  video = document.getElementsByTagName("video")[0];
  span1 = document.getElementById("first");
  span1.innerHTML = video.currentSrc;

  span2 = document.getElementById("progress");
  function span2Update(evt) {
    span2.innerHTML = video.currentSrc;
  }
  span3 = document.getElementById("loadedmetadata");
  function span3Update(evt) {
    span3.innerHTML = video.currentSrc;
  }
  video.addEventListener("progress", span2Update, false);
  video.addEventListener("loadedmetadata", span3Update, false);
</script>
```

Note how Opera and IE already display a loaded resource on start, while the others don't. This is because these two browsers have already parsed their DOM by the time they execute that JavaScript, while the others haven't. You cannot rely on reading the @currentSrc attribute before the loadedmetadata event has fired.

The behavior between the five browsers differs slightly on page reload. There are three ways in which to reload a page:

1. Hit "enter" on the URL bar.

2. Hit the "reload" button.

3. Hit "shift" and the "reload" button or "ctrl" and "reload" if you are in IE.

The first and second are supposed to create the same effect: reloading the web page and resources from cache, unless the cache timed out. The third is supposed to allow reloading a page and all its resources by bypassing the cache; i.e. reloading them from the origin server. However, because browsers often have a separate cache for media resources than for other browser resources, not every browser supports this functionality.

Firefox and Safari will always reload the media resource when reloading the web page, no matter what reload mechanism you choose. Thus, a new sequence of progress events will be fired. Opera and Chrome don't reload a media resource unless the media URI changes, which is why the progress event only fires when loading the media resource for the very first time. IE distinguishes between reloading from cache and reloading all resources from the origin, which happens either when hitting the "reload" or the "ctrl"-"reload" buttons. However, it always calls the progress event, no matter whether the resource is loaded from the cache or remotely.

It is clear to see that you need to use the loadedmetadata event for catching the right time to ask about which resource has been loaded from @currentSrc.

CurrentSrc on start: .

CurrentSrc after progress: http://192.168.1.132/HelloWorld.webm.

CurrentSrc after loadedmetadata: http://192.168.1.132/HelloWorld.webm.

CurrentSrc on start: .

CurrentSrc after progress: http://192.168.1.132/HelloWorld.mp4.

CurrentSrc after loadedmetadata: http://192.168.1.132/HelloWorld.mp4.

CurrentSrc on start: http://192.168.1.132/HelloWorld.webm.

CurrentSrc after progress: http://192.168.1.132/HelloWorld.webm.

CurrentSrc after loadedmetadata: http://192.168.1.132/HelloWorld.webm.

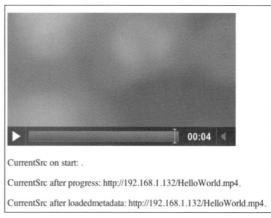

CurrentSrc on start: .

CurrentSrc after progress: http://192.168.1.132/HelloWorld.mp4.

CurrentSrc after loadedmetadata: http://192.168.1.132/HelloWorld.mp4.

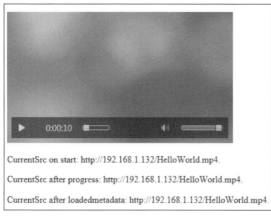

CurrentSrc on start: http://192.168.1.132/HelloWorld.mp4.

CurrentSrc after progress: http://192.168.1.132/HelloWorld.mp4.

CurrentSrc after loadedmetadata: http://192.168.1.132/HelloWorld.mp4.

Figure 4–1. Retrieving the @currentSrc value in Firefox, Safari (top row), Opera, Chrome (middle row), and IE (bottom)

@startTime

After a media resource is loaded, it is possible to know what the timestamp is of the earliest possible position that can be played back from the media resource. Typically, a media resource starts at timestamp 0, but some resources have a positive time offset that they start from—either because they may have been created as a fragment from a larger resource, or because they stem from a live stream that a user tuned into later, or because the browser is unable to obtain certain parts of the stream after it has expired from its buffer.

Thus, the read-only @startTime IDL attribute provides the earliest possible position in the stream or resource that a browser is able to return to.

Listing 4–5 shows as an example how to retrieve the @startTime attribute during page load time, after a loadedmetadata event and after an ended event. Figure 4–2 shows the results in Firefox and IE.

Listing 4–5. Getting the startTime value for a media element

```
<video controls autoplay width="400">
  <source src="HelloWorld.mp4"  type="video/mp4">
  <source src="HelloWorld.webm" type="video/webm">
  <source src="HelloWorld.ogv"  type="video/ogg">
</video>
<p>StartTime on start: <span id="startTime_first"></span>.</p>
<p>StartTime after loadedmetadata:
    <span id="startTime_loadedmetadata"></span>.</p>
<p>StartTime after timeupdate:
    <span id="startTime_timeupdate"></span>.</p>
<p>StartTime after ended: <span id="startTime_ended"></span>.</p>
<script type="text/javascript">
  video = document.getElementsByTagName("video")[0];
  span1 = document.getElementById("startTime_first");
  span1.innerHTML = video.startTime;
  span2 = document.getElementById("startTime_loadedmetadata");
  function span2Update(evt) {  span2.innerHTML = video.startTime; }
  span3 = document.getElementById("startTime_timeupdate");
  function span3Update(evt) {  span3.innerHTML = video.startTime; }
  span4 = document.getElementById("startTime_ended");
  function span4Update(evt) {  span4.innerHTML = video.startTime; }
  video.addEventListener("loadedmetadata", span2Update, false);
  video.addEventListener("timeupdate", span3Update, false);
  video.addEventListener("ended", span4Update, false);
</script>
```

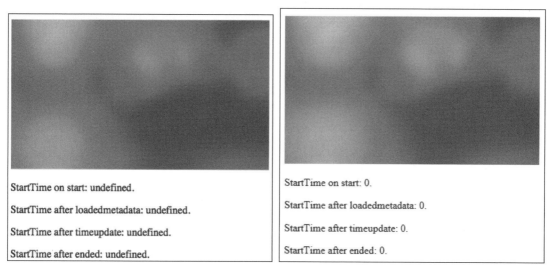

StartTime on start: undefined.

StartTime after loadedmetadata: undefined.

StartTime after timeupdate: undefined.

StartTime after ended: undefined.

StartTime on start: 0.

StartTime after loadedmetadata: 0.

StartTime after timeupdate: 0.

StartTime after ended: 0.

Figure 4–2. Retrieving the startTime value in Firefox and IE

All browsers implement @startTime in the way IE implements it—except for Firefox, whose implementation of the media timeline predates the @startTime attribute. According to their developers, you can safely assume @startTime is always 0 in Firefox.

More recently, an explicit definition of a timeline has entered the HTML5 specification, and the @startTime attribute has been removed. It can be replicated through the start time of the first range in the @seekable attribute's TimeRanges object and is therefore no longer necessary. At the same time, new attributes have been introduced: @initialTime and @startOffsetTime.

The new timeline specifies how to interpret times provided in media resources to the media timeline for the element; e.g. how to deal with time gaps in a resource or time offsets that are common in live streams.

The @startOffsetTime is a Date object and represents a mapping of the zero time in the media timeline to a date given in the media resource for this time. This is particularly important when dealing with live streaming and the time and date are actually given in the media resource.

The @initialTime stores the initial playback position for a media resource. In the absence of media data, @initialTime is zero, but may later turn into an offset time on the media timeline. It comes into play with the delivery of media fragments (see also Chapter 9, where we talk about media fragment URIs).

None of the browsers has implemented this new timeline and the new attributes.

@duration

When a media resource's metadata is loaded and before any media data is played back, you can find out about the duration of the resource. The read-only @duration IDL attribute returns the length of the media resource in seconds. During loading time, @duration will return the NaN value (Not-a-Number). If it is a live or an unbound stream, the duration is infinity, unless the stream ends, at which time the duration changes to that given through the last samples in the stream set in relation to @startTime. Also note that sometimes a UA is unable to get an accurate duration after loading the resource's metadata and will provide only an approximate duration, which it can update during playback as it learns more about the actual duration of the resource.

Every update of the @duration of the media resource causes a durationchange event to be fired, so you can always retrieve the exact @duration value that the UA is working with. This will also happen if a different resource is loaded.

Listing 4–6 shows an example of how to retrieve the @duration attribute during page load time, after a loadedmetadata event, a durationchange event and after a ended event. Figure 4–3 shows the results in the browsers.

Listing 4–6. Getting the duration value for a media element

```
<video controls autoplay width="400">
  <source src="HelloWorld.mp4"  type="video/mp4">
  <source src="HelloWorld.webm" type="video/webm">
  <source src="HelloWorld.ogv"  type="video/ogg">
</video>
<p>duration on start: <span id="duration_first"></span>.</p>
<p>duration after loadedmetadata:
    <span id="duration_loadedmetadata"></span>.</p>
<p>duration after durationchange:
    <span id="duration_durationchange"></span>.</p>
<p>duration after ended: <span id="duration_ended"></span>.</p>
<script type="text/javascript">
  video = document.getElementsByTagName("video")[0];
  span1 = document.getElementById("duration_first");
  span1.innerHTML = video.duration;
  span2 = document.getElementById("duration_loadedmetadata");
  function span2Update(evt) {  span2.innerHTML = video.duration; }
  span3 = document.getElementById("duration_durationchange");
  function span3Update(evt) {  span3.innerHTML = video.duration; }
  span4 = document.getElementById("duration_ended");
  function span4Update(evt) {  span4.innerHTML = video.duration; }
  video.addEventListener("loadedmetadata", span2Update, false);
  video.addEventListener("durationchange", span3Update, false);
  video.addEventListener("ended", span4Update, false);
</script>
```

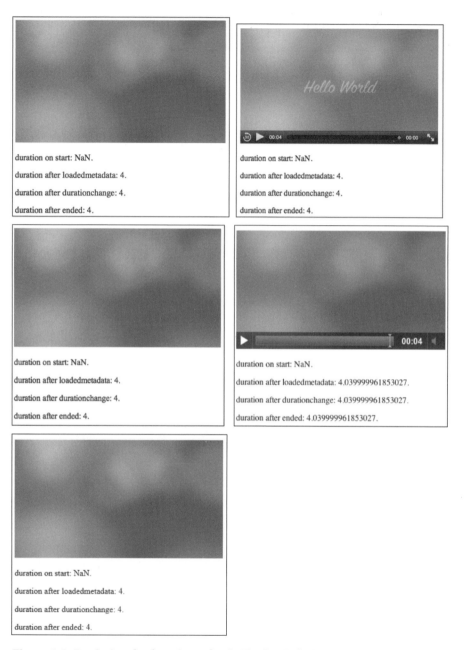

duration on start: NaN.

duration after loadedmetadata: 4.

duration after durationchange: 4.

duration after ended: 4.

duration on start: NaN.

duration after loadedmetadata: 4.

duration after durationchange: 4.

duration after ended: 4.

duration on start: NaN.

duration after loadedmetadata: 4.

duration after durationchange: 4.

duration after ended: 4.

duration on start: NaN.

duration after loadedmetadata: 4.039999961853027.

duration after durationchange: 4.039999961853027.

duration after ended: 4.039999961853027.

duration on start: NaN.

duration after loadedmetadata: 4.

duration after durationchange: 4.

duration after ended: 4.

Figure 4–3. *Retrieving the duration value in Firefox, Safari (top row), Opera, Chrome (middle row), and IE (bottom)*

Note that the attribute value in Google Chrome is more accurate than in the other browsers, since it returns duration as a double value of seconds. It seems the other MPEG-based browsers (IE and Safari) round the duration values. When testing with `FFmpeg`, the duration of the Ogg file turns out to be 3.96s, the WebM file is 4.00s and the MPEG-4 file 4.04s. Chrome, Opera, and Firefox return accurate durations.

More recently, the HTML5 specification has slightly changed the meaning of the `@duration` attribute. It now represents the end time of the media resource. This has not been implemented by any browser yet.

@volume

When reading the `@volume` IDL attribute of a media resource, the playback volume of the audio track is returned in the range 0.0 (silent) to 1.0 (loudest). On initial load of the media resource, its `@volume` is set to 1.0. After use of the media resource and change of its volume setting—either through user or script interaction—the `@volume` value may have changed. The browser may remember this setting for a later reload of the resource to allow a user to return to the volume adjustments made earlier.

The `@volume` IDL attribute can be set through JavaScript to change the volume of the media resource. A value between 0.0 and 1.0 inclusive is allowed. Anything else will raise an INDEX_SIZE_ERR exception. The playback volume will be adjusted correspondingly as soon as possible after setting the attribute. Note that the range may not be linear, but is determined by the browser. Further, the loudest setting may be lower than the system's loudest possible setting.

Whenever the volume of the media resource is changed—either through user interaction or JavaScript—a volumechanged event is fired.

Listing 4–7 shows an example of how to get and set the @volume attribute using an audio element. Every time the `timeupdate` event is raised, we reduce the volume by 0.05 until we reach a volume of less than 0.1. Then we reset the value to 1.0 and start successively pulling it down again like a sawtooth. Figure 4–4 shows the results in the browsers.

Listing 4–7. Getting and setting the volume value for a media element

```
<audio controls autoplay>
    <source src="HelloWorld.m4a" type="audio/aac">
    <source src="HelloWorld.mp3" type="audio/mp4">
    <source src="HelloWorld.ogg" type="audio/ogg">
</audio>

<p>volume on start: <span id="volume_first"></span>.</p>
<p>volume after volumechange: <span id="volumechange"></span>.</p>
<p>volume after timeupdate: <span id="timeupdate"></span>.</p>
<script type="text/javascript">
  audio = document.getElementsByTagName("audio")[0];
  span1 = document.getElementById("volume_first");
  span1.innerHTML = audio.volume;

  span2 = document.getElementById("volumechange");
  function span2Update(evt) {
    span2.innerHTML = audio.volume;
  }
  span3 = document.getElementById("timeupdate");
  function span3Update(evt) {
    if (audio.volume > 0.1) {
      audio.volume = audio.volume - 0.05;
    } else {
      audio.volume = 1.0;
    }
```

```
        span3.innerHTML = audio.volume;
    }
    audio.addEventListener("volumechange", span2Update, false);
    audio.addEventListener("timeupdate", span3Update, false);
</script>
```

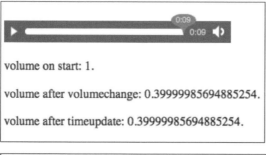

volume on start: 1.

volume after volumechange: 0.39999985694885254.

volume after timeupdate: 0.39999985694885254.

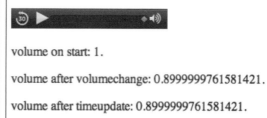

volume on start: 1.

volume after volumechange: 0.8999999761581421.

volume after timeupdate: 0.8999999761581421.

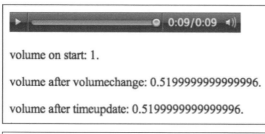

volume on start: 1.

volume after volumechange: 0.5199999999999996.

volume after timeupdate: 0.5199999999999996.

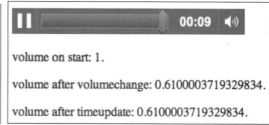

volume on start: 1.

volume after volumechange: 0.6100003719329834.

volume after timeupdate: 0.6100003719329834.

volume on start: 1.

volume after volumechange: 0.09999984502792358.

volume after timeupdate: 0.09999984502792358.

Figure 4–4. Retrieving and setting the volume value in Firefox, Safari (top row), Opera, Chrome (middle row), and IE (bottom)

Note that the frequency at which timeupdate is being called is different among the browsers and, as such, they all arrive at different volumes at the end of playback.

@muted

When reading the @muted IDL attribute of a media resource, it returns "true" if the audio channels are muted and "false" otherwise. On initial load of the media resource, it is not muted. After use of the media resource and change of its muted setting—either through user or script interaction—the @muted value may have changed. The browser may remember this setting for a later reload of the resource to allow a user to return to the mute adjustments made earlier. The @muted value overrides the @volume setting.

The @muted IDL attribute can be set through JavaScript to "true" to mute the audio playback for the media resource or "false" to unmute it.

Whenever the volume of the media resource is changed—either through user interaction or through JavaScript—a volumechanged event is fired. This event fires both on @volume and @muted changes. The @muted value is not changed when @volume changes; in particular, it is possible to change the volume setting while the media element is actually muted.

Listing 4–8 shows an example of how to get and set the @muted attribute. In this example we change the @muted setting every 20 timeupdate ticks. Note that we also show, together with the muted value, the number up to which the timeupdate loop has counted since the last timeupdate. Figure 4–5 shows the results in the browsers.

Listing 4–8. Getting and setting the muted value for a media element

```
<audio controls autoplay>
  <source src="HelloWorld.m4a" type="audio/aac">
  <source src="HelloWorld.mp3" type="audio/mp4">
  <source src="HelloWorld.ogg" type="audio/ogg">
</audio>
<p>muted on start: <span id="muted_first"></span>.</p>
<p>muted after volumechange: <span id="muted_volumechange"></span>.</p>
<p>muted after timeupdate: <span id="muted_timeupdate"></span>.</p>
<script type="text/javascript">
  audio = document.getElementsByTagName("audio")[0];
  span1 = document.getElementById("muted_first");
  span1.innerHTML = audio.muted;
  span2 = document.getElementById("muted_volumechange");
  function span2Update(evt) {   span2.innerHTML = audio.muted; }
  span3 = document.getElementById("muted_timeupdate");
  i=0;
  function span3Update(evt) {
    if (i>20) {
      audio.muted = !audio.muted;
      i=0;
    } else {
      i=i+1;
    }
    span3.innerHTML = i + " " + audio.muted;
  }
  audio.addEventListener("volumechange", span2Update, false);
  audio.addEventListener("timeupdate", span3Update, false);
</script>
```

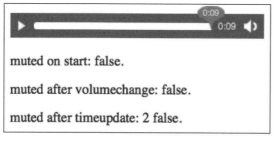

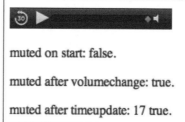

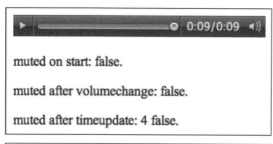

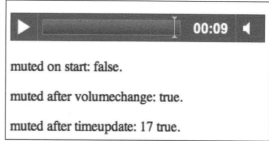

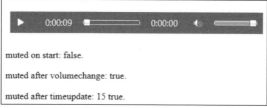

Figure 4–5. Retrieving and setting the muted value in Firefox, Safari (top row), Opera, Chrome (middle row), and IE (bottom)

For the 10sec file, Safari, Chrome and IE arrive at a state of `@muted="true"` while Firefox, Opera arrives at `@muted="false."` Note how the browsers explicitly display the muted state in their controls.

@videoWidth, @videoHeight

For video resources, there are read-only IDL attributes `@videoWidth` and `@videoHeight,` which return the intrinsic width and height of the video, or zero if the dimensions are not known at video load time. The intrinsic dimensions are calculated in CSS pixels, including information about the resource's dimensions, aspect ratio, resolution, etc., as defined by the resource's file format.

It is important to understand the difference between the `@width` and `@height` content attributes and these IDL attributes. With the `@width` and `@height` content attributes, you can set and get the displayed width of the video in CSS pixels or in percentage. In contrast, the read-only `@videoWidth` and `@videoHeight` IDL attributes refer to the width and height of the video itself as it comes from the decoding pipeline. Changing the `@width` and `@height` content attribute values has no effect on the value of the `@videoWidth` and `@videoHeight` attributes.

Listing 4–9 shows an example of how to get the `@videoWidth` and `@videoHeight` attributes. Figure 4–6 shows the results in Opera.

Listing 4–9. Getting the intrinsic videoWidth and videoHeight values for a video element

```
<video controls width="400">
  <source src="HelloWorld.mp4"  type="video/mp4">
  <source src="HelloWorld.webm" type="video/webm">
  <source src="HelloWorld.ogv"  type="video/ogg">
</video>
<p>dimensions on start: <span id="dimensions_first"></span>.</p>
<p>dimensions after loadedmetadata:
    <span id="dimensions_loadedmetadata"></span>.</p>
<script type="text/javascript">
  video = document.getElementsByTagName("video")[0];
  span1 = document.getElementById("dimensions_first");
  span1.innerHTML = video.videoWidth + " x " + video.videoHeight;
  span2 = document.getElementById("dimensions_loadedmetadata");
  function span2Update(evt) {
      span2.innerHTML = video.videoWidth + " x " + video.videoHeight;
  }
  video.addEventListener("loadedmetadata", span2Update, false);
</script>
```

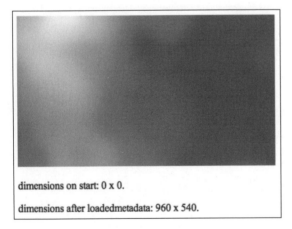

Figure 4–6. Retrieving the videoWidth and videoHeight values in Opera

All browsers show the same behavior for this property.

4.2.2 Playback-Related Attributes of Media Resources

The following IDL attributes, all related to playback position and control, are explained in this section:

- currentTime
- seeking
- paused
- ended
- defaultPlaybackRate
- playbackRate

@currentTime

The @currentTime IDL attribute returns the current playback position of the media resource in seconds. If a media element has a non-zero @startTime, the first value of @currentTime will be the value of @startTime. Under normal circumstances, the media resource starts at 0, in which case the @currentTime during uninterrupted playback will contain the time passed since starting playback of the media resource.

The @currentTime can also be set by JavaScript, which will initiate a seek by the browser to a new playback position. Depending on whether the resource is seekable and that position is available and reachable, the @currentTime is successfully changed or an exception is raised.

Seeking can be undertaken only when the media element's metadata has been loaded, so don't try changing the @currentTime before the readyState is at least HAVE_METADATA. A timeupdate event will be fired upon a successful seek.

A browser will interrupt any current seeking activities if you start a new seeking action. If you seek to a time where the data is not available yet, current playback (if any) will be stopped and you will have to wait until that data is available. A waiting event will be fired.

If you seek past the end of the media resource, you will be taken to the end. If you seek to a time before the @startTime of the media resource, you will be taken to the @startTime. If you seek to a time that is not seekable—i.e., it is not inside one of the time ranges in the @seekable attribute—the browser will position the seek to the nearest seekable position. If your seek position is exactly between two seekable positions, you will be positioned at the one closest to the current playback position.

Listing 4–10 shows an example of how to get and set the @currentTime attribute. After having played one third of the resource, we jump forward by a third, then the next timeupdate event shows where we jumped to. Figure 4–7 shows the results in the browsers.

Listing 4–10. *Getting and setting the currentTime value for a media element*

```
<video controls autoplay width="400">
  <source src="HelloWorld.mp4"  type="video/mp4">
  <source src="HelloWorld.webm" type="video/webm">
  <source src="HelloWorld.ogv"  type="video/ogg">
</video>
<p>currentTime on start: <span id="currentTime_first"></span>.</p>
<p>currentTime after timeupdate:
    <span id="currentTime_timeupdate"></span>.</p>
<p>currentTime after ended: <span id="currentTime_ended"></span>.</p>
<script type="text/javascript">
```

```
        video = document.getElementsByTagName("video")[0];
        span1 = document.getElementById("currentTime_first");
        span1.innerHTML = video.currentTime;
        span2 = document.getElementById("currentTime_timeupdate");
        function span2Update(evt) {
          span2.innerHTML = video.currentTime;
          video.removeEventListener("timeupdate", span2Update, false);
        }
        span3 = document.getElementById("currentTime_ended");
        function span3Update(evt) {  span3.innerHTML = video.currentTime; }
        function timeupdatecallback(evt) {
          if (video.currentTime > video.duration/3) {
            video.currentTime = 2*video.duration/3;
            video.removeEventListener("timeupdate", timeupdatecallback, false);
            video.addEventListener("timeupdate", span2Update, false);
          }
        }
        video.addEventListener("timeupdate", timeupdatecallback, false);
        video.addEventListener("ended", span3Update, false);
      </script>
```

currentTime on start: 0.

currentTime after timeupdate: 2.6659998893737793.

currentTime after ended: 4.

currentTime on start: 0.

currentTime after timeupdate: 2.6666667461395264.

currentTime after ended: 4.

currentTime on start: 0.

currentTime after timeupdate: 2.6666666666666665.

currentTime after ended: 4.

currentTime on start: 0.

currentTime after timeupdate: 2.6666666666666665.

currentTime after ended: 4.

currentTime on start: 0.

currentTime after timeupdate: 2.6666667461395263.

currentTime after ended: 4.039616584777832.

Figure 4–7. Retrieving and setting the currentTime value in Firefox, Safari (top row), Opera, Chrome (middle row), and IE (bottom)

All the browsers behave identically on a @currentTime update.

@seeking

The read-only @seeking IDL attribute is set by the browser to "true" during times of seeking and is "false" at all other times.

Listing 4–11 shows as an example how to get the @seeking attribute. Since seeking times are typically short, we have to catch the @seeking attribute value as soon as possible after starting to seek. Thus, we print it straight after changing @currentTime. Figure 4–8 shows the results in Safari.

Listing 4–11. Getting the seeking value for a media element

```
<video controls autoplay width="400">
  <source src="HelloWorld.mp4"  type="video/mp4">
  <source src="HelloWorld.webm" type="video/webm">
  <source src="HelloWorld.ogv"  type="video/ogg">
</video>
<p>seeking on start: <span id="seeking_first"></span>.</p>
<p>seeking after timeupdate: <span id="seeking_timeupdate"></span>.</p>
<p>seeking after ended: <span id="seeking_ended"></span>.</p>
<script type="text/javascript">
  video = document.getElementsByTagName("video")[0];
  span1 = document.getElementById("seeking_first");
  span1.innerHTML = video.seeking;
  span2 = document.getElementById("seeking_timeupdate");
  function span2Update(evt) {
    if (video.currentTime > video.duration/3) {
      video.currentTime = 2*video.duration/3;
      video.removeEventListener("timeupdate", span2Update, false);
      span2.innerHTML = video.seeking;
    }
  }
  span3 = document.getElementById("seeking_ended");
  function span3Update(evt) { span3.innerHTML = video.seeking; }
  video.addEventListener("timeupdate", span2Update, false);
  video.addEventListener("ended", span3Update, false);
</script>
```

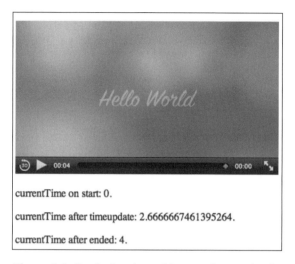

currentTime on start: 0.

currentTime after timeupdate: 2.6666667461395264.

currentTime after ended: 4.

Figure 4–8. Retrieving the seeking attribute value in Safari

You can see that @seeking is "true" just after seeking. All browsers exhibit the same behavior for this example.

@paused

The read-only @paused IDL attribute is set by the browser to "true" if the media playback is paused. Pausing can happen either through user interaction on the interface or through JavaScript. Initially, @paused is "true" and is only set to "false" when the media resource is supposed to start playing.

It is not possible to assume that the video is playing when @paused is "false." Even when @paused is "false," it is possible the media resource is in a state of buffering, in an error state, or has reached the end and is waiting for more media data to be appended. Because there is no explicit @playing IDL attribute, you need to use the @paused value and some other hints to determine if the browser is currently playing back a media resource. The combined hints are:

- @paused is "false."

- @ended is "false."

- The readyState is HAVE_FUTURE_DATA or HAVE_ENOUGH_DATA.

- @error is null.

There are also events that can help you ensure that playback continues working: the playing event is fired when playback starts and as long as no waiting or ended or error event is fired and @paused is "false," you can safely assume that you are still playing.

When the @paused IDL attribute changes value, a timeupdate event is fired.

Listing 4–12 shows as an example how to get the value of the @paused attribute and how to deduce an assumption for a playing status. Halfway through the media resource, we briefly pause the video to catch the states and then start playback again. Figure 4–9 shows the results in Chrome and IE.

Listing 4–12. Getting the paused value for a media element

```
<video controls autoplay width="400">
  <source src="HelloWorld.mp4"  type="video/mp4">
  <source src="HelloWorld.webm" type="video/webm">
  <source src="HelloWorld.ogv"  type="video/ogg">
</video>
<p>paused on start: <span id="paused_first"></span>.</p>
<p>paused after pause(): <span id="paused_timeupdate"></span>.</p>
<p>paused after play(): <span id="paused_playing"></span>.</p>
<p>paused after ended: <span id="paused_ended"></span>.</p>
<script type="text/javascript">
  video = document.getElementsByTagName("video")[0];
  span1 = document.getElementById("paused_first");
  function playing() {
    return !video.paused && !video.ended && video.error==null &&
       (video.readyState==video.HAVE_FUTURE_DATA ||
        video.readyState==video.HAVE_ENOUGH_DATA);
  }
  span1.innerHTML = video.paused + " (playing: " + playing() + ")";
  span2 = document.getElementById("paused_timeupdate");
  function span2Update(evt) {
    if (video.currentTime > video.duration/2) {
      video.pause();
      video.removeEventListener("timeupdate", span2Update, false);
      span2.innerHTML = video.paused + " (playing: " + playing() + ")";
      video.play();
      span3 = document.getElementById("paused_playing");
      span3.innerHTML = video.paused + " (playing: " + playing() + ")";
    }
  }
  span4 = document.getElementById("paused_ended");
  function span4Update(evt) {
      span4.innerHTML = video.paused + " (playing: " + playing() + ")";
  }
  video.addEventListener("timeupdate", span2Update, false);
  video.addEventListener("ended", span4Update, false);
</script>
```

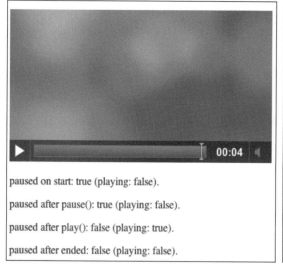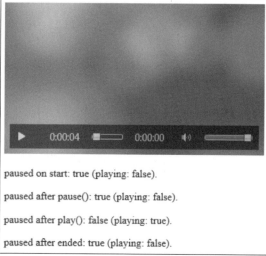

Figure 4–9. Retrieving the paused attribute value and also a playing status in Chrome and IE.

Firefox, Safari, Opera, and Chrome all behave the same with the state of *@paused*. IE, however, doesn't respect the idea that at the end of playback the state should be set to @paused="false" to wait for further data to arrive. Instead, IE rewinds to the beginning of the resource and pauses the video.

@ended

The read-only @ended IDL attribute is set by the browser to "true" if the media playback has ended and the direction of playback is forward (see @playbackRate); otherwise @ended is "false."

Note that @ended will not be set to "true" when the @loop content attribute is set to "true," the current playback position reaches the end of the media resource and the playback direction is forward. Instead, the browser will seek to the @startTime of the media resource and continue playback.

When @ended is set to "true," the browser will fire both a timeupdate event and an ended event.

Since Firefox does not implement @loop, you can imitate looping by catching the ended event and then setting @currentTime to 0.

Interestingly, when the playback direction is backward and the playback position reaches the @startTime of the media resource, the value of the @loop content attribute is irrelevant and playback will stop. Only a timeupdate event will be fired.

Listing 4–13 shows as an example how to get the @ended attribute. Figure 4–10 shows the results in Safari.

Listing 4–13. Getting the ended value for a media element

```
<video controls autoplay width="400">
  <source src="HelloWorld.mp4"  type="video/mp4">
  <source src="HelloWorld.webm" type="video/webm">
  <source src="HelloWorld.ogv"  type="video/ogg">
</video>
<p>ended on start: <span id="ended_first"></span>.</p>
<p>ended after ended: <span id="ended_ended"></span>.</p>
<script type="text/javascript">
```

103

```
    video = document.getElementsByTagName("video")[0];
    span1 = document.getElementById("ended_first");
    span1.innerHTML = video.ended;
    span2 = document.getElementById("ended_ended");
    function span2Update(evt) { pan2.innerHTML = video.ended; }
    video.addEventListener("ended", span2Update, false);
</script>
```

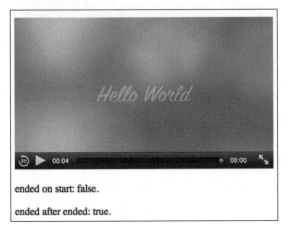

Figure 4–10. *Retrieving the paused attribute value and also a playing status in Safari*

All browsers exhibit the same behavior for this example.

@defaultPlaybackRate, @playbackRate

The @defaultPlaybackRate IDL attribute returns the speed at which the media resource is meant to be played back as a multiple of its intrinsic speed. Initially, it is set to 1.0, which is normal playback speed.

The attribute is mutable but changing it has no direct effect on playback. Rather, it is a default value to which the @playbackRate is initialized or returns to after it has been changed for fast-forwarding or reversing.

The @playbackRate IDL attribute returns the speed at which the media resource actually plays back as a multiple of its intrinsic speed. You can implement fast forward and fast rewind with @playbackRate.

Initially, @playbackRate is set to the value of @defaultPlaybackRate. If @playbackRate is positive or 0, then the direction of playback is forward. If it's negative, the direction is backward. If the @playbackRate is 0, playback doesn't move forward even though the media resource is not paused.

When playing backward, the browser mutes the audio. When @playbackRate is forward, but very slow (i.e. @playbackRate is close to 0) or fast pace (i.e. @playbackRate is pretty big), the browser mutes the audio, too. For fast forward with @playbackRate around the value of @defaultPlaybackRate, the audio is turned on, but the browser is encouraged to adjust the pitch to the original level to render the audio faithfully.

Fast-forward and rewinding are implemented by changing the @playbackRate relative to the @defaultPlaybackRate. Anything with a larger absolute value is faster; anything with a smaller absolute value is slower. This means that while a media resource plays, its current playback position increases monotonically at @playbackRate/@defaultPlaybackRate percent of the original speed.

When a user activates the "play" button in the browser controls, the @playbackRate IDL attribute's value is reset to the value of the @defaultPlaybackRate before starting playback.

When the @defaultPlaybackRate or the @playbackRate attribute values are changed, a rateChange event is fired.

Note that if you are playing back at a high @playbackRate, the download and decoding of the media resource may not be able to keep up and you may get stalled as buffering takes place.

Listing 4–14 shows an example of how to make use of the @defaultPlaybackRate and the @playbackRate attributes. First, we set the default to 0.8. When half the video is played back, we change the playback direction to backwards and set the speed to 2. Figure 4–11 shows the results in the browsers.

Listing 4–14. Getting the defaultPlaybackRate and playbackRate values for a media element

```
<video controls autoplay width="400">
  <source src="HelloWorld.mp4"  type="video/mp4">
  <source src="HelloWorld.webm" type="video/webm">
  <source src="HelloWorld.ogv"  type="video/ogg">
</video>
<p>default/PlaybackRate on start:
  <span id="defaultPlaybackRate_first"></span>.</p>
<p>default/PlaybackRate as set:
  <span id="defaultPlaybackRate_set"></span>.</p>
<p>default/PlaybackRate after timeupdate:
  <span id="defaultPlaybackRate_timeupdate"></span>.</p>
<p>default/PlaybackRate after ended:
  <span id="defaultPlaybackRate_ended"></span>.</p>
<script type="text/javascript">
  video = document.getElementsByTagName("video")[0];
  span1 = document.getElementById("defaultPlaybackRate_first");
  span1.innerHTML = video.defaultPlaybackRate + ", " +
                    video.playbackRate;
  video.defaultPlaybackRate = 0.8;
  span2 = document.getElementById("defaultPlaybackRate_set");
  span2.innerHTML = video.defaultPlaybackRate + ", " +
                    video.playbackRate;
  span3 = document.getElementById("defaultPlaybackRate_timeupdate");
  function span3Update(evt) {
    if (video.currentTime > video.duration/2) {
      video.playbackRate = -2;
      span3.innerHTML = video.defaultPlaybackRate + ", " +
                        video.playbackRate;
      video.removeEventListener("timeupdate", span2Update, false);
    }
  }
  span4 = document.getElementById("defaultPlaybackRate_ended");
  function span4Update(evt) {
    span4.innerHTML = video.defaultPlaybackRate + ", " +
                      video.playbackRate;
  }
  video.addEventListener("timeupdate", span3Update, false);
  video.addEventListener("ended", span4Update, false);
</script>
```

default/PlaybackRate on start: undefined, undefined.

default/PlaybackRate as set: 0.8, undefined.

default/PlaybackRate after timeupdate: 0.8, -2.

default/PlaybackRate after ended: 0.8, -2.

default/PlaybackRate on start: 1, 1.

default/PlaybackRate as set: 0.800000011920929, 1.

default/PlaybackRate after timeupdate: 0.800000011920929, -2.

default/PlaybackRate after ended: .

default/PlaybackRate on start: 1, 1.

default/PlaybackRate as set: 0.8, 1.

default/PlaybackRate after timeupdate: 0.8, -2.

default/PlaybackRate after ended: 0.8, -2.

default/PlaybackRate on start: 1, 1.

default/PlaybackRate as set: 0.800000011920929, 1.

default/PlaybackRate after timeupdate: 0.800000011920929, -2.

default/PlaybackRate after ended: 0.800000011920929, -2.

default/PlaybackRate on start: 1, 1.

default/PlaybackRate as set: 0.800000011920929, 1.

default/PlaybackRate after timeupdate: 0.800000011920929, 0.

default/PlaybackRate after ended: 0.800000011920929, 0.

Figure 4–11. Retrieving and setting playback rate attribute values in Firefox, Safari (top row), Opera, Chrome (middle row), and IE (bottom)

As can be seen from the images in Figure 4–10, all browsers but Safari reach the end of the media resource (they all display something after the ended event). In fact, they play back the media resource at the normal playback speed, and none starts playing backward nor at a faster pace.

Only Safari reacts correctly to these attributes and changes the playback speed and playback direction. It's quite impressive, actually, to see the video go backwards.

That none of the other browsers has implemented support of this attribute yet may be related to the codec and media frameworks in use. The media frameworks in use in Chrome, Opera, IE, and Firefox possibly require new functionality to play the codecs backward. In any case, at the time of this writing, only Safari, using the QuickTime framework and MPEG-4 files, was able to correctly display the standardized functionality.

4.2.3 States of the Media Element

The following IDL attributes, which represent web browser managed states of a media element, are explained in this section:

- networkState
- readyState
- error
- buffered TimeRanges
- played TimeRanges
- seekable TimeRanges

@networkState

The @networkState IDL attribute represents the current state of network activity of the media element. The available states are the following:

- NETWORK_EMPTY (0):
  no @currentSrc has been identified. This may be because the element has yet to be initialized, or because the resource selection hasn't found an @src attribute or <source> elements and is waiting for a load() function call to set it.

- NETWORK_IDLE (1):
  an @currentSrc has been identified and resource fetching is possible, but the browser has suspended network activity while waiting for user activity. This typically happens after the browser has downloaded the media element metadata on a resource that is not set to @autoplay. It also happens when the media resource has been partly downloaded, and the network buffering is suspended for some reason. These could include a connection interruption, media resource file corruption, a user abort, or for the simple fact that the browser has pre-buffered more than enough media data ahead of the playback position so is waiting for the user to catch up. Finally, it also occurs when a resource is completely downloaded. A suspend event is fired as the browser enters the NETWORK_IDLE state.

- NETWORK_LOADING (2):
  the browser is trying to download media resource data. The first time this happens on a media resource as part of the resource selection, the loadstart event is fired. If the @networkState changes at a later stage back to NETWORK_LOADING and the browser is fetching media data, a progress event is fired periodically. If media

data is unexpectedly not arriving from the network while trying to load, a stalled event is fired.

- NETWORK_NO_SOURCE (3):
the resource selection has identified a @currentSrc, but the resource has failed to load or the URL couldn't be resolved, or there is no resource provided; i.e. no @src or valid <source> children.

Listing 4–15 shows an example of how the different @networkState values can be reached – in theory. The states are displayed before load, after loading the resource metadata, after a progress event, and after changing the video's @src halfway through the video to a nonexistent resource. Figure 4–12 shows the results in the browsers.

Listing 4–15. Getting the networkState values for a media element

```
<video controls autoplay width="400">
  <source src="HelloWorld.mp4"  type="video/mp4">
  <source src="HelloWorld.webm" type="video/webm">
  <source src="HelloWorld.ogv"  type="video/ogg">
</video>
<p>networkState on start: <span id="networkState_first"></span>.</p>
<p>networkState after loadedmetadata:
  <span id="networkState_loadedmetadata"></span>.</p>
<p>networkState after progress:
  <span id="networkState_progress"></span>.</p>
<p>networkState after timeupdate:
  <span id="networkState_timeupdate"></span>.</p>
<script type="text/javascript">
  video = document.getElementsByTagName("video")[0];
  span1 = document.getElementById("networkState_first");
  span1.innerHTML = video.networkState;
  span2 = document.getElementById("networkState_loadedmetadata");
  function span2Update(evt) {
      span2.innerHTML = video.networkState;
  }
  span3 = document.getElementById("networkState_progress");
  function span3Update(evt) {
      span3.innerHTML = video.networkState;
  }
  span4 = document.getElementById("networkState_timeupdate");
  function span4Update(evt) {
    if (video.currentTime > video.duration/2) {
      video.src = "notavail.mp4";
      video.load();
      span4.innerHTML = video.networkState;
    }
  }
  video.addEventListener("loadedmetadata", span2Update, false);
  video.addEventListener("progress", span3Update, false);
  video.addEventListener("timeupdate", span4Update, false);
</script>
```

networkState on start: 3.

networkState after loadedmetadata: 1.

networkState after progress: 1.

networkState after timeupdate: 3.

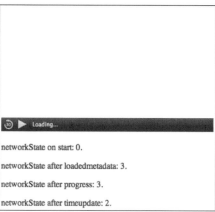

networkState on start: 0.

networkState after loadedmetadata: 3.

networkState after progress: 3.

networkState after timeupdate: 2.

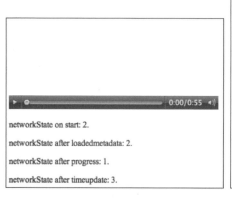

networkState on start: 2.

networkState after loadedmetadata: 2.

networkState after progress: 1.

networkState after timeupdate: 3.

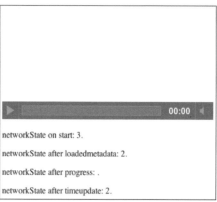

networkState on start: 3.

networkState after loadedmetadata: 2.

networkState after progress: .

networkState after timeupdate: 2.

networkState on start: 0.

networkState after loadedmetadata: 2.

networkState after progress: 2.

networkState after timeupdate: .

Figure 4–12. Retrieving the networkState attribute values in Firefox, Safari (top row), Opera, Chrome (middle row), and IE (bottom)

As can be seen, the browsers have some diverging interpretations of the specification probably because they were implemented at different stages of the specification's evolution.

At the start, we can find the browsers in all possible networks states: Firefox and Chrome start in @networkState NETWORK_NO_SOURCE (3), IE in NETWORK_LOADING (2), Opera in NETWORK_IDLE (1), and Safari in NETWORK_EMPTY (0).

After the metadata is loaded, Opera, Chrome, and IE set the @networkState to NETWORK_LOADING (2), Firefox to NETWORK_IDLE (1), and Safari to NETWORK_NO_SOURCE (3). It seems if a media resource is buffered, NETWORK_IDLE is the correct state; if it's not buffered, NETWORK_LOADING seems right, but Safari's state seems inexplicable.

Chrome never seems to throw the progress event. Opera and Firefox agree that they are in NETWORK_IDLE state when hit by a progress event. Safari thinks it is still in NETWORK_NO_SOURCE state, and IE is in NETWORK_LOADING state even though all downloading is done for this player. It also keeps a frame behind.

After trying to load the new media resource in vain, Safari and Google Chrome enter the NETWORK_LOADING state, while Firefox and Opera are in NETWORK_NO_SOURCE state. It seems IE doesn't raise a timeupdate event.

Clearly, not all states can be relied on to be set consistently across browsers. So as you do your implementations, be sure to test this well if you need this feature, then event raising is probably more reliable than the states.

@readyState

The @readyState IDL attribute represents the current state of the media element in relation to its playback position. The available states are the following:

- HAVE_NOTHING (0):
  no information regarding the video resource is available, including nothing about its playback position. This is typically the case before the media resource starts downloading. Media elements whose @networkState attribute is set to NETWORK_EMPTY are always in the HAVE_NOTHING @readyState.

- HAVE_METADATA (1):
  the setup information of the media resource has been received, such that the decoding pipeline is set up, the width and height of a video resource are known, and the duration of the resource (or a good approximation of it) is available. Seeking and decoding is now possible, even though no actual media data is available yet for the current playback position. As the HAVE_METADATA state is reached, a loadedmetadata event is fired.

- HAVE_CURRENT_DATA (2):
  decoded media data for the current playback position is available, but either not enough to start playing back continuously or the end of the playback direction has been reached. If this state is reached for the first time, a loadeddata event is fired. Note that this state may not be taken, but rather a HAVE_FUTURE_DATA or HAVE_ENOUGH_DATA state may be directly achieved after HAVE_METADATA, in which case the loadeddata event is fired upon reaching them for the first time. This state will also be reached when waiting for enough data to download for playback; e.g. after a seek or after the buffered data ran out—in this case, a waiting and a timupdate event are fired.

- HAVE_FUTURE_DATA (3):
  decoded media data for the current playback position and the next position is available; e.g. the current video frame and the one following it. If this state is reached for the first time, a canplay event is fired. If the element is not paused and not seeking and HAVE_FUTURE_DATA is reached, a playing event is fired. If the

browser actually starts playback at this stage, it may still need to stop soon afterward to buffer more data.

- HAVE_ENOUGH_DATA (4):
enough decoded media data is available for the current and next playback positions. The network download rate is fast enough that the browser estimates data will be fetched and decoded at the @defaultPlaybackRate sufficiently to allow continuous playback to the end of the media resource without stopping for further buffering. If this state is reached without going through HAVE_FUTURE_DATA, a canplay event is fired. If the element is not paused and not seeking and this state is reached without going through HAVE_FUTURE_DATA, a playing event is fired. If the HAVE_ENOUGH_DATA state is reached for the first time, a canplaythrough event is fired.

Listing 4–16 has an example of how the different @readyState values can be reached. We have taken a longer video so that there is a possibility for the browsers not to load all the data from the start. We check the state at specific events: after starting to load the video, after the metadata is loaded, after a timeupdate event, and after a progress event. Figure 4–13 shows the results in the browsers.

Listing 4–16. Getting the readyState values for a media element

```
<video controls width="400">
   <source src="video1.mp4"  type="video/mp4">
   <source src="video1.webm" type="video/webm">
   <source src="video1.ogv"  type="video/ogg">
</video>
<p>readyState on start: <span id="readyState_first"></span>.</p>
<p>readyState after loadedmetadata:
   <span id="readyState_loadedmetadata"></span>.</p>
<p>readyState after progress:
   <span id="readyState_progress"></span>.</p>
<p>readyState after timeupdate:
   <span id="readyState_timeupdate"></span>.</p>
<script type="text/javascript">
   video = document.getElementsByTagName("video")[0];
   span1 = document.getElementById("readyState_first");
   span1.innerHTML = video.readyState;
   span2 = document.getElementById("readyState_loadedmetadata");
   function span2Update(evt) {
       span2.innerHTML = video.readyState;
   }
   span3 = document.getElementById("readyState_progress");
   function span3Update(evt) {
       span3.innerHTML = video.readyState;
   }
   span4 = document.getElementById("readyState_timeupdate");
   function span4Update(evt) {
       span4.innerHTML = video.readyState;
   }
   video.addEventListener("loadedmetadata", span2Update, false);
   video.addEventListener("progress", span3Update, false);
   video.addEventListener("timeupdate", span4Update, false);
</script>
```

Figure 4–13. *Retrieving the readyState attribute values in Firefox, Safari (top row), Opera, Chrome (middle row), and IE (bottom)*

At the start, all browsers are in a HAVE_NOTHING (0) state.

After the video element has been initialized, Firefox and Safari go into the HAVE_FUTURE_DATA (3) state, Opera and Chrome into the HAVE_ENOUGH_DATA (4), and IE into HAVE_CURRENT_DATA (2). IE's choice seems odd, given that the browser is actually playing back the video.

As we press the play button and the video starts playing, the timeupdate event provides us with HAVE_ENOUGH_DATA (4) ready state on Safari, Opera and Chrome, with HAVE_FUTURE_DATA (3) in Firefox, and again with HAVE_CURRENT_DATA (2) in IE.

As we reach a progress event (which for IE, Opera and Chrome implies loading a previously noncached resource), Firefox, Safari and Chrome show HAVE_ENOUGH_DATA (4) upon the progress event, Opera says HAVE_NOTHING (0), and IE sticks with HAVE_CURRENT_DATA (2).

Clearly some alignment between the browser interpretations of the @readyState is still necessary.

@error

The @error IDL attribute represents the latest error state of the media element as a MediaError object.

The MediaError object looks as follows:

```
interface MediaError {
  const unsigned short MEDIA_ERR_ABORTED = 1;
  const unsigned short MEDIA_ERR_NETWORK = 2;
  const unsigned short MEDIA_ERR_DECODE = 3;
  const unsigned short MEDIA_ERR_SRC_NOT_SUPPORTED = 4;
  readonly attribute unsigned short code;
};
```

If there is no error, @error will be null, otherwise @error.code will have the error state. The available states are as follows:

- MEDIA_ERR_ABORTED (1):
  this error is raised when the fetching process for the media resource was aborted by the browser at the user's request; e.g. when browsing to another web page. The @networkState will be either NETWORK_EMPTY or NETWORK_IDLE, depending on when the download was aborted. An abort event is fired.

- MEDIA_ERR_NETWORK (2):
  this error is raised when any kind of network error caused the browser to stop fetching the media resource after the resource was established to be usable; e.g. when the network connection is interrupted. The @networkState will be either NETWORK_EMPTY or NETWORK_IDLE, depending on when the download was aborted. An error event is fired.

- MEDIA_ERR_DECODE (3):
  this error is raised when decoding of a retrieved media resource failed and video playback had to be aborted; e.g. because the media data was corrupted or the media resource used a feature that the browser does not support. The @networkState will be either NETWORK_EMPTY or NETWORK_IDLE, depending on when the download was aborted. An error event is fired.

- MEDIA_ERR_SRC_NOT_SUPPORTED (4):
  this error is raised when the media resource in the @src attribute failed to load or the URL could not be resolved. The media resource may not load if the server or the network failed or because the format is not supported. The @networkState will be either NETWORK_EMPTY or NETWORK_IDLE, depending on when the download was aborted. An error event is fired.

Listing 4–17 has an example for catching an @error value. We catch an error after loading a nonexistent media resource. Figure 4–14 shows the results in Firefox.

Listing 4–17. Getting the error values for a media element

```
<video controls autoplay width="400">
  <source src="HelloWorld.mp4"  type="video/mp4">
  <source src="HelloWorld.webm" type="video/webm">
  <source src="HelloWorld.ogv"  type="video/ogg">
</video>
<p>error on start: <span id="error_first"></span>.</p>
<p>error after timeupdate: <span id="error_timeupdate"></span>.</p>
<p>error after error: <span id="error_error"></span>.</p>
<script type="text/javascript">
  video = document.getElementsByTagName("video")[0];
  span1 = document.getElementById("error_first");
  span1.innerHTML = (video.error ? video.error.code : "none");
  span2 = document.getElementById("error_timeupdate");
  function span2Update(evt) {
    if (video.currentTime > video.duration/2) {
      video.src = "notavail.mp4";
      video.load();
      span2.innerHTML = (video.error ? video.error.code : "none");
    }
  }
  span3 = document.getElementById("error_error");
  function span3Update(evt) {
      span3.innerHTML = (video.error ? video.error.code : "none");
  }
  video.addEventListener("timeupdate", span2Update, false);
  video.addEventListener("error", span3Update, false);
</script>
```

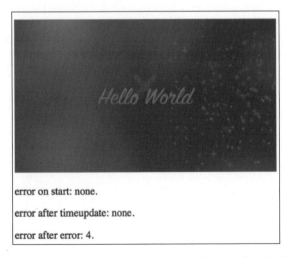

error on start: none.

error after timeupdate: none.

error after error: 4.

Figure 4–14. Retrieving the error attribute values in Firefox

The browsers throw an `error` event after which `@error.code` is `MEDIA_ERR_SRC_NOT_SUPPORTED`. All browsers have the same behavior.

@buffered

The `@buffered` IDL attribute retains the ranges of the media resource that the browser has buffered. The value is stored in a normalized `TimeRanges` object, which represent a list of ranges (intervals or periods) of time.

The `TimeRanges` object looks as follows:

```
interface TimeRanges {
  readonly attribute unsigned long length;
  float start(in unsigned long index);
  float end(in unsigned long index);
};
```

The IDL attributes of the `TimeRanges` object have the following meaning:

- `@length`: contains the number of ranges in the object, counting from 0 to `@length` - 1.

- `start(i)`: returns the start time for range number i in seconds from the start of the timeline.

- `end(i)`: returns the end time for range number i in seconds from the start of the timeline.

- `start(i)` and `end(i)` raise `INDEX_SIZE_ERR` exceptions if called with an index greater than or equal to `@length`.

A normalized `TimeRanges` object is one that consists only of ranges that:

- Aren't empty: `start(i) < end(i)` for all i.

- Are ordered, don't overlap, and don't touch: `start(i) > end(j)` for all j<i.

- If adjacent ranges would need to be created, they are instead folded into one bigger range.

The timeline of the `@buffered` IDL attribute is the timeline of the media resource.

Typically, the `@buffered` IDL attribute contains a single time range that starts at the `@startTime` of the media resource and grows as media data is downloaded until all of it has been received. However, for a large resource where seeking is undertaken to later points in the resource, the browser may store multiple byte ranges, thus creating multiple `TimeRanges`.

Note that browsers are free to discard previously buffered data, so time ranges that may be available earlier are not guaranteed to be still available at a later time.

Listing 4–18 retrieves the `@buffered` value at different playback states and prints the ranges. Figure 4–15 shows the results in the four browsers.

Listing 4–18. Getting the buffered ranges for a media element

```
<video controls width="400">
  <source src="video1.mp4"  type="video/mp4">
  <source src="video1.webm" type="video/webm">
  <source src="video1.ogv"  type="video/ogg">
</video>
<p>buffered on start: <span id="buffered_first"></span>.</p>
<p>buffered after loadedmetadata:
```

```
      <span id="buffered_loadedmetadata"></span>.</p>
<p>buffered after seeking: <span id="buffered_seeking"></span>.</p>
<p>buffered after timeupdate: <span id="buffered_timeupdate"></span>.</p>
<script type="text/javascript">
    function printTimeRanges(tr) {
      if (tr == null) return "undefined";
      s= tr.length + ": ";
      for (i=0; i<tr.length; i++) {
        s += tr.start(i) + " - " + tr.end(i) + "; ";
      }
      return s;
    }
    video = document.getElementsByTagName("video")[0];
    span1 = document.getElementById("buffered_first");
    span1.innerHTML = printTimeRanges(video.buffered);
    span2 = document.getElementById("buffered_loadedmetadata");
    function span2Update(evt) {
        span2.innerHTML = printTimeRanges(video.buffered);
        span3 = document.getElementById("buffered_seeking");
        video.currentTime = video.duration/2;
        video.play();
        span3.innerHTML = printTimeRanges(video.buffered);
    }
    span4 = document.getElementById("buffered_timeupdate");
    function span4Update(evt) {
      span4.innerHTML = printTimeRanges(video.buffered);
    }
    video.addEventListener("loadedmetadata", span2Update, false);
    video.addEventListener("timeupdate", span4Update, false);
</script>
```

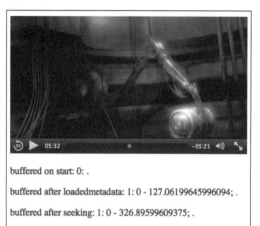

buffered on start: 0: .

buffered after loadedmetadata: 1: 0 - 127.06199645996094; .

buffered after seeking: 1: 0 - 326.89599609375; .

buffered after timeupdate: 1: 0 - 653.7919921875; .

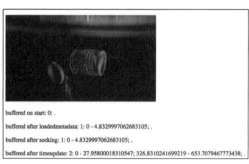

buffered on start: 0: .

buffered after loadedmetadata: 1: 0 - 4.8329997062683105; .

buffered after seeking: 1: 0 - 4.8329997062683105; .

buffered after timeupdate: 2: 0 - 27.95800018310547; 326.8310241699219 - 653.7079467773438; .

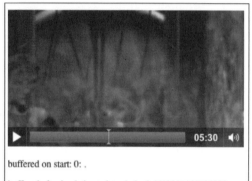

buffered on start: 0: .

buffered after loadedmetadata: 1: 0 - 0.4410000145435333; .

buffered after seeking: 1: 0 - 0.4410000145435333; .

buffered after timeupdate: 1: 0 - 479.6910095214844; .

buffered on start: 0: .

buffered after loadedmetadata: 0: .

buffered after seeking: 0: .

buffered after timeupdate: 0: .

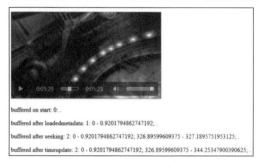

buffered on start: 0: .

buffered after loadedmetadata: 1: 0 - 0.9201794862747192; .

buffered after seeking: 2: 0 - 0.9201794862747192; 326.89599609375 - 327.1895751953125; .

buffered after timeupdate: 2: 0 - 0.9201794862747192; 326.89599609375 - 344.25347900390625; .

Figure 4–15. *Retrieving the buffered attribute values in Firefox, Safari (top row), Opera, Chrome (middle row), and IE (bottom)*

117

As the screenshots show, Opera hasn't implemented the @buffered attribute yet and doesn't even initialize the structure. All others – Firefox, Safari, Chrome, and IE – provide the attribute and update its content.

The attribute also exposes some of the buffering strategy. Safari seems to load as much of the media data as possible (note that this example is on a fast connection), while Firefox only prebuffers the next roughly 25 seconds and doesn't continue loading more until the end of this buffer is reached.

@played

The @played IDL attribute retains the ranges of the media resource the browser has played. The value is stored in a normalized TimeRanges object (see @buffered attribute). The timeline of the @played IDL attribute is the timeline of the media resource.

Typically, the @played IDL attribute contains a single time range that starts at the @startTime of the media resource and grows as more media data is downloaded and played until all the media data has been received. However, for a large resource where seeking is undertaken to alter points in the resource, the browser may store multiple byte ranges, thus creating multiple time ranges.

Listing 4–19 retrieves the @played value at different playback states and prints the ranges basically the same way as the @buffered example. Figure 4–16 shows the results in the browsers.

Listing 4–19. Getting the played ranges for a media element

```
<video controls width="400">
  <source src="video1.mp4"  type="video/mp4">
  <source src="video1.webm" type="video/webm">
  <source src="video1.ogv"  type="video/ogg">
</video>
<p>played on start: <span id="played_first"></span>.</p>
<p>played after loadedmetadata:
  <span id="played_loadedmetadata"></span>.</p>
<p>played after seeking: <span id="played_seeking"></span>.</p>
<p>played after timeupdate: <span id="played_timeupdate"></span>.</p>
<script type="text/javascript">
  function printTimeRanges(tr) {
    if (tr == null) return "undefined";
    s = tr.length + ": ";
    for (i=0; i<tr.length; i++) {
      s += tr.start(i) + " - " + tr.end(i) + "; ";
    }
    return s;
  }
  video = document.getElementsByTagName("video")[0];
  span1 = document.getElementById("played_first");
  span1.innerHTML = printTimeRanges(video.played);
  span2 = document.getElementById("played_loadedmetadata");
  function span2Update(evt) {
      span2.innerHTML = printTimeRanges(video.played);
      span3 = document.getElementById("played_seeking");
      video.currentTime = video.duration/2;
      video.play();
      span3.innerHTML = printTimeRanges(video.played);
  }
  span4 = document.getElementById("played_timeupdate");
  function span4Update(evt) {
    span4.innerHTML = printTimeRanges(video.played);
```

```
      }
      video.addEventListener("loadedmetadata", span2Update, false);
      video.addEventListener("timeupdate", span4Update, false);
    </script>
```

Figure 4–16. Retrieving the played attribute values in Firefox, Safari (top row), Opera, Chrome (middle row), and IE (bottom).

As before, it seems that neither Firefox nor Opera has implemented support for the @played IDL attribute. Chrome, Safari and IE support the attribute and report the played time ranges correctly. Note that if the user seeks to different time ranges and plays them back, several time ranges will be reported in the @played attribute. We'll leave this as an exercise to the user.

@seekable

The @seekable IDL attribute retains the ranges of the media resource to which the browser can seek. The value is stored in a normalized TimeRanges object (see @buffered attribute). The timeline of the @seekable IDL attribute is the timeline of the media resource.

Typically, the @seekable IDL attribute contains a single time range that starts at the @startTime of the media resource and ends at the media resource @duration. If the duration is not available from the start, such as on an infinite stream, the time range may change continuously and just keep a certain window available.

Listing 4–20 retrieves the @seekable value at different playback states and prints the ranges basically the same way as the @buffered example. Figure 4–17 shows the results in the browsers.

Listing 4–20. Getting the seekable ranges for a media element

```
<video controls width="400">
  <source src="video1.mp4"  type="video/mp4">
  <source src="video1.webm" type="video/webm">
  <source src="video1.ogv"  type="video/ogg">
</video>
<p>seekable on start: <span id="seekable_first"></span>.</p>
<p>seekable after loadedmetadata:
  <span id="seekable_loadedmetadata"></span>.</p>
<script type="text/javascript">
  function printTimeRanges(tr) {
    if (tr == null) return "undefined";
    s = tr.length + ": ";
    for (i=0; i<tr.length; i++) {
      s += tr.start(i) + " - " + tr.end(i) + "; ";
    }
    return s;
  }
  video = document.getElementsByTagName("video")[0];
  span1 = document.getElementById("seekable_first");
  span1.innerHTML = printTimeRanges(video.seekable);
  span2 = document.getElementById("seekable_loadedmetadata");
  function span2Update(evt) {
    span2.innerHTML = printTimeRanges(video.seekable);
  }
  video.addEventListener("loadedmetadata", span2Update, false);
</script>
```

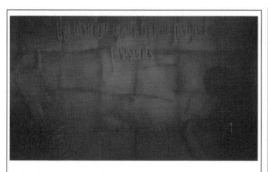

seekable on start: undefined.

seekable after loadedmetadata: undefined.

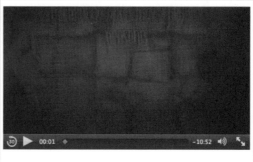

seekable on start: 0: .

seekable after loadedmetadata: 1: 0 - 653.7919921875; .

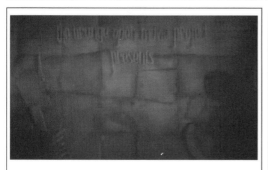

seekable on start: 0: .

seekable after loadedmetadata: 0: .

seekable on start: 0: .

seekable after loadedmetadata: 1: 0 - 653.7916870117188; .

played on start: 0: .

played after loadedmetadata: 0: .

played after seeking: 0: .

played after timeupdate: 1: 326.89599609375 - 329.20001220703125; .

Figure 4–17. *Retrieving the seekable attribute values in Firefox, Safari (top row), Opera, Chrome (middle row), and IE (bottom)*

As before, it seems that neither Firefox nor Opera has implemented support for the @seekable IDL attribute. Chrome, Safari and IE support the attribute and report the full duration of the media resource as seekable once the resource's metadata is loaded. You can simply assume for Firefox and Opera that the media resource as loaded is seekable from @startTime=0 to @duration.

4.3 Control Methods in the API

The following JavaScript control methods defined on media elements are explained in this section:

- load()
- play()
- pause()
- canPlayType()

load()

The load() control method, when executed on a media element, causes all activity on a media resource to be suspended (including resource selection and loading, seeking and playback), all network activity to be seized, the element to be reset (including removal of pending callbacks and events), and the resource selection and loading process to be restarted.

In a typical scenario for a successful load(), roughly the following sequence of steps will happen:

- Initialization:
    - @networkState is set to NETWORK_EMPTY.
    - @readyState is set to HAVE_NOTHING.
    - @paused is set to "true."
    - @seeking is set to "false."
    - @ended is set to "false."
    - @currentTime is set to 0.
    - @error is set to null.
    - @buffered, @played, and @seekable are set to empty.
    - @playbackRate is set to the value of @defaultPlaybackRate.
- Resource selection:
    - @currentSrc is set from the given @src value or the <source> elements.
    - @networkState is set to NETWORK_LOADING.
    - the loadstart event is fired.
- Resource fetching:
    - begin downloading the media resource identified in the @currentSrc attribute.

- progress event is fired roughly every 350ms or for every byte received (whichever is less frequent).

- @preload and @autoplay values help determine how much to download.

- when the resource's metadata has been downloaded:

    - @startTime is determined.

    - @currentTime is set to @startTime.

    - @duration is determined.

    - the durationchange event is fired.

    - @videoWidth and @videoHeight are determined (if video element).

    - @seekable is determined.

    - @readyState is set to HAVE_METADATA.

    - the loadedmetadata event is fired.

- seek to the appropriate start time given in the media resource or the @currentSrc URI:

    - @currentTime is set to this start time.

    - the timeupdate event is fired.

- potentially more media data is downloaded (and decoded):

    - @readyState changes to HAVE_CURRENT_DATA or higher.

    - the loadeddata event is fired.

    - the canplay event is fired for any @readyState higher than HAVE_FUTURE_DATA.

    - @buffered is updated.

- @networkState is set to NETWORK_IDLE.

- playback start, if @autoplay is "true":

    - download more data until @readyState is HAVE_FUTURE_DATA or higher (preferably HAVE_ENOUGH_DATA so playback doesn't get stalled).

    - @paused is set to "false."

    - the play event is fired.

    - the playing event is fired.

    - playback is started.

Note that many error and network state situations are also dealt with through the loading process. For example, if the network download stalls and the browser hasn't received data for more than about 3 seconds, a stalled event will be fired.

Several previous examples in this chapter have made use of the load() control method; see e.g. Listings 4–15 and 4–17. We will not include another example here.

play()

The play() control method executed on a media element sets the @paused IDL attribute to "false" and starts playback of the media resource, downloading and buffering media data as required.

In a typical scenario for a successful play(), roughly the following sequence of steps will happen:

- if @networkState is NETWORK_EMPTY—i.e. no @currentSrc has been determined yet (e.g. because the @src of the element was empty as the element was set up, but now the attribute was set through JavaScript and the resource can be fetched)— "resource selection" and "resource fetching," as described for load() above, are executed.

- if @ended is "true" and the playback direction is forward, the browser seeks to @startTime.

- @currentTime is set to @startTime.

- timeupdate event is fired.

- "start playback" as described for load() above is executed.

We'll look at an example use of play() together with pause().

pause()

The pause() control method, when executed on a media element, sets the @paused IDL attribute to "true" and stops playback of the media resource.

In a typical scenario for a successful pause(), roughly the following sequence of steps will happen:

if @networkState is NETWORK_EMPTY—i.e. no @currentSrc has been determined yet—"resource selection" and "resource fetching," as described for load() above, are executed. @currentSrc may not have been determined yet because the @src of the element was empty as the element was set up, but now the attribute was set through JavaScript and the resource can be fetched.

- pause playback:

- @paused is set to "true."

- timeupdate event is fired.

- pause event is fired.

- downloading of more media data is potentially suspended and a suspend event is fired if the browser is far ahead of the current playback position.

Listing 4–21 makes use of both, play() and pause(). At first, no media resource is specified for a video element. Then, we set the @src attribute, depending on what format a browser supports, and call play(). Later we call pause() halfway through playing. Figure 4–18 shows the results in the browsers.

Listing 4–21. Using the play() and pause() control methods for a media element

```
<video controls width="400">
</video>
<p>currentSrc on start: <span id="currentSrc_first"></span>.</p>
<p>currentSrc after loadedmetadata:
  <span id="currentSrc_loadedmetadata"></span>.</p>
<p>currentTime on pause: <span id="currentTime_pause"></span>.</p>
<script type="text/javascript">
  video = document.getElementsByTagName("video")[0];
```

```
  source = document.getElementsByTagName("source");
  span1 = document.getElementById("currentSrc_first");
  span1.innerHTML = video.currentSrc;
  if (video.canPlayType("video/ogg") != "") {
    video.src = "HelloWorld.ogv";
  } else if (video.canPlayType("video/webm") != "") {
    video.src = "HelloWorld.webm";
  } else if (video.canPlayType("video/mp4") != "") {
    video.src = "HelloWorld.mp4";
  }
  video.play();
  span2 = document.getElementById("currentSrc_loadedmetadata");
  function span2Update(evt) { span2.innerHTML = video.currentSrc; }
  function callpause(evt) {
    if (video.currentTime > video.duration/2) {
      video.pause();
    }
  }
  span3 = document.getElementById("currentTime_pause");
  function span3Update(evt) {   span3.innerHTML = video.currentTime;   }
  video.addEventListener("loadedmetadata", span2Update, false);
  video.addEventListener("timeupdate", callpause, false);
  video.addEventListener("pause", span3Update, false);
</script>
```

currentSrc on start: .

currentSrc after loadedmetadata: http://localhost/HelloWorld.webm.

currentTime on pause: 2.0929999351501465.

currentSrc on start: .

currentSrc after loadedmetadata: http://localhost/HelloWorld.mp4.

currentTime on pause: 2.003370761871338.

currentSrc on start: .

currentSrc after loadedmetadata: http://localhost/HelloWorld.webm.

currentTime on pause: 2.08.

currentSrc on start: .

currentSrc after loadedmetadata: http://localhost/HelloWorld.mp4.

currentTime on pause: 2.2565059661865234.

currentSrc on start: .

currentSrc after loadedmetadata: http://192.168.1.132/HelloWorld.mp4.

currentTime on pause: 2.005401611328125.

Figure 4–18. Using the play() and pause() control methods in Firefox, Safari (top row), Opera, Chrome (middle row), and IE (bottom)

All browsers support this functionality.

canPlayType()

The canPlayType(in DOMString type) control method for a media element takes a string as a parameter that is of a MIME type and returns whether the browser is confident that it can play back that media type.

Possible return values are:

- the empty string "":
  the browser is confident it cannot decode and render this type of media resource in a media element.

- "maybe":
  the browser is not sure if it can or cannot render this type of media resource in a media element.

- "probably":
  the browser is confident that it can decode and render this type of media resource in a media element; because this implies knowledge about whether the codecs in a container format are supported by the browser. Browsers are encouraged to only return "probably" for a MIME type that includes the codecs parameter.

The previous example in Listing 4–21 has made use of the canPlayType() control method, and it has also been used in Chapter 2 in Listings 2–28 and 2–29.

4.4 Events

In the following table we summarize all the available events, many of which we have already used in previous examples. This is just an overview table to find everything in one place.

Event	Is dispatched when...	Preconditions
loadstart	the browser begins looking for media data, as part of the resource selection upon media element load, or load(), play(), or pause().	@networkState is NETWORK_LOADING for the first time.
progress	the browser is fetching media data.	@networkState is NETWORK_LOADING.
suspend	the browser has paused fetching media data, but does not have the entire media resource downloaded yet.	@networkState is NETWORK_IDLE.
abort	the browser was stopped from fetching the media data before it is completely downloaded, but not due to an error—rather due to a user action, such as browsing away.	@error is MEDIA_ERR_ABORTED. @networkState is either NETWORK_EMPTY or NETWORK_IDLE, depending on when the download was aborted.
error	an error occurred while fetching the media data.	@error is MEDIA_ERR_NETWORK or higher. @networkState is either NETWORK_EMPTY or NETWORK_IDLE, depending on when the download was aborted.

Event	Is dispatched when...	Preconditions
emptied	a media element has just lost the network connection to a media resource, either because of a fatal error during load that's about to be reported or because the load() method was invoked while the resource selection algorithm was already running.	`@networkState` is `NETWORK_EMPTY` for the first time and all the IDL attributes are in their initial states.
stalled	the browser tried to fetch media data, but data has not arrived for more than 3 seconds.	`@networkState` is `NETWORK_LOADING`.
play	playback has begun upon media element load with an `@autoplay` attribute through user interaction or after the `play()` method has returned.	`@paused` is newly "false."
pause	playback has been paused either through user interaction, or after the `pause()` method has returned.	`@paused` is newly "true".
loadedmetadata	the browser has just set up the decoding pipeline for the media resource and determined the `@duration` and dimensions.	`@readyState` is `HAVE_METADATA` or greater for the first time.
loadeddata	the browser can render the media data at the current playback position for the first time.	`@readyState` is `HAVE_CURRENT_DATA` or greater for the first time.
waiting	playback has stopped because the next media data is not yet available from the network, but the browser expects that frame to become available in due course; i.e. less than 3 seconds. This can be after a seek or when the network is unexpectedly slow.	`@readyState` is newly equal to or less than `HAVE_CURRENT_DATA`, and `@paused` is "false." Either `@seeking` is "true," or the current playback position is not contained in any of the ranges in `@buffered`.
playing	playback has started.	`@readyState` is newly equal to or greater than `HAVE_FUTURE_DATA`, `@paused` is "false," `@seeking` is "false," or the current playback position is contained in one of the ranges in `@buffered`.
canplay	the browser can start or resume playback of the media resource, but without being certain of being able to play through at the given playback rate without a need for further buffering.	`@readyState` newly increased to `HAVE_FUTURE_DATA` or greater.

Event	Is dispatched when...	Preconditions
canplaythrough	the browser is certain that with the given media data, the rate at which the network delivers further media data and the given playback rate, the media resource can play through without further buffering.	@readyState is newly equal to HAVE_ENOUGH_DATA.
seeking	the browser is seeking and the seek operation is taking long enough that the browser has time to fire the event.	@seeking is "true" and @readyState is less than HAVE_FUTURE_DATA.
seeked	the browser is finished seeking.	@seeking has changed to "false."
timeupdate	the current playback position changed as part of normal playback every 15 to 250ms. It is also fired when seeking, or when fetching a new media resource. It is also fired when playback has ended, is paused, is stopped due to an error or because the media resource needs to buffer from the network.	@seeking is newly "true" OR @startTime is newly set OR @ended is newly "true" OR @paused is newly "true" OR @readyState newly changed to a value lower than HAVE_FUTURE_DATA without @ended is "true" OR @error is newly non-null with @readyState being HAVE_METADATA or more OR @seeking is "false," @paused is "false," @ended is "false," @readyState is at least HAVE_FUTURE_DATA, and the last timeupdate was fired more than 15-250ms ago
ended	playback has stopped because the end of the media resource was reached.	@ended is newly "true" and @currentTime is equal to @startTime plus @duration.
ratechange	either the default playback rate or the playback rate has just been updated.	@defaultPlaybackRate or @playbackRate is newly changed.
durationchange	the duration has just been changed upon media element load, or after an explicit change of @src and media resource fetching, or when the browser has a better estimate; e.g. during streaming.	@readyState is HAVE_METADATA or greater for the first time.
volumechange	either the volume or the muted state of the media element changed.	@volume or @muted changed.

4.5 Custom Controls

The JavaScript API's foremost use case will be to roll your own controls with a style that looks identical across all browsers. Because this is such a common use case, we provide you with an example on how to do so. This includes a skeleton of the HTML code, some CSS, and the required JavaScript calls to control it.

We want to build the player displayed in Figure 4–19. It is inspired by an accessible YouTube player implemented by Christian Heilmann and available at http://icant.co.uk/easy-youtube/.

Design inspiration and buttons from http://icant.co.uk/easy-youtube/
Thanks go to Chris Heilmann

Figure 4–19. A custom video player using the JavaScript API

The player consists of several interface elements. It has a progress display (the bar underneath the video), behind which it shows the seconds played and the video duration. Below that is a collection of buttons to start playing (a play/pause toggle), rewind by 5sec, stop playback (and reset to file start), increase volume by 10 percent, reduce volume by 10 percent, and mute/unmute. To the right of the video is the volume display. It is grayed out when muted, and the volume level is shown as a percentage in height.

We start implementing this player by providing a skeleton of the HTML code that creates this player. Listing 4–22 shows the skeleton.

Listing 4–22. An HTML markup skeleton for the video player in Figure 4–19

```
<div id="player">
  <div id="video">
    <video width="400" height="225">
      <source src="video2.mp4"  type="video/mp4">
      <source src="video2.webm" type="video/webm">
      <source src="video2.ogv"  type="video/ogg">
    </video>
```

```
      <div id="positionview">
        <div id="transportbar"><div id="position"></div></div>
        <div id="time">
          <span id="curTime">00:00</span>/<span id="duration">00:00</span>
        </div>
      </div>
    </div>
    <div id="volumecontrol">
      <div id="volumebar"><div id="volume"></div></div>
      <div id="vol"></div>
    </div>
    <div style="clear: both;"></div>
    <div id="controls">
      <div><input id="play"    type="image" src="0.gif" alt="Play"></div>
      <div><input id="repeat"  type="image" src="0.gif" alt="Repeat"></div>
      <div><input id="stop"    type="image" src="0.gif" alt="Stop"></div>
      <div><input id="louder"  type="image" src="0.gif" alt="Louder"></div>
      <div><input id="quieter" type="image" src="0.gif" alt="Quieter">
      </div>
      <div><input id="mute" type="image" src="0.gif" alt="Mute"></div>
    </div>
  </div>
```

A `<div>` encapsulates the complete player code such that we can later give it a style that shows it as an entity. Inside the #player div are three main divs: #video, #volumecontrol, and #controls. The #video part contains the video element, as well as the transport bar and time displays. The #volumecontrol contains the volume bar and volume number display. The #controls contains all the buttons.

Note that the video element does not have a @controls attribute—as we want to run these controls ourselves. Also notice how the `<input>` elements that represent the buttons have been made accessible by making them of type "image" and giving them an @alt attribute value. Since we are going to provide the actual buttons in CSS through a single PNG, we have to put a placeholder 1x1 px GIF into the @src attribute of the `<input>` elements so that they do not show up as broken images.

Next, we move on to styling this HTML skeleton. Listing 4–23 shows an extract of the CSS in use.

Listing 4–23. *CSS for the HTML skeleton in Listing 4–22 and the video player in Figure 4–18*

```
<style type="text/css">
#player {
  padding: 10px;
  border:    5px solid black;
  border-radius: 15px;
  box-shadow: 10px 10px 5px gray;
  box-sizing: content-box;
  max-width: 455px;
}
#positionview {
  width: 400px; height: 40px;
}
#transportbar {
  height: 20px;
  width: 300px;
  position: relative;
  float: left;
```

```
    border: 2px solid black;
  }
  #position {
    background: #D7BC28;
    height: 20px;
    width: 0px;
  }
  #time {
    position: relative;
    float: right;
  }
  #video {
    position: relative;
    float: left;
    padding: 0;
    margin: 0;
  }
  // include your own CSS for the volume control here and
  // style every button with an offset on buttons.png (we only show one)
  #controls div input {
    background:url(buttons.png) no-repeat top left;
    border:none;
    height: 60px;
    width: 60px;
    padding: 5px;
    display: inline-block;
  }
  #controls div #repeat {
    background-position:0 -901px;
  }
  </style>
```

The player div gets a nice border, rounded corners, and a shadow to make it stand out. For the position display we have an outer <div> and an inner <div>, where the outer one provides the box into which the playback position can grow and the inner one grows with the playback speed of the video. The buttons all use the same PNG with an offset and a 60x60 px cropping area.

Finally we add the JavaScript that will make it all work in Listing 4–24.

Listing 4–24. *JavaScript for the HTML skeleton in Listing 4–22 and the video player in Figure 4–19*

```
<script type="text/javascript">
  video = document.getElementsByTagName("video")[0];
  position  = document.getElementById("position");
  curTime   = document.getElementById("curTime");
  duration  = document.getElementById("duration");
  volume    = document.getElementById("volume");
  vol       = document.getElementById("vol");
  play      = document.getElementById("play");
  repeat    = document.getElementById("repeat");
  stop      = document.getElementById("stop");
  louder    = document.getElementById("louder");
  quieter   = document.getElementById("quieter");
  mute      = document.getElementById("mute");
```

```
video.addEventListener("loadedmetadata", init, false);
function init(evt) {
  duration.innerHTML = video.duration.toFixed(2);
  vol.innerHTML      = video.volume.toFixed(2);
}

video.addEventListener("timeupdate", curTimeUpdate, false);
function curTimeUpdate(evt) {
  curTime.innerHTML = video.currentTime.toFixed(2);
  position.style.width = 300*video.currentTime/video.duration + "px";
}

video.addEventListener("volumechange", dispVol, false);
function dispVol(evt) {
  vol.innerHTML = video.volume.toFixed(2);
}

play.addEventListener("click", togglePlay, false);
function togglePlay(evt) {
  if (video.paused == false) {
    video.pause();
    play.style.backgroundPosition = "0 0";
  } else {
    video.play();
    play.style.backgroundPosition = "0 -151px";
  }
}

repeat.addEventListener("click", rewind, false);
function rewind(evt) {
  video.currentTime = video.currentTime - 2.0;
}

stop.addEventListener("click", restart, false);
function restart(evt) {
  video.pause();
  play.style.backgroundPosition = "0 0";
  video.currentTime = 0;
}

louder.addEventListener("click", volInc, false);
function volInc(evt) {
  changeVolume(video.volume+0.1);
}

quieter.addEventListener("click", volDec, false);
function volDec(evt) {
  changeVolume(video.volume-0.1);
}

mute.addEventListener("click", toggleMute, false);
function toggleMute(evt) {
  video.muted = !video.muted;
```

```
      if (video.muted) {
        volume.className = 'disabled';
      } else {
        volume.className = '';
      }
    }

    function changeVolume(changeTo) {
      if(video.muted){
        toggleMute();
      }
      if(changeTo > 1.0) {
        changeTo = 1.0;
      } else if (changeTo < 0.0) {
        changeTo = 0.0;
      }
      volume.style.height = 225*changeTo +'px';
      volume.style.marginTop = 225-(225*changeTo) + 'px';
      video.volume = changeTo;
    }
</script>
```

The full JavaScript for the player is replicated here. Take a minute to go through the code. Note how every button has an onclick event handler and there are extra event handlers for the loadedmetadata, timeupdate, and volumechange events. You will notice many familiar IDL attributes: video.duration, video.volume, video.currentTime, video.paused, and video.muted are all used here to provide the functions behind the buttons. Finally, you will also notice the play() and pause() control methods.

4.5 Summary

In this chapter we introduced the JavaScript API of the <video> and <audio> elements.

We have approached this in a structured way, starting with the IDL attributes that represent the content attributes from the HTML markup, such as @src, @width, and @height. Then we discussed the IDL attributes that represent resource features, such as @currentSrc, @duration, and @volume. Then we looked at the playback related IDL attributes such as @currentTime, @paused, and @ended.

After the IDL attributes, we introduced the states of a media resource, including networkState, readyState, and played, buffered, or seekable TimeRanges.

After the states came the control methods load(), play(), pause(), and canPlayType().

We finished analyzing the JavaScript API with a listing of the events that the media elements fire. There is a fair number, including loadedmetadata, canplay, playing, pause, seeking, volumechange, durationchange, and ended.

We concluded the chapter with a practical use case of the JavaScript API: running your own custom controls.

We now have all the tools at hand to successfully use <audio> and <video> in HTML5 applications. The next chapters will analyze how <audio> and <video> interact with other elements and JavaScript functionalities in HTML5, including SVG, the Canvas, and WebWorkers.

CHAPTER 5

■■■

HTML5 Media and SVG

SVG stands for Scalable Vector Graphics and is a language used to describe two-dimensional graphical objects in XML. In the past, SVG has been a standalone format used in web browsers through Adobe Flash as an embedded resource or as an image resource. Nowadays, all modern browsers support SVG natively, including Internet Explorer 9.

The main use of SVG on the Web is to allow the creation of interactive graphics with many objects that can be viewed at any zoom-factor without loss of resolution. Maps, technical diagrams, and hierarchical system diagrams are typically good examples of uses of SVG.

SVG Features

The current version of SVG supported in browsers is SVG 1.1.[1] The next version, SVG 1.2[2], also exists as a working draft and has a large number of additional features specified in so-called modules. In particular, it has a "Media" module[3] that contains <audio> and <video> elements. Of all the modern web browsers, only Opera supports some of the additional SVG 1.2 features, including the Media module.

In this chapter, we will look at how SVG 1.1 features can be used to manipulate HTML5 video. Because <video> has a visual dimension, SVG applies to it. It doesn't really apply to <audio>, though you can render SVG graphics together with audio elements. We will focus on SVG 1.1 features, but also look at the SVG 1.2 Media module to see what additional functionalities it provides.

We cannot give an in-depth introduction to SVG here, but since we will use only a few of the elements, it will be easy to follow. For a bit of a background, here is a list of the different types of elements that exist in SVG 1.1:

- structural elements (<svg>, <defs>, <desc>, <title>, <metadata>, <symbol>, <use>, <g>, <switch>, <a>, <view>).

- shapes (<circle>, <ellipse>, <rect>, <line>, <polyline>, <polygon>, <path>, <cursor>).

- text (<text>, <tspan>, <tref>, <textPath>, <altGlyph>, <altGlyphDef>, <altGlyphItem>, <glyphRef>, <font> and font features).

- styling (<style>, <marker>, <linearGradient>, <radialGradient>, <stop>, <pattern>).

- effects (<clipPath>, <mask>, <filter> and filter effects).

---

[1] See http://www.w3.org/TR/SVG/intro.html for specification.

[2] See http://www.w3.org/TR/SVG12/

[3] See http://www.w3.org/TR/2004/WD-SVG12-20041027/media.html

- animations (<animate>, <set>, <animateMotion>, <animateTransform>, <animateColor>, <mpath>).

- <script>, <image> and <foreignObject>.

If you are looking for some good resources to help you get started with using SVG in the different browsers, we highly recommend the following links:

- Firefox: https://developer.mozilla.org/En/SVG_in_Firefox

- WebKit (Chrome and Safari): http://webkit.org/projects/svg/status.xml

- Opera: http://www.opera.com/docs/specs/opera95/svg/

- IE: http://blogs.msdn.com/b/ie/archive/2010/03/18/svg-in-ie9-roadmap.aspx

This Wikipedia article is very useful to check which browser has implementation support for which 1.1 feature: http://en.wikipedia.org/wiki/Comparison_of_layout_engines_(Scalable_Vector_Graphics).

5.1 Use of SVG with <video>

There are three different ways in which the <video> element and SVG can interact: inline SVG, SVG for masking, and video in SVG.

Inline SVG

With HTML5, SVG has been natively integrated into web pages through its own <svg> element or as a referenced CSS property. Thus, you can now create web pages with **inline SVG** graphics, where the SVG graphics are fully integrated with the rest of the page; e.g. following CSS styling, allowing JavaScript to interact with SVG objects, drawing graphics, or creating effects on hover-over of certain SVG objects. Also, you can use inline SVG to modify given graphics and videos; e.g. cropping them, adding a filter, or adding animations.

Note that only Firefox, IE, and Chrome support SVG inline for **HTML** pages at this time; i.e. they allow the use of the <svg> element inside the HTML page. Safari and Opera support inline SVG only for **XHTML** pages, because XML can deal with the namespace inclusion. Where we want to use SVG elements to control a video element through JavaScript, we use XHTML with inline SVG at this stage. Also note that IE's support of SVG is still very sketchy, in particular for some of the features we use in this chapter.

SVG for Masking

A major use of SVG with HTML pages is as an advanced styling and effects tool. In Firefox, we have the CSS attributes[4] filter, mask, and clip-path to use inline or external SVG fragments for effects. In the WebKit-based browsers, it is possible to use external SVG files as a CSS mask through the -webkit-mask CSS attribute. Inline SVG cannot be used in -webkit-mask. Opera and IE at this stage have no means of using an SVG in CSS for extra effects, whether defined inline or in an external SVG file.

---

[4] Also proposed to W3C for standardization http://people.mozilla.com/~roc/SVG-CSS-Effects-Draft.html

Video in SVG

All browsers except for IE are capable of supporting <video> inside an SVG definition, either natively as a SVG 1.2 feature as is the case with Opera or through the `<foreignObject>` feature of SVG. IE hasn't implemented any SVG 1.2 feature yet, which means it does not yet support <video> or `<foreignObject>`.

Our examples

The examples in this chapter will make use of all three ways of using SVG with HTML and <video>.

We use HTML and XHTML where we demonstrate only inline SVG elements together with a direct hook into the video element through JavaScript; e.g. for custom controls. This works in all browsers.

For demonstrating the use of SVG effects such as masking on video, we will use HTML and an external SVG file. In the HTML file, we will incorporate different CSS code for WebKit-based browsers (Safari and Google Chrome) and for Firefox. Unfortunately, this leaves Opera and IE out of these examples.

Where we want to experiment with both inline SVG elements and SVG effects, we can use only Firefox and thus we will use inline SVG.

Finally, we will also look at the use of video in SVG, but only as inline SVG with XHTML either through the `<video>` or the `<foreignObject>` element. This currently is probably the most cross-browser compatible means of using SVG effects for video, even though it still leaves IE out in the cold. It can be expected that IE will implement `<foreignObject>` or possibly even `<video>` in SVG relatively soon.

5.2 Basic Shapes and <video>

At the most basic level, SVG allows the creation of basic shapes and outlines:

- <circle>
- <ellipse>
- <rect>
- <line>
- <polyline>
- <polygon>
- <path>

Shapes as a mask

We can use any of the shapes as a mask to overlay onto video. This means we can clip a video to a complex shape defined by SVG. For this, we use an SVG image (in WebKit browsers) or an SVG fragment (in Firefox) as a mask through CSS. Listing 5–1 shows an example using the SVG file in Listing 5–2. The SVG file contains a circle that is applied as a mask on the video. Figure 5–1 shows the result in Firefox and Safari.

Listing 5–1. Styling a video using an external SVG resource as a mask

```
<video class="target" height="270px" width="480px" controls >
    <source src="HelloWorld.mp4"  type="video/mp4">
    <source src="HelloWorld.webm" type="video/webm">
    <source src="HelloWorld.ogv"  type="video/ogg">
</video>
<style>
  .target {
    mask: url("basic_example_c5_1.svg#c1");
    -webkit-mask: url("basic_example_c5_1.svg");
  }
</style>
```

Listing 5–2. The SVG resource used by Listing 5–1

```
<?xml version="1.0" standalone="no"?>
<!DOCTYPE svg PUBLIC "-//W3C//DTD SVG 1.1//EN"
          "http://www.w3.org/Graphics/SVG/1.1/DTD/svg11.dtd">
<svg version="1.1" xmlns="http://www.w3.org/2000/svg"
     xmlns:xlink="http://www.w3.org/1999/xlink">
  <defs>
    <mask id="c1" maskUnits="userSpaceOnUse"
                  maskContentUnits="userSpaceOnUse">
      <circle id="circle" cx="240" cy="135" r="135" fill="white"/>
    </mask>
  </defs>
  <use xlink:href="#circle"/>
</svg>
```

Figure 5–1. Applying an SVG mask to a video in Firefox and Safari

Opera and IE don't yet have support for applying SVG images as masks to HTML elements through CSS. They simply display the full video and we, therefore, have not included screenshots here. We will later look at how we can achieve this same effect with Opera, but we don't have a solution for IE.

Chrome is a special case. The example actually once worked in Chrome 6.0.xxx versions, but with the eventual version used for this book, it was broken and displayed just the same full video as Opera and IE. It seems that SVG masking has stopped working for <video>, even though it continues to work for <img>. A bug has been filed.[5]

You will note in the code that Firefox requires a link directly to a SVG fragment, addressed through a fragment URL (#), while the WebKit-based browsers link to the full SVG resource. Therefore, we provide two different specifications in the SVG resource: the <mask> element is for Firefox and the <use> element is for the WebKit-based browsers. The <use> element allows us to avoid repeating the definition of the circle. Instead, we just reference it, which requires inclusion of the xlink namespace. The <use> element basically instantiates the circle as a mask for WebKit-based browsers, while Firefox requires only the definition.

An interesting observation with all the masked videos is that as the video controls are turned on, it is possible to control playback by mouse clicks and guessing where in the hidden area are the play button and transport bar. This shows that mouse events penetrate the masked area—something to pay attention to since it might create unexpected side effects for users. It might be better to run your own controls instead.

Note that the <mask> element in SVG has two means of styling: you can set the @maskUnits and @maskContentUnits either to "userSpaceOnUse" or "objectBoundingBox." When you use "userSpaceOnUse," you can define the dimensions as absolute dimensions and position the mask within the boundaries of the object anywhere. If you decide instead to use "objectBoundingBox." the circle centre coordinates cx and cy as well as the radius r are interpreted as percentages in relation to the x and y dimensions of the object.

Listing 5–3 shows two different versions of the SVG using <mask> with "objectBoundingBox" in Firefox and results in the rendering in Figure 5–2. We've put this SVG inline, so you can see how it is done. The masks are defined in a <defs> element as they are not meant to be visible by themselves.

Listing 5–3. Two SVG masks as used by Firefox with "objectBoundingBox"

```
<video class="target1" height="270px" width="480px" controls >
    <source src="HelloWorld.webm" type="video/webm">
    <source src="HelloWorld.ogv"  type="video/ogg">
</video>
<video class="target2" height="270px" width="480px" controls >
    <source src="HelloWorld.webm" type="video/webm">
    <source src="HelloWorld.ogv"  type="video/ogg">
</video>
<style>
  .target1 { mask: url("#c1"); }
  .target2 { mask: url("#c2"); }
</style>
<svg version="1.1" xmlns="http://www.w3.org/2000/svg">
  <defs>
    <mask id="c1" maskUnits="objectBoundingBox"
                  maskContentUnits="objectBoundingBox">
      <circle cx="0.5" cy="0.5" r="0.5" fill="white"/>
    </mask>
    <mask id="c2" maskUnits="objectBoundingBox"
                  maskContentUnits="objectBoundingBox">
      <circle cx="0.25" cy="0.25" r="0.5" fill="white"/>
    </mask>
  </defs>
</svg>
```

---

[5] See http://code.google.com/p/chromium/issues/detail?id=63055

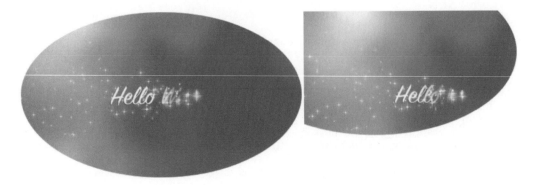

Figure 5–2. *Applying a circle SVG mask to a video in Firefox using the object's bounding box as reference*

The stretched circle in the second video is displaced with its center at 25% of the video's width and height.

When using `<svg>` inline, the `@namespace` attribute on the `<svg>` element is required because SVG runs in a separate namespace. Thus, if you want to manipulate an element inside the `<svg>` namespace through JavaScript, you need to use the namespace versions of the functions. Listing 5–4 shows an example where the SVG mask with the circle is extended with a rectangle shape. The resulting rendering in Firefox is shown in Figure 5–3. None of the other browsers supports this yet.

Listing 5–4. *Manipulating inline SVG with JavaScript in Firefox*

```
<video class="target" height="270px" width="480px" controls >
    <source src="HelloWorld.webm" type="video/webm">
    <source src="HelloWorld.ogv"  type="video/ogg">
</video>
<style>
  .target { mask: url("#c1"); }
</style>
<svg version="1.1" xmlns="http://www.w3.org/2000/svg">
  <defs>
    <mask id="c1" maskUnits="objectBoundingBox"
                  maskContentUnits="objectBoundingBox">
      <circle cx="0.25" cy="0.25" r="0.5" fill="white"/>
    </mask>
  </defs>
</svg>
<script>
  var rect = document.createElementNS("http://www.w3.org/2000/svg",
                                      "rect");
  rect.setAttribute("x", "0.5"); rect.setAttribute("y", "0.5");
  rect.setAttribute("width", "0.5"); rect.setAttribute("height", "0.5");
  rect.setAttribute("fill", "white");
  var mask = document.getElementById("c1");
  mask.appendChild(rect);
</script>
```

Figure 5–3. Adding a rectangle to the SVG mask on a video in Firefox using JavaScript

5.3 SVG Text and <video>

Another basic SVG construct consists of text elements:

- <text>
- <tspan>
- <tref>
- <textPath>
- <altGlyph>
- <altGlyphDef>
- <altGlyphItem>
- <glyphRef>
- <font> and font features

In this section we will use SVG text as a mask for video.

Listing 5–5 shows an example video with a text mask using the SVG file in Listing 5–6. The SVG file contains a circle applied as a mask to the video. Figure 5–4 shows the result in Firefox and Safari.

Listing 5–5. Styling a video using an external SVG resource as a mask

```
<video class="target" height="270px" width="480px" controls autoplay>
    <source src="HelloWorld.mp4"  type="video/mp4">
    <source src="HelloWorld.webm" type="video/webm">
    <source src="HelloWorld.ogv"  type="video/ogg">
</video>
<style>
  .target {
    mask: url("basic_example_c5_4.svg#textClip");
    -webkit-mask: url("basic_example_c5_4.svg");
```

```
        }
    </style>
```

Listing 5–6. The SVG resource used by Listing 5–5

```
<?xml version="1.0" standalone="no"?>
<!DOCTYPE svg PUBLIC "-//W3C//DTD SVG 1.1//EN"
          "http://www.w3.org/Graphics/SVG/1.1/DTD/svg11.dtd">
<svg version="1.1" xmlns="http://www.w3.org/2000/svg"
                   xmlns:xlink="http://www.w3.org/1999/xlink">
    <defs>
      <mask id="textClip" maskUnits="userSpaceOnUse"
                          maskContentUnits="userSpaceOnUse">
        <text id="text1" x="40" y="120" dx="0,5,5,5,0" dy="10,0,0,0,-20"
              rotate="-20 -30 -40 -50 0 0 -10" font-size="120" fill="white"
              font-family="Verdana" font-weight="bold">
          <tspan x="40">HELLO</tspan>
          <tspan x="0" dy="120">WORLD</tspan>
        </text>
      </mask>
    </defs>
    <use xlink:href="#text1"/>
</svg>
```

Figure 5–4. Applying a SVG text mask to a video in Firefox and Safari

The mask consists of two lines of text in `<tspan>` elements starting at a x=40 px and y=120 px offset with a dx and dy distances and individual letter rotations. Again, Opera and IE don't yet support SVG in CSS and Chrome is broken due to a bug.

You might have noticed that the SVG masks are all filled with the color "white." This is because of the way in which masking is specified.

In WebKit browsers, the image (even the SVG image) is interpreted as an alpha mask, which is an image that contains alpha values ranging from 0 to 1. Any color, including black and white, is masked as a fully transparent area; colors with a higher transparency result in less transparency in the mask.

In Firefox by contrast, the mask value is calculated from both the color and alpha channel values as per the SVG specification.[6] A linear luminance value is computed from the color channel values and then

---

[6] See http://www.w3.org/TR/SVG/masking.html#Masking

multiplied by the alpha channel value. For a black picture, all color channel values are thus 0, which is why a mask from a black picture results in nothing in Firefox. So make sure to fill your mask with a nonblack color. For full transparency, use white as in the examples above.

5.4 SVG Styling for <video>

With CSS3, much of the advanced styling functionalities of SVG have found entry into HTML. However, some of the advanced features of SVG, such as masks, clipPaths, filters and animations, can be styled only in SVG.

SVG Play/Pause Toggle

One particularly nice application of SVG for video is to run your own video controls. Listing 5–7 shows an example of a video without native controls, but with a SVG play/pause toggle that hooks into the video JavaScript API and uses the page's CSS. Because this uses inline SVG and hooks into the JavaScript of the web page, we need to use XHTML to allow it to render in all browsers. Figure 5–5 shows the result.

Listing 5–7. Running your own controls in SVG

```
<!DOCTYPE html>
<html xmlns="http://www.w3.org/1999/xhtml" lang="en" xml:lang="en">
  <head>
    <style>
      .svginside > * {
        position: absolute;
      }
      .svgbutton path {
        pointer-events: none;
      }
    </style>
    <script>
/* <![CDATA[ */
var vid;
window.onload = function() {
  vid = document.getElementsByTagName("video")[0];
  vid.addEventListener("ended", updateButton, true);
  vid.addEventListener("play", updateButton, true);
  updateButton();
}
function updateButton() {
  document.querySelector("#controls .play").style.display =
      isPlaying(vid) ? "none" : "block";
  document.querySelector("#controls .pause").style.display =
      !isPlaying(vid) ? "none" : "block";
}
function isPlaying(video) {
  return (!video.paused && !video.ended);
}
function togglevideo() {
  !isPlaying(vid) ? vid.play() : vid.pause();
  updateButton();
```

```
        } /* ]]> */
      </script>
    </head>
    <body>
    <div id="controls" class="svginside">
      <video height="270px" width="480px">
        <source src="HelloWorld.mp4"  type="video/mp4"/>
        <source src="HelloWorld.webm" type="video/webm"/>
        <source src="HelloWorld.ogv"  type="video/ogg"/>
      </video>
      <svg height="270px" width="480px" xmlns="http://www.w3.org/2000/svg"
          xmlns:xlink="http://www.w3.org/1999/xlink" >
        <g class="svgbutton">
          <circle stroke="black" fill="transparent" fill-opacity="0"
                  stroke-width="12" cx="240" cy="135" r="40"
                  onclick="togglevideo();"/>
          <path class="play" fill="black" d="M 230 120 v 30 l 25 -15 Z"/>
          <path class="pause" stroke-width="12" stroke="black"
                d="M 230 120 v 30 m 16 -30 v 30"/>
        </g>
      </svg>
    </div>
    </body>
  </html>
```

Note that because this is XHTML, you need to put the JavaScript into a CDATA section.

The XHTML page contains first a list of JavaScript functions. There is a function to toggle the play and pause state of the video, one to identify which state it actually is in, one to update the image upon toggling play/pause, and one to initialize the hook-up of toggle button events to the functions. Then we display the video and the SVG toggle button overlay, which consists of a circle, a path that draws the play image, and a path that draws the pause image. The SVG is positioned absolutely by nailing the video down to 480x270, and the circle, pause and play buttons are centered on that. By taking away pointer events from the play triangle and the pause rectangles, we give all the pointer events to the circle to call the toggleVideo function.

We also created the same version of this web page as an HTML page, which works in Firefox, Chrome, and IE, but not in Safari and Opera.

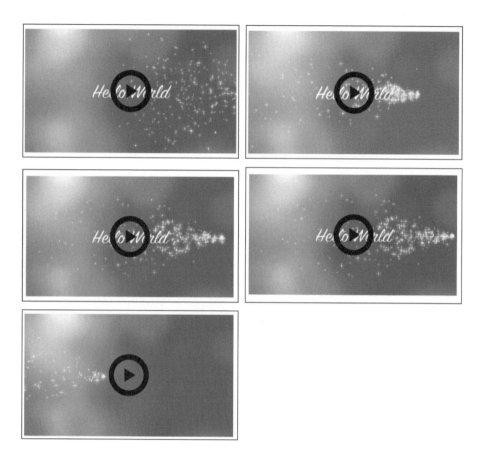

Figure 5–5. Running your own SVG controls for a video

SVG Gradients

Being able to use SVG gradients on SVG masks, clipPaths, and other SVG effects is another styling advantage of SVG over CSS. Listing 5–8 shows an example of an SVG mask for a video that has a gradient applied to everything that's not masked. The HTML file required for this is very similar to the one in Listing 5–1. Figure 5–6 shows the result.

Listing 5–8. A SVG mask with a gradient

```
<?xml version="1.0" standalone="no"?>
<!DOCTYPE svg PUBLIC "-//W3C//DTD SVG 1.1//EN"
          "http://www.w3.org/Graphics/SVG/1.1/DTD/svg11.dtd">
<svg version="1.1" xmlns="http://www.w3.org/2000/svg"
                   xmlns:xlink="http://www.w3.org/1999/xlink">
  <defs>
    <mask id="c1" maskUnits="userSpaceOnUse"
```

```
                       maskContentUnits="userSpaceOnUse">
        <g id="group">
          <linearGradient id="grad" gradientUnits="objectBoundingBox"
                          x2="0" y2="1">
            <stop stop-color="white" offset="0"/>
            <stop stop-color="white" stop-opacity="0" offset="1"/>
          </linearGradient>
          <circle id="circle" cx="240" cy="135" r="135" fill="white"/>
          <rect x="0" y="0" width="480" height="270" fill="url(#grad)"/>
        </g>
      </mask>
    </defs>
    <use xlink:href="#group"/>
  </svg>
```

Figure 5–6. An SVG mask and a gradient applied to a video in Safari and Firefox shows the same effect

The SVG mask is defined by a circle in the center of the video and a rectangle over the whole height. The rectangle is filled with the gradient, which starts at the top boundary of the image and increases toward a final value of white at the bottom. Two mask shapes come together, so the mask multiplies these two together before applying it to the video.

It certainly makes a lot of sense in the above example to run your own controls instead of having the semi-transparent default controls shine through the mask. One can imagine creating a video player that plays back a series of videos and uses SVG and JavaScript to provide transition effects, such as wipes or fades.

SVG Pattern

In the next example, we use a circle as a pattern to blend in more than the central circle of the video. Listing 5–9 shows the SVG mask. The HTML file required for this is very similar to the one in Listing 5–1. Figure 5–7 shows the result.

Listing 5–9. An SVG mask with a pattern

```
<?xml version="1.0" standalone="no"?>
<!DOCTYPE svg PUBLIC "-//W3C//DTD SVG 1.1//EN"
          "http://www.w3.org/Graphics/SVG/1.1/DTD/svg11.dtd">
<svg version="1.1" xmlns="http://www.w3.org/2000/svg"
                   xmlns:xlink="http://www.w3.org/1999/xlink">
  <defs>
    <mask id="c1" maskUnits="userSpaceOnUse"
                  maskContentUnits="userSpaceOnUse">
      <g id="group">
        <pattern id="pat" patternUnits="userSpaceOnUse" x="0" y="0"
                 width="20" height="20">
          <circle cx="6" cy="6" r="5" fill="white" stroke="white"/>
        </pattern>
        <rect x="0" y="0" width="480" height="246" fill="url(#pat)"/>
        <circle id="circle" cx="240" cy="122" r="122" fill="white"/>
        <rect x="0" y="246" width="480" height="25" fill="white"/>
      </g>
    </mask>
  </defs>
  <use xlink:href="#group"/>
</svg>
```

Figure 5–7. A patterned mask applied to a video in Firefox and Safari

First we have a rectangle over the complete video to which the small circle pattern is applied. Over this we mask the big circle for the video center. Finally, we also have a small rectangle that roughly covers the video controls and provides for better usability. In browsers where the controls disappear during pause time, this looks rather funny, as can be seen in the Firefox example. It, however, works mostly with Safari.

5.5 SVG Effects for <video>

We've already seen multiple examples of masks. Other interesting SVG effects are clip-paths and filters.

Clip-paths restrict the region to which paint can be applied, creating a custom viewport for the referencing element. This also means that pointer events are not dispatched on the clipped regions of the shape. This is in contrast to masks, where only visibility and transparency of the masked regions is changed, but the masked regions still exist and can be interacted with.

SVG Clip-Path

Listing 5–10 shows an example use of clip-path on a video. We need the controls to be able to interact with the video. This currently will work only in Firefox in HTML since it is the only browser that supports inline SVG, which is necessary for the controls. You can get Safari to display it, too, but you need to move to XHTML and use the -webkit-mask CSS property; see Listing 5–11. See Figure 5–8 for the result.

Listing 5–10. An SVG clip-path used with the controls from Listing 5–7

```
<?xml version="1.0" standalone="no"?>
<!DOCTYPE svg PUBLIC "-//W3C//DTD SVG 1.1//EN"
          "http://www.w3.org/Graphics/SVG/1.1/DTD/svg11.dtd">
<svg version="1.1" xmlns="http://www.w3.org/2000/svg"
                   xmlns:xlink="http://www.w3.org/1999/xlink">
  <defs>
    <clipPath id="c1" maskUnits="userSpaceOnUse"
                      maskContentUnits="userSpaceOnUse">
      <polygon id="poly" fill="white"
               transform="translate(-180,-90) scale(1.2)"
               points="350,75  379,161 469,161 397,215
                       423,301 350,250 277,301 303,215
                       231,161 321,161" />
    </clipPath>
  </defs>
  <use xlink:href="#poly"/>
</svg>
```

Listing 5–11. Addition to the HTML page in Listing 5–7

```
<style>
  video {
    clip-path: url("basic_example_c5_8.svg#c1");
    -webkit-mask: url("basic_example_c5_8.svg");
  }
</style>
```

Figure 5–8. A clip-path in the form of a star applied to a video in Firefox and Safari with SVG controls

The HTML page from example Listing 5–5 is extended with a CSS feature called clip-path. This feature links to the SVG block that contains the <clipPath>. In our example, that clipPath contains a polygon that describes a star, which creates a cut-out from the video. Onto this, the controls of Listing 5–7 are rendered to enable interaction with the video.

SVG Filters

Now let's move on to the most interesting functionality that SVG can provide for the video element: filters. Filters are composed from filter effects, which are a series of graphics operations applied to a given source graphic to produce a modified graphical result. They typically are applied to images and videos to expose different details from the graphical image than are typically seen by the human eye or to improve a particular image feature—be that for image/video analysis or for artistic purposes.

A long list of filter effects, also called filter primitives, is defined in the SVG specification[7]:

- Blending two images together: <feBlend>.

- Color matrix transformation: <feColorMatrix>.

- Component-wise remapping of pixel data: <feComponentTransfer> using one of the following component transfer functions: identity, table, discrete, linear, gamma on one of the color channels through <feFuncR>, <feFuncG>, <feFuncB>, <feFuncA>.

- Combine two input images pixel-wise: <feComposite>.

- Matrix convolution of pixels with their neighbors: <feConvolveMatrix>.

- Light image using the alpha channel as a bump map: <feDiffuseLighting>, <feSpecularLighting>.

- Spatially displace an image based on a second image: <feDisplacementMap>.

- Create filled rectangle: <feFlood>.

- Gaussian blur on input image: <feGaussianBlur>.

- Load external graphic into filter into RGBA raster: <feImage>.

- Collapse input image layers into one: <feMerge> with a list of <feMergeNode>.

- Dilate (fatten)/erode (thin) artwork: <feMorphology>.

- Offset image: <feOffset>.

- Fill rectangle with repeated pattern of input image: <feTile>.

- Create turbulence or fractal noise: <feTurbulence>.

- Light source effects: <feDistantLight>, <fePointLight>, <feSpotLight>.

Firefox, Opera, IE, and the WebKit-based browsers support all of these filter effects for SVG, but the use in HTML is supported only by Firefox[8]. Firefox made use of the CSS filter property for this, which was previously supported only by IE.

---

[7] See http://www.w3.org/TR/SVG/filters.html#FilterPrimitivesOverview

Listing 5–12 shows application of a **blur filter** to the video element, defined in an inline SVG. Figure 5–9 shows the result in Firefox.

Listing 5–12. An SVG-defined blur filter applied to a video

```
<video class="target" height="270px" width="480px" controls >
   <source src="HelloWorld.webm" type="video/webm">
   <source src="HelloWorld.ogv"  type="video/ogg">
</video>
<svg height="0">
   <defs>
     <filter id="f1">
        <feGaussianBlur stdDeviation="3"/>
     </filter>
   </defs>
</svg>
<style>
   .target {
      filter: url("#f1");
   }
</style>
```

Figure 5–9. A blur filter applied to a video in Firefox

In CSS you use the `filter` property to refer to the SVG `<filter>` element. The Gaussian blur effect is the only filter primitive used here. It is possible to combine more filter effects in one filter. Note that the filter is also applied to the default controls, so it is necessary to run your own controls.

---

[8] See https://developer.mozilla.org/En/Applying_SVG_effects_to_HTML_content

Let's look at a few more filters. Listing 5–13 shows several filters:

- f1: a **color matrix**, which turns the video black and white.
- f2: a **component transfer**, which inverts all the color components.
- f3: a **convolution matrix**, which brings out the borders of color patches.
- f4: a **displacement map**, which displaces the video pixels along the x and y axes using the R color component.
- f5: a **color matrix**, which lightens the colors and moves them towards pastel.

Figure 5–10 shows the results of the filters used with the HTML code in Listing 5–12 in Firefox, applied to a somewhat more interesting video. The first image is a reference frame without a filter applied.

Listing 5–13. Several SVG filter definitions

```
<filter id="f1">
  <feColorMatrix values="0.3 0.3 0.3 0 0
                         0.3 0.3 0.3 0 0
                         0.3 0.3 0.3 0 0
                         0   0   0   1 0"/>
</filter>

<filter id="f2">
  <feComponentTransfer>
    <feFuncR type="table" tableValues="1 0"/>
    <feFuncG type="table" tableValues="1 0"/>
    <feFuncB type="table" tableValues="1 0"/>
  </feComponentTransfer>
</filter>

<filter id="f3">
  <feConvolveMatrix order="3" kernelMatrix="1    -1  1
                                           -1 -0.01 -1
                                            1    -1  1"
                    edgeMode="duplicate"/>
</filter>

<filter id="f4" x="0%" y="0%" height="100%" width="100%">
  <feDisplacementMap scale="100" in2="SourceGraphic"
                     xChannelSelector="R"/>
</filter>

<filter id="f5">
  <feColorMatrix values="1 0 0 0 0
                         0 1 0 0 0
                         0 0 1 0 0
                         0 1 0 0 0"
                 style="color-interpolation-filters:sRGB"/>
</filter>
```

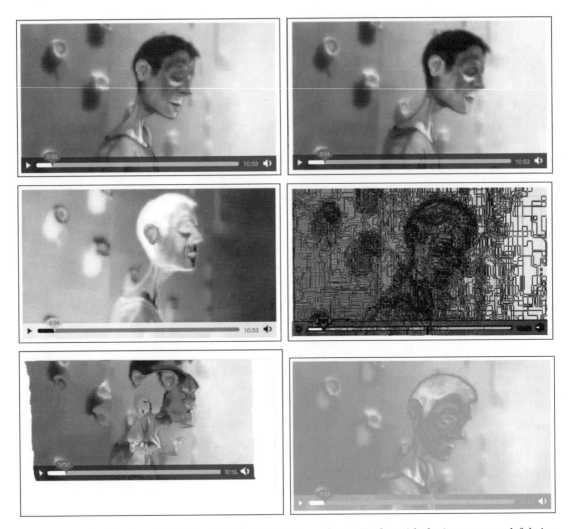

Figure 5–10. Application of the filters in Listing 5–13 to a video in Firefox with the image at top left being the reference image and the filters f1 to f5 applied from top right to bottom right.

Finally, we want to make a few **combined filters**. Listing 5–14 shows several combined filters:

- f1: a blue flood on the black color.
- f2: a canvas-style rendering.
- f3: two layers of blur and convolution merged.
- f4: a line mask on the re-colored video.

Figure 5–11 shows the results of the filters used with the HTML code in Listing 5–12 in Firefox.

Listing 5–14. Several composite SVG filter definitions

```
<filter id="f1" x="0%" y="0%" width="100%" height="100%">
  <feFlood  flood-color="blue" result="A"/>
  <feColorMatrix type="matrix" in="SourceGraphic" result="B"
              values="1   0  0  0 0
                      0   1  0  0 0
                      0   0  1  0 0
                      1   1  1  0 0"/>
  <feMerge>
    <feMergeNode in="A"/>
    <feMergeNode in="B"/>
  </feMerge>
</filter>

<filter id="f2">
  <feGaussianBlur in="SourceAlpha" stdDeviation="4" result="A"/>
  <feOffset in="A" dx="4" dy="4" result="B"/>
  <feSpecularLighting in="A" surfaceScale="5" specularConstant=".75"
                      specularExponent="20" lighting-color="#bbbbbb"
                      result="C">
    <fePointLight x="-5000" y="-10000" z="20000"/>
  </feSpecularLighting>
  <feComposite in="C" in2="SourceAlpha" operator="in" result="C"/>
  <feComposite in="SourceGraphic" in2="C" operator="arithmetic"
             k1="0" k2="1" k3="1" k4="0" result="D"/>
  <feMerge>
    <feMergeNode in="B"/>
    <feMergeNode in="D"/>
  </feMerge>
</filter>

<filter id="f3">
  <feGaussianBlur in="SourceGraphic" stdDeviation="6" result="A"/>
  <feConvolveMatrix order="3" edgeMode="none" result="B"
                    kernelMatrix="1 -1  1 -1 -0.01 -1 1 -1 1"/>
  <feMerge>
    <feMergeNode in="A"/>
    <feMergeNode in="B"/>
  </feMerge>
</filter>

<filter id="f4">
  <feColorMatrix values="1 1 0 0 0
                         0 0 1 0 0
                         0 0 0 1 0
                         0 0 0 0 1"
          style="color-interpolation-filters:sRGB" result="A"/>
  <feConvolveMatrix filterRes="100 100" preserveAlpha="true" in="A"
          style="color-interpolation-filters:sRGB"
          order="3" kernelMatrix="0 -1 0   -1 4 -1   0 -1 0" />
</filter>
```

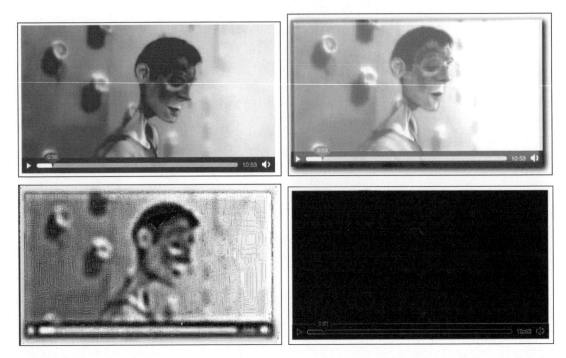

Figure 5–11. Application of the filters in Listing 5–14 to a video in Firefox with the image at top left being the reference image and the filters f1 to f5 applied from top right to bottom right.

5.6 SVG Animations and <video>

We now briefly move on to SVG animations, which allow us to animate basically all the SVG effects and features we have experimented with. Animation functionality in SVG originates from SMIL's animation module[9]

SVG animate

The **<animate>** element is used to animate a single attribute or property over a time interval. Listing 5–15 has an example for animating the circular mask used in Listing 5–2. The HTML page for this example is identical to the one in Listing 5–1. Figure 5–12 has the rendering in Firefox and Safari.

---

[9] See http://www.w3.org/TR/2001/REC-smil-animation-20010904/

Listing 5–15. An animated circle in SVG

```
<?xml version="1.0" standalone="no"?>
<!DOCTYPE svg PUBLIC "-//W3C//DTD SVG 1.1//EN"
          "http://www.w3.org/Graphics/SVG/1.1/DTD/svg11.dtd">
<svg version="1.1" xmlns="http://www.w3.org/2000/svg"
                   xmlns:xlink="http://www.w3.org/1999/xlink">
  <defs>
    <mask id="c1" maskUnits="userSpaceOnUse"
                  maskContentUnits="userSpaceOnUse">
      <circle id="circle" cx="240" cy="135" r="135" fill="white">
        <animate attributeName="r" values="150;240;150" dur="3s"
                 repeatCount="10" />
      </circle>
    </mask>
  </defs>
  <use xlink:href="#circle"/>
</svg>
```

Figure 5–12. Applying an animated SVG mask to a video in Firefox and Safari

In the example, the circular mask on the video is animated from a radius of 150 px to 240 px and back, which makes for a sliding width mask on the exposed video. This animation is executed 10 times before the mask falls back to the original circle of 135 px radius as used in Listing 5–1.

SVG Animate Color and Transform

Note that the <animate> element allows animation of only simple attributes. To animate color-related attributes, you need to use **<animateColor>** and to animate the @transform attribute, you need to use **<animateTransform>**.

SVG Animate Motion

With the **<animateMotion>** element, it is possible to move an element along a certain path defined by **<mpath>**. Listing 5–16 has an example for animating a small circular mask in searchlight fashion over the video. The HTML page for this example is identical to the one in Listing 5–1. Figure 5–13 has the rendering in Firefox and Safari.

Listing 5–16. A motion animation in SVG used as a mask

```
<?xml version="1.0" standalone="no"?>
<!DOCTYPE svg PUBLIC "-//W3C//DTD SVG 1.1//EN"
          "http://www.w3.org/Graphics/SVG/1.1/DTD/svg11.dtd">
<svg version="1.1" xmlns="http://www.w3.org/2000/svg"
                   xmlns:xlink="http://www.w3.org/1999/xlink">
  <defs>
    <mask id="c1" maskUnits="userSpaceOnUse"
              maskContentUnits="userSpaceOnUse">
      <circle id="circle" cx="120" cy="70" r="50" fill="white">
        <animateMotion path="M 0 20 C 150 30 250 250 50 70"
                       begin="0s" dur="6s" fill="freeze" />
      </circle>
    </mask>
  </defs>
  <use xlink:href="#circle"/>
</svg>
```

Figure 5–13. Applying a motion animated SVG mask to a video in Firefox and Safari

In the example, a path is defined inside the `<animateMotion>` element. This could have been done in a separate `<path>` element with an `<mpath>` subelement referencing it. However, the path was simple enough to simply retain in the element.

5.7 Media in SVG

We've had plenty of examples now where SVG was used inline or as an externally referenced CSS mask to provide effects into an HTML video element. In this subsection we turn this upside down and take a look at using the HTML5 video element inside SVG resources. While this is strictly speaking the development of SVG content and not of HTML, we will still take a look, because the SVG markup can be used inline in HTML.

Video in SVG

Let's start with the simple first step of displaying video in SVG. Opera has the <video> element of SVG 1.2 implemented, so you can just use <video> inside SVG. The other browsers require the use of the <foreignObject> feature of SVG.

Listing 5–17 shows an XHTML file with inline SVG that just displays a video. The renderings in all browsers except IE are shown in Figure 5–14. IE doesn't understand <video> or <foreignObject> yet, so it shows nothing.

Listing 5–17. Inline SVG with a video element in XHTML

```
<!DOCTYPE html>
<html xmlns="http://www.w3.org/1999/xhtml" lang="en" xml:lang="en">
  <body>
    <svg version="1.1" xmlns="http://www.w3.org/2000/svg"
        xmlns:xlink="http://www.w3.org/1999/xlink" width="480px"
        height="270px">
    <g id="video">
      <foreignObject width="480px" height="270px">
        <body xmlns="http://www.w3.org/1999/xhtml" style="margin:0;">
          <video class="target" height="270" width="480"
                  controls="controls">
            <source src="HelloWorld.mp4"  type="video/mp4"/>
            <source src="HelloWorld.webm" type="video/webm"/>
            <source src="HelloWorld.ogv"  type="video/ogg"/>
          </video>
        </body>
      </foreignObject>
      <video class="target" height="270" width="480" controls="controls"
          xlink:href="HelloWorld.ogv">
      </video>
    </g>
  </svg>
  </body>
</html>
```

Figure 5–14. *Rendering inline SVG with video in Firefox (top left), Safari (top right), Opera (bottom left), and Google Chrome (bottom right).*

Notice how it is necessary to put two video elements in the inline SVG: the first in a `<foreignObject>` is interpreted on Firefox, Safari and Google Chrome, while the second one is interpreted by Opera. It has an `@xref:href` instead of an `@src` attribute because it is native XML/SVG rather than a foreign object. Because of this, it also doesn't deal with `<source>` elements, and it doesn't actually display controls, but is always autoplay.[10]

Also note that we had to put a 0 margin on the `<body>` element in SVG since some browsers—in particular Firefox—have a default margin on inline SVG.

This example works in all browsers except for IE.

Masking Video in SVG

Now we can try to replicate the example of Listing 5–1 inside SVG; i.e. put a circular mask on the video. Listing 5–18 has the XHTML code and Figure 5–15 the renderings.

Listing 5–18. *Inline SVG with a video element in XHTML and a circular mask*

```
<svg version="1.1" xmlns="http://www.w3.org/2000/svg"
    xmlns:xlink="http://www.w3.org/1999/xlink" width="480px"
```

---

[10] See http://www.w3.org/TR/SVGMobile12/multimedia.html#VideoElement

```
    height="270px">
<defs>
  <mask id="c1" maskUnits="userSpaceOnUse"
                maskContentUnits="userSpaceOnUse">
    <circle id="circle" cx="240" cy="135" r="135" fill="white"/>
  </mask>
</defs>
<g>
  <defs>
    <g id="video">
      <foreignObject width="480px" height="270px">
        <body xmlns="http://www.w3.org/1999/xhtml" style="margin:0;">
          <video class="target" height="270" width="480"
                 controls="controls">
              <source src="HelloWorld.mp4"  type="video/mp4"/>
              <source src="HelloWorld.webm" type="video/webm"/>
              <source src="HelloWorld.ogv"  type="video/ogg"/>
          </video>
        </body>
      </foreignObject>
      <video class="target" height="270" width="480"
             controls="controls" xlink:href="HelloWorld.ogv">
      </video>
    </g>
  </defs>
  <use xlink:href="#video" mask="url(#c1)"/>
</g>
</svg>
```

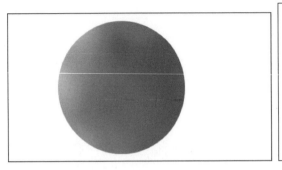

Figure 5–15. Rendering inline SVG with circular filter on video in Firefox and Opera

The WebKit-based browsers don't seem to be able yet to apply a mask on a `<foreignObject>`. IE doesn't support either masks or `<foreignObject>`. Opera works fine, so this provides the opportunity to mix the implementation of Listing 5–1 with the implementation here to gain the same effect in all browsers except IE.

To finish off this chapter, let's look at some more effects now provided in inline SVG on the video elements.

SVG Reflection

Listing 5–19 shows the inline SVG code for a **reflection** created by copying the video in a <use> statement, mirroring through a scale(1 -1) transform, moving it below the video through a translate(0 - 540) transform, and applying a gradient to the copied video. Figure 5–16 shows the renderings in Firefox and Opera.

Listing 5–19. SVG code for a video reflection

```
<svg version="1.1" xmlns="http://www.w3.org/2000/svg"
     xmlns:xlink="http://www.w3.org/1999/xlink"
     width="480px" height="540px">
  <defs>
    <linearGradient id="grad" y2="1" x2="0">
      <stop offset="0.2" stop-color="white" stop-opacity="0"/>
      <stop offset="1"   stop-color="white" stop-opacity=".4"/>
    </linearGradient>
    <mask id="c1" maskContentUnits="objectBoundingBox">
      <rect width="1" height="1" fill="url(#grad)"/>
    </mask>
  </defs>
  <g id="reflection">
    <g id="video">
      <foreignObject width="480px" height="270px">
        <body xmlns="http://www.w3.org/1999/xhtml" style="margin:0;">
          <video height="270" width="480" autoplay="autoplay">
            <source src="HelloWorld.mp4"  type="video/mp4"/>
            <source src="HelloWorld.webm" type="video/webm"/>
            <source src="HelloWorld.ogv"  type="video/ogg"/>
          </video>
```

```
            </body>
          </foreignObject>
          <video height="270" width="480" xlink:href="HelloWorld.ogv"/>
        </g>
        <use xlink:href="#video" transform="scale(1 -1) translate(0 -540)"
            mask="url(#c1)"/>
      </g>
    </svg>
```

Figure 5–16. Rendering inline SVG with reflection on video in Firefox (left) and Opera (right)

Opera's presentation is much smoother than Firefox's, which seems to do a lot of processing. As we can see from the screenshot, it seems that Firefox has two different renderings of the video data, since the video and its reflection are not synchronized. In contrast, the <use> element just seems to copy the data from the <video> element. Opera can possibly do some optimization since it is using <video> as a native SVG element, while Firefox has to deal with the <video> in an HTML <foreignObject>. It seems to be an advantage to have a native <video> element in SVG. It could be a good idea, however, to synchronize the markup of the <video> element in SVG and HTML, in particular introduce a <source> element.

SVG Edge Detection

Listing 5–20 shows the inline SVG code for **edge detection** created through a convolution matrix. Figure 5–17 shows the renderings in Firefox and Opera.

161

Listing 5–20. SVG code for edge detection

```
<svg version="1.1" xmlns="http://www.w3.org/2000/svg"
     xmlns:xlink="http://www.w3.org/1999/xlink"
     width="480px" height="540px">
<defs>
  <filter id="c1">
    <feConvolveMatrix order="3" kernelMatrix="1  1 1
                                              1 -8 1
                                              1  1 1"
                      preserveAlpha="true"/>
  </filter>
</defs>
<video height="270px" width="480px" xlink:href="HelloWorld.ogv"
       filter="url(#c1)"/>
<defs>
  <g id="video">
    <foreignObject width="480px" height="270px">
      <body xmlns="http://www.w3.org/1999/xhtml" style="margin:0;">
        <video height="270px" width="480px" autoplay="autoplay">
          <source src="HelloWorld.mp4"  type="video/mp4"/>
          <source src="HelloWorld.webm" type="video/webm"/>
          <source src="HelloWorld.ogv"  type="video/ogg"/>
        </video>
      </body>
    </foreignObject>
  </g>
</defs>
<use xlink:href="#video" filter="url(#c1)"/>
</svg>
```

Figure 5–17. Rendering inline SVG with edge detection on video in Firefox (left) and Opera (right)

The filter can be directly applied to the native SVG 1.2 <video> element in Opera. In Firefox, we need to define the <foreignObject> and then apply the filter to the object through a <use> statement.

5.8. Summary

In this chapter we analyzed how the HTML5 <video> element can interoperate with objects defined in SVG. First, we looked at using objects specified in SVG as masks on top of the <video> element. In Safari we can reference external SVG "images" in the -webkit-mask CSS property. This also used to work in Chrome, but is currently broken. In Firefox we can use the mask CSS property with a direct fragment reference to the <mask> element inside the SVG "image." Use of URI fragments in the way in which Firefox supports them is not standardized yet.

Firefox is also able to reference inline defined SVG masks through the fragment-addressing approach. This means <mask> elements inside the same HTML file in an <svg> element can be used as masks, too. IE and Chrome also support inline definition of <svg> elements in HTML, but since they don't support the fragment-addressing approach inside the mask CSS property, they cannot use this for masking onto HTML <video> elements.

The same approach with the mask and -webkit-mask CSS properties is also used later for applying CSS animations to HTML5 <video> in Firefox and Safari.

We then moved on to using SVG inline for defining controls. If we define them in XHTML, all browsers, including IE, display them. You can create some of the prettiest controls with SVG. Because Safari and Opera do not support inline <svg> in HTML yet, we have to use XHTML. It is expected that these browsers will move toward a native HTML5 parser in the near future, which will then enable <svg> support inline in HTML pages, too.

Next we looked at how Firefox managed to apply SVG filter effects to HTML elements. It uses the CSS filter property for this and again references SVG objects with a fragment reference. In this way you can apply some of the amazing filter effects that are available in SVG to <video>, including blur, black-and -white, false-color effects, pastel colors, and contours.

We rounded out the chapter by using the SVG <video> and <foreignObject> elements to play back <video> directly in SVG. Such SVG was further included as inline SVG in an HTML page through <svg>. This enabled us also to make use of masking and other effects on <video> in Opera, since it is the only browser with native <video> element support in SVG.

CHAPTER 6

■ ■ ■

HTML5 Media and Canvas

While the SVG environment is a declarative graphics environment dealing with vector-based shapes, the HTML Canvas provides a script-based graphics environment revolving around pixels or bitmaps. In comparison with SVG, it is faster to manipulate data entities in Canvas, since it is easier to get directly to individual pixels. On the other hand, SVG provides a DOM and has an event model not available to Canvas. Thus, applications that need graphics with interactivity will typically choose SVG, while applications that do a lot of image manipulation will more typically reach for Canvas. The available transforms and effects in both are similar, and the same visual results can be achieved with both, but with different programming effort and potentially different performance.

When comparing performance between SVG and Canvas,[1] typically the drawing of a lot of objects will eventually slow down SVG, which has to maintain all the references to the objects, while for Canvas it's just more pixels to draw. So, when you have a lot of objects to draw and it's not really important that you continue to have access to the individual objects but are just after pixel drawings, you should use Canvas.

In contrast, the size of the drawing area of Canvas has a huge impact on the speed of a `<canvas>`, since it has to draw more pixels. So, when you have a large area to cover with a smaller number of objects, you should use SVG.

Note that the choice between Canvas and SVG is not fully exclusive. It is possible to bring a Canvas into an SVG image by converting it to an image using a function called `toDataURL()`. This can be used, for example, when drawing a fancy and repetitive background for a SVG image. It may often be more efficient to draw that background in the Canvas and include it into the SVG image through the `toDataURL()` function.

So, let's focus on Canvas in this chapter. Like SVG, the Canvas is predominantly a visually oriented medium — it doesn't do anything with audio. Of course, you can combine background music with an awesome graphical display by simply using the `<audio>` element as part of your pages, as beautifully executed, for example, by 9elements[2] with a visualization of Twitter chatter through colored and animated circles on a background of music.

Seeing as you already have experience with JavaScript, Canvas will not be too difficult to understand. It's almost like a JavaScript library with drawing functionality. It supports, in particular, the following function categories:

- Canvas handling: creating a drawing area, a 2D context, saving and restoring state.

- Drawing basic shapes: rectangles, paths, lines, arcs, Bezier, and quadratic curves.

- Drawing text: drawing fill text and stroke text, and measuring text.

---

[1] See http://www.borismus.com/canvas-vs-svg-performance/

[2] See http://9elements.com/io/?p=153

- Using images: creating, drawing, scaling and slicing images.

- Applying styles: colors, fill styles, stroke styles, transparency, line styles, gradients, shadows, and patterns.

- Applying transformations: translating, rotating, scaling, and transformation matrices.

- Compositing: clipping and overlap drawing composition.

- Applying animations: execute drawing functions over time by associating time intervals and timeouts.

6.1 Video in Canvas

The first step to work with video in Canvas is to grab the pixel data out of a `<video>` element into a Canvas element.

drawImage()

The `drawImage()`function accepts a video element as well as an image or a Canvas element. Listing 6–1 shows how to use it directly on a video.

Listing 6–1. Introducing the video pixel data into a canvas

```
<video controls height="270px" width="480px" >
  <source src="HelloWorld.mp4"  type="video/mp4">
  <source src="HelloWorld.webm" type="video/webm">
  <source src="HelloWorld.ogv"  type="video/ogg">
</video>
<canvas width="400" height="300" style="border: 1px solid black;">
</canvas>
<script>
  window.onload = function() {
    initCanvas();
  }
  var context;
  function initCanvas() {
    video = document.getElementsByTagName("video")[0];
    canvas = document.getElementsByTagName("canvas")[0];
    context = canvas.getContext("2d");
    video.addEventListener("timeupdate", paintFrame, false);
  }
  function paintFrame() {
    context.drawImage(video, 0, 0, 160, 80);
  }
</script>
```

The HTML markup is simple. It contains only the `<video>` element and the `<canvas>` element into which we are painting the video data. To this end, we register an event listener on the video element and with every "timeupdate" event the currently active frame of the video is drawn using `drawImage()` at canvas offset (0,0) with the size 160x80. The result is shown in Figure 6–1.

Figure 6–1. *Painting a video into a canvas with every timeupdate event in Firefox, Safari (top row), Opera, Chrome (middle row), and IE (bottom)*

A few differences can be noticed between the browsers as we play back this example. As the page is loaded, Safari displays the first frame directly in the Canvas, while Chrome, Opera, IE, and Firefox don't and only start painting when the play button is pressed. This is obviously linked to the difference in dispatching the "timeupdate" event described in Chapter 4.

It is important to understand that the "timeupdate" event does not fire for every frame, but only every few frames—roughly every 100-250ms.[3] There currently is no function to allow you to reliably grab every frame. We can, however, create a painting loop that is constantly grabbing a frame from the video as quickly as possible or after a given time interval. We use the setTimeout() function for this with a timeout of 0 to go as quickly as possible.

Because the setTimeout() function calls a function after a given number of milliseconds and we normally would run the video at 24 (PAL) or 30 (NTSC) frames per second, a timeout of 41ms or 33ms would theoretically be more than appropriate. However, we cannot actually know how much time was spent processing and what picture the video has arrived at. We may as well tell it to go as fast as possible in these examples. For your application, you might want to tune the frequency down to make your web page less CPU intensive.

In this situation, we use the "play" event to start the painting loop when the user starts playback and run until the video is paused or ended. Another option would be to use the "canplay" or "loadeddata" events to start the display independently of a user interaction.

We have implemented this approach in Listing 6–2. To make it a bit more interesting, we also displace each subsequent frame by 10 pixels in the x and y dimension within the borders of the Canvas box. The results are shown in Figure 6–2.

---

[3] Firefox used to fire the event at a much higher rate previously. The HTML5 specification allows between 15 and 250ms, but all browsers since Firefox 4 are taking a conservative approach.

Listing 6–2. Painting video frames at different offsets into the canvas

```
<video controls height="270px" width="480px" >
  <source src="HelloWorld.mp4"  type="video/mp4">
  <source src="HelloWorld.webm" type="video/webm">
  <source src="HelloWorld.ogv"  type="video/ogg">
</video>
<canvas width="400" height="300" style="border: 1px solid black;">
</canvas>
<script>
  window.onload = function() {
    initCanvas();
  }
  var context, video;
  var x = 0, xpos = 10;
  var y = 0, ypos = 10;
  function initCanvas() {
    video = document.getElementsByTagName("video")[0];
    canvas = document.getElementsByTagName("canvas")[0];
    context = canvas.getContext("2d");
    video.addEventListener("play", paintFrame, false);
  }
  function paintFrame() {
    context.drawImage(video, x, y, 160, 80);
    if (x > 240) xpos = -10;
    if (x < 0) xpos = 10;
    x = x + xpos;
    if (y > 220) ypos = -10;
    if (y < 0) ypos = 10;
    y = y + ypos;
    if (video.paused || video.ended) {
      return;
    }
    setTimeout(function () {
        paintFrame();
    }, 0);
  }
</script>
```

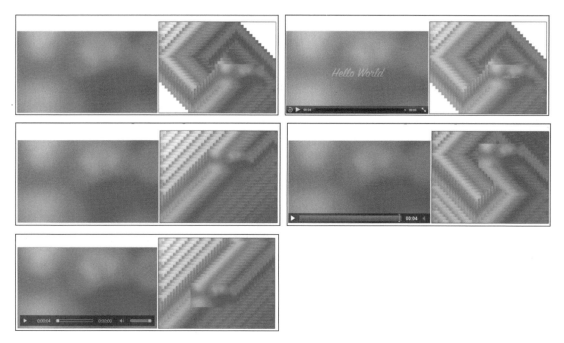

Figure 6–2. *Painting a video into a canvas with the setTimeout event in Firefox, Safari (top row), Opera,*
Chrome (middle row), and IE (bottom)

You may notice that the different browsers managed to draw a different number of video frames during the playback of the complete four-second clip. This is a matter of the speed of the JavaScript engine. Chrome is the clear winner in this race with the browser versions used here, followed by IE and Opera. Firefox and Safari came last and reached almost exactly the same number of frames. The speed of JavaScript engines is still being worked on in all browsers, so these rankings continuously change. The exact browser versions in use for this book are given in the Preface.

Extended drawImage()

Thus far we have used the `drawImage()` function to directly draw the pixels extracted from a video onto the Canvas, including a scaling that the Canvas does for us to fit into the given width and height dimensions. There is also a version of `drawImage()` that allows extracting a rectangular subregion out of the original video pixels and painting them onto a region in the Canvas.

An example of such an approach is tiling, where the video is split into multiple rectangles and re-drawn with a gap between the rectangles. A naïve implementation of this is shown in Listing 6–3. We only show the new `paintFrame()` function since the remainder of the code is identical to Listing 6–2.

Listing 6–3. *Naïve implementation of video tiling into a canvas*

```
function paintFrame() {
  in_w = 960; in_h = 540;
  w = 320; h = 160;
  // create 4x4 tiling
```

```
tiles = 4; gap = 5;
for (x = 0; x < tiles; x++) {
  for (y = 0; y < tiles; y++) {
    context.drawImage(video, x*in_w/tiles,    y*in_h/tiles,
                             in_w/tiles,      in_h/tiles,
                        x*(w/tiles+gap), y*(h/tiles+gap),
                             w/tiles,          h/tiles);
  }
}
if (video.paused || video.ended) {
  return;
}
setTimeout(function () {
    paintFrame();
}, 0);
}
```

The drawImage() function with this many parameters allows extraction of a rectangular region from any offset in the original video and drawing of this pixel data into any scaled rectangular region in the Canvas. Figure 6–3, as taken out of the HTML5 specification[4], explains how this function works, where the parameters are as follows: drawImage(image, sx, sy, sw, sh, dx, dy, dw, dh). In Listing 6–3 it is used to subdivide the video into tiles of size in_w/tiles by in_h/tiles, which are scaled to size w/tiles by h/tiles and placed with a gap.

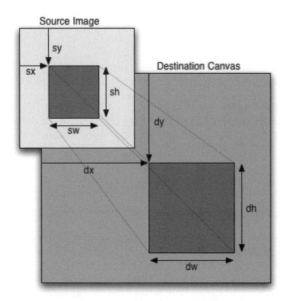

Figure 6–3. Extracting a rectangular region from a source video into a scaled rectangular region in the Canvas

---

[4] See http://www.whatwg.org/specs/web-apps/current-work/

It is important to understand that the original video `resource` is used to extract the region from the video and not the potentially scaled video in the video `element`. If this is disregarded, you may be calculating with the width and height of the scaled video and extract the wrong region. Also note that it is possible to scale the extracted region by placing it into a destination rectangle with different dimensions. The result of running Listing 6–3 is shown in Figure 6–4 by example in IE. All browsers show the same behavior.

Figure 6–4. Tiling a video into a canvas in IE

This implementation is naïve because it assumes that the video frames are only extracted once into the Canvas for all calls of `drawImage()`. This is, however, not the case, as can be noticed when we turn up the number of tiles that are painted. For example, when we set the variable `tiles` to a value of 32, we notice how hard the machine suddenly has to work. Each call to `drawImage()` for the video element retrieves all the pixel data again.

There are two ways to overcome this. Actually, there is potentially a third, but this one doesn't yet work in all browsers. Let's start with that one, so we understand what may be possible in future.

getImageData(), putImageData()

Option 1 consists of drawing the video pixels into the Canvas, then picking up the pixel data from the Canvas with `getImageData()` and writing it out again with `putImageData()`. Since `putImageData()` has parameters to draw out only sections of the picture again, you should in theory be able to replicate the same effect as above. Here is the signature of the function: `putImageData(imagedata, dx, dy [, sx, sy, sw, sh ])`.

No scaling will happen to the image, but otherwise the mapping is as in Figure 6–3. You can see the code in Listing 6–4—again, only the `paintFrame()` function is provided since the remainder is identical with Listing 6–2.

Listing 6–4. Reimplementation of video tiling into a canvas with getImageData

```
function paintFrame() {
  w = 320; h = 160;
  context.drawImage(video, 0, 0, w, h);
  frame = context.getImageData(0, 0, w, h);
  context.clearRect(0, 0, w, h);
```

```
/* create 4x4 tiling */
tiles = 4;
gap = 5;
for (x = 0; x < tiles; x++) {
  for (y = 0; y < tiles; y++) {
    context.putImageData(frame, x*(w/tiles+gap), y*(h/tiles+gap),
                         x*w/tiles, y*h/tiles, w/tiles, h/tiles);
  }
}
if (video.paused || video.ended) {
  return;
}
setTimeout(function () {
    paintFrame();
}, 0);
}
```

In this version, the `putImageData()` function uses parameters to specify the drawing offset, which includes the gap and the size of the cut-out rectangle from the video frame. The frame has already been received through `getImageData()` as a resized image. Note that the frame drawn with `drawImage()` needs to be cleared before redrawing with `putImageData()`. The result of running Listing 6–4 is shown in Figure 6–5.

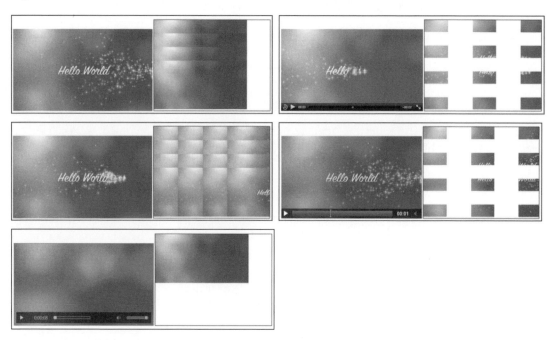

Figure 6–5. Attempted tiling of a video into a Canvas using putImageData() in Firefox, Safari (top row), Opera, Chrome (middle row), and IE (bottom)

Note that you have to run this example from a web server, not from a file on your local computer. The reason is that getImageData() does not work cross-site and security checks will ensure it only works on the same http domain. That leaves out local file access.

Unfortunately, all browsers still have bugs implementing this function. Firefox and Opera do not provide the cutting functionality and instead just display the full frame at every offset. Firefox actually fails the script as soon as putImageData() tries to write outside the Canvas dimensions. These bugs are being worked on. The WebKit-based browsers have an interesting interpretation of the function: dx and dy are applied to the top left corner of the image and then the cut-out is applied. Thus, the resulting gap is not just the size of the gap, but increased by the size of the tiles. There is a problem with IE using getImageData() in the Canvas on video and writing it back out with putImageData(). IE extracts one frame, but then breaks in putImageData(). Thus, we cannot recommend using the cut-out functionality of putImageData() at this point to achieve tiling.

getImageData(), simple putImageData()

Option 2 is to perform the cut-outs ourselves. Seeing as we have the pixel data available through getImageData(), we can create each of the tiles ourselves and use putImageData() with only the offset attributes to place the tiles. Listing 6–5 shows an implementation of the paintFrame() function for this case.

Note that Opera doesn't support the createImageData() function, so we create an image of the required size using getImageData() on Opera. Because we cleared the rectangle earlier, this is not a problem.

Also note that none of this works in IE yet, since IE doesn't support this combination of getImageData() and putImageData() on videos yet.

Listing 6–5. Reimplementation of video tiling into a canvas with createImageData

```
function paintFrame() {
  w = 320; h = 160;
  context.drawImage(video, 0, 0, w, h);
  frame = context.getImageData(0, 0, w, h);
  context.clearRect(0, 0, w, h);

  // create 16x16 tiling
  tiles = 16;
  gap = 2;
  nw = w/tiles;   // tile width
  nh = h/tiles;   // tile height

  // Loop over the tiles
  for (tx = 0; tx < tiles; tx++) {
    for (ty = 0; ty < tiles; ty++) {

      // Opera doesn't implement createImageData, use getImageData
      output = false;
      if (context.createImageData) {
        output = context.createImageData(nw, nh);
      } else if (context.getImageData) {
        output = context.getImageData(0, 0, nw, nh);
      }

      // Loop over each pixel of output file
```

```
        for (x = 0; x < nw; x++) {
          for (y = 0; y < nh; y++) {
            // index in output image
            i = x + nw*y;
            // index in frame image
            j = x + w*y        // corresponding pixel to i
                + tx*nw        // which tile along the x axis
                + w*nh*ty;     // which tile along the y axis
            // go through all 4 color values
            for (c = 0; c < 4; c++) {
              output.data[4*i+c] = frame.data[4*j+c];
            }
          }
        }

        // Draw the ImageData object.
        context.putImageData(output, tx*(nw+gap), ty*(nh+gap));
      }
    }

    if (video.paused || video.ended) {
      return;
    }
    setTimeout(function () {
        paintFrame();
    }, 0);
  }
```

Because we now have to prepare our own pixel data, we loop through the pixels of the output image and fill it from the relevant pixels of the video frame image. We do this for each tile separately and place one image each. Figure 6–6 shows the results with a 16x16 grid of tiles.

This could obviously be improved by just writing a single image and placing the gap in between the tiles. The advantage of having an image for each tile is that you can more easily manipulate the individual tile—rotate, translate, or scale it, for example—but you will need to administer the list of tiles; i.e. keep a list of pointers to them. The advantage of having a single image is that it will be rendered faster; otherwise this is not really an improvement over Option 1.

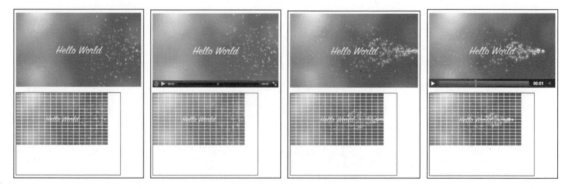

Figure 6–6. Attempted tiling of a video into a canvas using putImageData() in Firefox, Safari, Opera, and Google Chrome (from left to right).

Scratch Canvas

Since the drawImage() function also takes a Canvas as input, Option 3 is to draw the video frames into a scratch canvas and then use drawImage() again with input from that second canvas. The expectation is that the image in the Canvas is already in a form that can just be copied over into the display Canvas rather than having continuing pixel conversions as is necessary in Option 1, where scaling is happening, or Listing 6–3, where the conversion happens by pulling in pixels from the video. Listing 6–6 has the code. The output is identical to Figure 6–4.

Listing 6–6. Reimplementation of video tiling into a Canvas with two Canvases

```
<video controls height="270px" width="480px" >
  <source src="HelloWorld.mp4"  type="video/mp4">
  <source src="HelloWorld.webm" type="video/webm">
  <source src="HelloWorld.ogv"  type="video/ogg">
</video>
<canvas width="400" height="300" style="border: 1px solid black;">
</canvas>
<canvas id="scratch" width="320" height="160"
        style="display: none;"></canvas>
<script>
  window.onload = function() {
    initCanvas();
  }
  var context, sctxt, video;
  function initCanvas() {
    video = document.getElementsByTagName("video")[0];
    canvases = document.getElementsByTagName("canvas");
    canvas = canvases[0];
    scratch = canvases[1];
    context = canvas.getContext("2d");
    sctxt = scratch.getContext("2d");
    video.addEventListener("play", paintFrame, false);
  }
  function paintFrame() {
    // set up scratch frames
    w = 320; h = 160;
    sctxt.drawImage(video, 0, 0, w, h);
    // create 4x4 tiling
    tiles = 4;
    gap = 5;
    tw = w/tiles; th = h/tiles;
    for (x = 0; x < tiles; x++) {
      for (y = 0; y < tiles; y++) {
        context.drawImage(scratch, x*tw, y*th, tw, th,
                          x*(tw+gap), y*(th+gap), tw, th);
      }
    }
    if (video.paused || video.ended) {
      return;
    }
    setTimeout(function () {
        paintFrame();
```

175

```
        }, 0);
    }
</script>
```

Notice that there is now a second Canvas in the HTML. It has to be defined large enough to be able to contain the video frame. If you do not give it a width and height attribute, it will default to 300x150 and you may lose data around the edges. But you have to make it "display:none" such that it doesn't also get displayed. The video frames get decoded into this scratch canvas and rescaled only this once. Then the tiles are drawn into the exposed Canvas using the extended drawImage() function as in Listing 6–3.

This is the most efficient implementation of the tiling since it doesn't have to repeatedly copy the frames from the video, and it doesn't have to continuously rescale the original frame size. It also works across all browsers, including IE.

An amazing example of tiling together with further Canvas effects such as transformations is shown in "blowing up your video" by Sean Christmann[5].

6.2 Styling

Now that we know how to handle video in a Canvas, let's do some simple manipulations to the pixels that will have a surprisingly large effect.

Pixel Transparency to Replace the Background

Listing 6–7 shows a video where all colors but white are made transparent before being projected onto a Canvas with a background image.

Listing 6–7. Making certain colors in a video transparent through a Canvas

```
function paintFrame() {
    w = 480; h = 270;
    context.drawImage(video, 0, 0, w, h);
    frame = context.getImageData(0, 0, w, h);
    context.clearRect(0, 0, w, h);
    output = context.createImageData(w, h);

    // Loop over each pixel of output file
    for (x = 0; x < w; x++) {
        for (y = 0; y < h; y++) {
            // index in output image
            i = x + w*y;
            for (c = 0; c < 4; c++) {
                output.data[4*i+c] = frame.data[4*i+c];
            }
            // make pixels transparent
            r = frame.data[i * 4 + 0];
            g = frame.data[i * 4 + 1];
            b = frame.data[i * 4 + 2];
            if (!(r > 200 && g > 200 && b > 200))
```

---

[5] See http://craftymind.com/factory/html5video/CanvasVideo.html

```
        output.data[4*i + 3] = 0;
      }
    }
    context.putImageData(output, 0, 0);
    if (video.paused || video.ended) {
      return;
    }
    setTimeout(function () {
      paintFrame();
    }, 0);
  }
```

Listing 6–7 shows the essential painting function. The rest of the page is very similar to Listing 6–2 with the addition of a background image to the <canvas> styling. All pixels are drawn exactly the same way, except for the fourth color channel of each pixel, which is set to 0 depending on the color combination of the pixel. Figure 6–7 shows the result with the "Hello World" text and the stars being the only remaining nontransparent pixels.

This example works in all browsers except IE. The IE bug—where image data read from <video> through getImageData() cannot be written out via putImageData()—ears its head here, too.

Figure 6–7. Projecting a masked video onto a background image in the Canvas.

This technique can also be applied to a blue or green screen video to replace the background[6].

---

[6] See http://people.mozilla.com/~prouget/demos/green/green.xhtml for an example by Paul Rouget.

Scaling Pixel Slices for a 3D Effect

Videos are often placed in a 3D display to make them look more like real-world screens. This requires scaling the shape of the video to a trapeze where both width and height are scaled. In a Canvas, this can be achieved by drawing vertical slices of the video picture with different heights and scaling the width using the drawImage() function. Listing 6–8 shows an example.

Listing 6–8. Rendering a video in the 2D canvas with a 3D effect

```
function paintFrame() {
    // set up scratch frame
    w = 320; h = 160;
    sctxt.drawImage(video, 0, 0, w, h);

    // width change from -500 to +500
    width = -500;
    // right side scaling from 0 to 200%
    scale = 1.4;

    // canvas width and height
    cw = 1000; ch = 400;
    // number of columns to draw
    columns = Math.abs(width);
    // display the picture mirrored?
    mirror = (width > 0) ? 1 : -1;

    // origin of the output picture
    ox = cw/2; oy= (ch-h)/2;
    // slice width
    sw = columns/w;
    // slice height increase steps
    sh = (h*scale-h)/columns;

    // Loop over each pixel column of the output picture
    for (x = 0; x < w; x++) {
        // place output columns
        dx = ox + mirror*x*sw;
        dy = oy - x*sh/2;

        // scale output columns
        dw = sw;
        dh = h + x*sh;

        // draw the pixel column
        context.drawImage(scratch, x, 0, 1, h, dx, dy, dw, dh);
    }
    if (video.paused || video.ended) {
        return;
    }
    setTimeout(function () {
        paintFrame();
```

```
        }, 0);
    }
```

For this example we use a 1000x400 Canvas and a second scratch Canvas as in Listing 6–6 into which we pull the pixel data. We show only the paintFrame() function in Listing 6–8. As we pull the video frame into the scratch frame, we perform the scaling to the video size at which we want to undertake the effect. For this scaling we have the variables "width" and "scale". You can change these easily, for example, to achieve a book page turning effect (change "width" for this) or an approaching/retreating effect (change "scale" for this). The next lines define some variables important to use in the loop that places the pixel slices.

Figure 6–8 shows the result using different "width" and "scale" values in the different browsers. All browsers, including IE, support this example.

The width and scale variables in Figure 6–8 were changed between the screenshots to show some of the dynamics possible with this example. For Firefox we used (width,scale)=(500,2.0), for Safari (200,1.4), for Opera (50,1.1), for Chrome (-250,1.2), and for IE (-250,2).

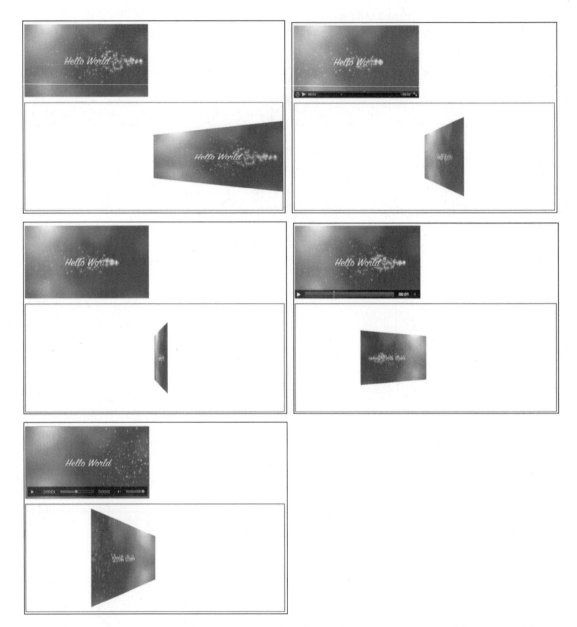

Figure 6–8. *Rendering video in a 3D perspective in Firefox, Safari (top row), Opera, Chrome (middle row), and IE (bottom).*

Ambient CSS Color Frame

Another nice effect that the Canvas can be used for is what is typically known as an ambient color frame for the video. In this effect, a colored frame is created around the video, and the color of that frame is adjusted according to the average color of the video.

Listing 6–9 shows an example implementation of such an ambient color frame.

Listing 6–9. Calculation of average color in a Canvas and display of ambient color frame

```
<style type="text/css">
#ambience {
  -moz-transition-property: all;
  -moz-transition-duration: 1s;
  -moz-transition-timing-function: linear;
  -webkit-transition-property: all;
  -webkit-transition-duration: 1s;
  -webkit-transition-timing-function: linear;
  -o-transition-property: all;
  -o-transition-duration: 1s;
  -o-transition-timing-function: linear;
  padding: 40px;
  width: 496px;
  outline: black solid 10px;
}
video {
  padding: 3px;
  background-color: white;
}
canvas {
  display: none;
}
</style>
<div id="ambience">
  <video controls height="270px" width="480px">
    <source src="video1.mp4"  type="video/mp4">
    <source src="video1.webm" type="video/webm">
    <source src="video1.ogv"  type="video/ogg">
  </video>
</div>
<canvas id="scratch" width="320" height="160"></canvas>
<script>
  window.onload = function() {
    initCanvas();
  }
  var sctxt, video, ambience;
  function initCanvas() {
    ambience = document.getElementById("ambience");
    video = document.getElementsByTagName("video")[0];
    scratch = document.getElementById("scratch");
    sctxt = scratch.getContext("2d");
    video.addEventListener("play", paintAmbience, false);
  }
  function paintAmbience() {
```

```
        // set up scratch frame
        sctxt.drawImage(video, 0, 0, 320, 160);
        frame = sctxt.getImageData(0, 0, 320, 160);
        // get average color for frame and transition to it
        color = getColorAvg(frame);
        ambience.style.backgroundColor =
            'rgb('+color[0]+','+color[1]+','+color[2]+')';
        if (video.paused || video.ended) {
          return;
        }
        // don't do it more often than once a second
        setTimeout(function () {
            paintAmbience();
        }, 1000);
      }
    function getColorAvg(frame) {
        r = 0;
        g = 0;
        b = 0;
        // calculate average color from image in canvas
        for (var i = 0; i < frame.data.length; i += 4) {
          r += frame.data[i];
          g += frame.data[i + 1];
          b += frame.data[i + 2];
        }
        r = Math.ceil(r / (frame.data.length / 4));
        g = Math.ceil(g / (frame.data.length / 4));
        b = Math.ceil(b / (frame.data.length / 4));
        return Array(r, g, b);
      }
  </script>
```

Listing 6–9 is pretty long, but also fairly easy to follow. We set up the CSS style environment such that the video is framed by a <div> element whose background color will be dynamically changed. The video has a 3px white padding frame to separate it from the color-changing <div>. Because we are performing the color changes only once every second, but we want the impression of a smooth color transition, we use CSS transitions to make the changes over the course of a second.

The Canvas being used is invisible since it is used only to pull an image frame every second and calculate the average color of that frame. The background of the <div> is then updated with that color. Figure 6–9 shows the result at different times in a video.

Figure 6–9. *Rendering of an ambient CSS color frame in Firefox(top left), Safari (top right), Opera (bottom left), and Google Chrome (bottom right)*

If you are reading this in the print version, in Figure 6–9 you may see only different shades of gray as the backgrounds of the videos. However, they are actually khaki, blue, gray and red.

Note that because of the IE bug on `getImageData()` and `putImageData()` on video, this example doesn't work in IE.

Other nice examples of ambient color backgrounds are available from Mozilla[7] and Splashnology.[8]

Video as Pattern

The Canvas provides a simple function to create regions tiled with images, another Canvas, or frames from a video: the `createPattern()` function. This will take an image and replicate it into the given region until that region is filled with it. If your video doesn't come in the size that your pattern requires, you will need to use a scratch Canvas to resize the video frames first. Listing 6–10 shows how it's done.

---

[7] See http://videos.mozilla.org/serv/blizzard/35days/silverorange-ambient-video/ambient.xhtml

[8] See http://www.splashnology.com/blog/html5/382.html

Listing 6–10. Filling a rectangular canvas region with a video pattern

```
<video style="display: none;">
  <source src="HelloWorld.mp4"  type="video/mp4">
  <source src="HelloWorld.webm" type="video/webm">
  <source src="HelloWorld.ogv"  type="video/ogg">
</video>
<canvas width="800" height="400" style="border: 1px solid black;">
</canvas>
<canvas id="scratch" width="160" height="80" style="display:none;">
</canvas>
<script>
  window.onload = function() {
    initCanvas();
  }
  var context, sctxt, video;
  function initCanvas() {
    video = document.getElementsByTagName("video")[0];
    canvas = document.getElementsByTagName("canvas")[0];
    context = canvas.getContext("2d");
    scratch = document.getElementById("scratch");
    sctxt = scratch.getContext("2d");
    video.addEventListener("play", paintFrame, false);
    if (video.readyState >= video.HAVE_METADATA) {
      startPlay();
    } else {
      video.addEventListener("loadedmetadata", startPlay, false);
    }
  }
  function startPlay() {
    video.play();
  }
  function paintFrame() {
    sctxt.drawImage(video, 0, 0, 160, 80);
    pattern = context.createPattern(scratch, 'repeat');
    context.fillStyle = pattern;
    context.fillRect(0, 0, 800, 400);
    if (video.paused || video.ended) {
      return;
    }
    setTimeout(function () {
        paintFrame();
    }, 10);
  }
</script>
```

Note how we are using the play() function to start video playback, but only if the video is ready for playback; otherwise, we have to wait until the video reports through the "loadedmetadata" event that its decoding pipeline is ready for it. This is why we are checking the state and potentially adding a callback for the "loadedmetadata" event.

Every time the paintFrame() function is called, the current image in the video is grabbed and used as the replicated pattern in createPattern(). The HTML5 Canvas specification states that if the image (or Canvas frame or video frame) is changed after the `createPattern()` function call where it is used, that will not affect the pattern.

Because there is no means of specifying scaling on the pattern image being used, we have to first load the video frames into the scratch Canvas, then create the pattern from this scratch Canvas and apply it to the drawing region.

We do not want the pattern painting to slow down the rest of the web page; thus we call this function again only after a 10ms wait. Figure 6–10 shows the rendering in Opera. Since all browsers show the same behavior, this is representative for all browsers.

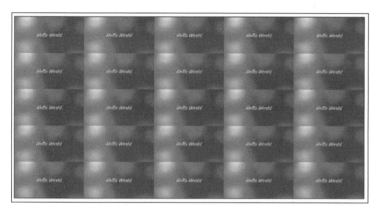

Figure 6–10. Rendering of a video pattern in Opera.

6.3 Compositing

When painting video frames on a Canvas, the frame pixels will be combined (also called: composited) with the existing background on the Canvas. The function applied for this composition is defined by the "`globalCompositeOperation`" property of the Canvas.[9] By default, what is being drawn onto the Canvas is drawn over the top of what is already there. But this property can be changed to allow for more meaningful use of the existing content on the Canvas.

Mozilla provides a very nice overview at https://developer.mozilla.org/samples/canvas-tutorial/6_1_canvas_composite.html to check what your browser does with each composite operation type. Some browsers don't implement all the functionalities yet, so be careful what you choose. We look at two examples here, one where we use a gradient for compositing and one where we use a path.

Gradient Transparency Mask

Gradient masks are used to gradually fade the opacity of an object. We have already seen in Chapter 5, Listing 5-8, how we can use a liner gradient image defined in SVG as a mask for a video to make video pixels increasingly transparent along the gradient. We could place page content behind the video and the video would sit on top of that content and would be transparent where the gradient was opaque. We used the CSS properties -webkit-mask and mask for this, but it doesn't (yet) work in Opera.

---

[9] See http://www.whatwg.org/specs/web-apps/current-work/multipage/the-canvas-element.html#dom-context-2d-globalcompositeoperation

With Canvas, we now repeat this exercise with a bit more flexibility, since we can set individual pixels in the middle of doing all this. We're reusing the previous example and are actually painting the video into the middle of a Canvas now. That video is blended into the ambient background through use of a radial gradient. Listing 6–11 shows the key elements of the code.

Listing 6–11. Introducing a gradient transparency mark into the ambient video

```
<style type="text/css">
#ambience {
  -moz-transition-property: all;
  -moz-transition-duration: 1s;
  -moz-transition-timing-function: linear;
  -webkit-transition-property: all;
  -webkit-transition-duration: 1s;
  -webkit-transition-timing-function: linear;
  -o-transition-property: all;
  -o-transition-duration: 1s;
  -o-transition-timing-function: linear;
  width: 390px; height: 220px;
  outline: black solid 10px;
}
#canvas {
  position: relative;
  left: 30px; top: 30px;
}
</style>
<div id="ambience">
  <canvas id="canvas" width="320" height="160"></canvas>
</div>
<video style="display: none;">
  <source src="video1.mp4"  type="video/mp4">
  <source src="video1.webm" type="video/webm">
  <source src="video1.ogv"  type="video/ogg">
</video>
<canvas id="scratch" width="320" height="160" style="display: none;">
</canvas>
<script>
  window.onload = function() {
    initCanvas();
  }
  var context, sctxt, video, ambience;
  function initCanvas() {
    ambience = document.getElementById("ambience");
    video = document.getElementsByTagName("video")[0];
    canvas = document.getElementsByTagName("canvas")[0];
    context = canvas.getContext("2d");
    context.globalCompositeOperation = "destination-in";
    scratch = document.getElementById("scratch");
    sctxt = scratch.getContext("2d");
    gradient = context.createRadialGradient(160,80,0, 160,80,150);
    gradient.addColorStop(0, "rgba( 255, 255, 255, 1)");
    gradient.addColorStop(0.7, "rgba( 125, 125, 125, 0.8)");
    gradient.addColorStop(1, "rgba( 0, 0, 0, 0)");
```

```
    video.addEventListener("play", paintAmbience, false);
    if (video.readyState >= video.HAVE_METADATA) {
      startPlay();
    } else {
      video.addEventListener("loadedmetadata", startPlay, false);
    }
  }
  function startPlay() {
    video.play();
  }
  function paintAmbience() {
    // set up scratch frame
    sctxt.drawImage(video, 0, 0, 320, 160);
    // get average color for frame and transition to it
    frame = sctxt.getImageData(0, 0, 320, 160);
    color = getColorAvg(frame);
    ambience.style.backgroundColor =
            'rgba('+color[0]+','+color[1]+','+color[2]+',0.8)';
    // paint video image
    context.putImageData(frame, 0, 0);
    // throw gradient onto canvas
    context.fillStyle = gradient;
    context.fillRect(0,0,320,160);
    if (video.paused || video.ended) {
      return;
    }
    setTimeout(function () {
      paintAmbience();
    }, 0);
  }
```

We do not repeat the getColorAvg() function, which we defined in Listing 6–9.

We achieve the video masking with a gradient through the change of the globalCompositeOperation property of the display Canvas to "destination-in." This means that we are able to use a gradient that is pasted on top of the video frame to control the transparency of the pixels of the video frame. We create a radial gradient in the setup function and reuse that for every video frame.

Figure 6–11 shows the results in the browsers except for IE, which doesn't display this example because of the bug with getImageData() and putImageData().

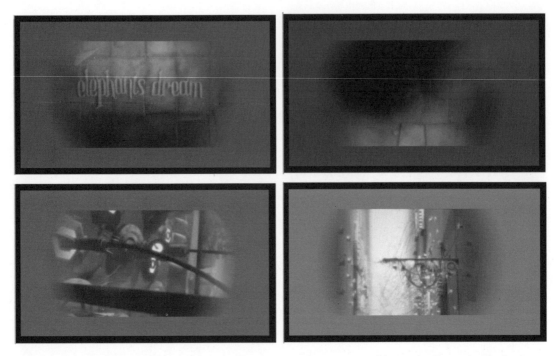

Figure 6–11. Rendering of video with a transparency mask onto an ambient color frame in Firefox(top left), Safari (top right), Opera (bottom left), and Chrome (bottom right)

Clipping a Region

Another useful compositing effect is to clip out a region from the Canvas for display. This will cause everything else drawn onto the Canvas afterwards to be drawn only in the clipped-out region. For this, a path is drawn that may also include basic shapes. Then, instead of drawing these onto the Canvas with the `stroke()` or `fill()` methods, we draw them using the `clip()` method, creating the clipped region(s) on the Canvas to which further drawings will be confined. Listing 6–12 shows an example.

Listing 6–12. Using a clipped path to filter out regions of the video for display

```
<canvas id="canvas" width="320" height="160"></canvas>
<video style="display: none;">
  <source src="HelloWorld.mp4"  type="video/mp4">
  <source src="HelloWorld.webm" type="video/webm">
  <source src="HelloWorld.ogv"  type="video/ogg">
</video>
<script>
  window.onload = function() {
    initCanvas();
  }
  var context, video;
  function initCanvas() {
```

```
      video = document.getElementsByTagName("video")[0];
      canvas = document.getElementsByTagName("canvas")[0];
      context = canvas.getContext("2d");
      context.beginPath();
      // speech bubble
      context.moveTo(75,25);
      context.quadraticCurveTo(25,25,25,62.5);
      context.quadraticCurveTo(25,100,50,100);
      context.quadraticCurveTo(100,120,100,125);
      context.quadraticCurveTo(90,120,65,100);
      context.quadraticCurveTo(125,100,125,62.5);
      context.quadraticCurveTo(125,25,75,25);
      // outer circle
      context.arc(180,90,50,0,Math.PI*2,true);
      context.moveTo(215,90);
      // mouth
      context.arc(180,90,30,0,Math.PI,false);
      context.moveTo(170,65);
      // eyes
      context.arc(165,65,5,0,Math.PI*2,false);
      context.arc(195,65,5,0,Math.PI*2,false);
      context.clip();
      video.addEventListener("play", drawFrame, false);
      if (video.readyState >= video.HAVE_METADATA) {
        startPlay();
      } else {
        video.addEventListener("loadedmetadata", startPlay, false);
      }
    }
    function startPlay() {
      video.play();
    }
    function drawFrame() {
      context.drawImage(video, 0, 0, 320, 160);
      if (video.paused || video.ended) {
        return;
      }
      setTimeout(function () {
          drawFrame();
      }, 0);
    }
  }
</script>
```

In this example, we don't display the video element, but only draw its frames onto the Canvas. During setup of the Canvas, we define a clip path consisting of a speech bubble and a smiley face. We then set up the event listener for the "play" event and start playback of the video. In the callback, we only need to draw the video frames onto the Canvas. This is a very simple and effective means of masking out regions. Figure 6–12 shows the results in Chrome. It works in all browsers the same way, including IE.

Figure 6–12. Rendering of video on a clipped Canvas in Google Chrome.

6.4 Drawing Text

We can also use text as a mask for video, such that the filling on some text is the video. Listing 6–13 shows how it is done with a Canvas.

Listing 6–13. Text filled with video

```
<canvas id="canvas" width="320" height="160"></canvas>
<video style="display: none;">
  <source src="HelloWorld.mp4"  type="video/mp4">
  <source src="HelloWorld.webm" type="video/webm">
  <source src="HelloWorld.ogv"  type="video/ogg">
</video>
<script>
  window.onload = function() {
    initCanvas();
  }
  var context, video;
  function initCanvas() {
    video = document.getElementsByTagName("video")[0];
    canvas = document.getElementsByTagName("canvas")[0];
    context = canvas.getContext("2d");
    // paint text onto canvas as mask
    context.font = 'bold 70px sans-serif';
    context.textBaseline = 'top';
    context.fillText('Hello World!', 0, 50, 320);
    context.globalCompositeOperation = "source-atop";
    video.addEventListener("play", paintFrame, false);
    if (video.readyState >= video.HAVE_METADATA) {
      startPlay();
```

```
    } else {
      video.addEventListener("loadedmetadata", startPlay, false);
    }
  }
  function startPlay() {
    video.play();
  }
  function paintFrame() {
    context.drawImage(video, 0, 0, 320, 160);
    if (video.paused || video.ended) {
      return;
    }
    setTimeout(function () {
      paintFrame();
    }, 0);
  }
</script>
```

We have a target Canvas and a hidden video element. In JavaScript, we first paint the text onto the Canvas. Then we use the "globalCompositeOperation" property to use the text as a mask for all video frames painted onto the Canvas afterwards. Note that we used "source-atop" as the compositing function; "source-in" works in Opera and WebKit-browsers, but Firefox refuses to mask the video and simply displays the full frames. IE unfortunately doesn't yet support the global composition for video images. Figure 6–13 shows the results in the other browsers that all support this functionality.

Figure 6–13. Rendering of video as a filling of text in Firefox(top left), Safari (top right), Opera (bottom left), and Google Chrome (bottom right).

Note that the text rendering with the optional maxWidth parameter on the fillText() function doesn't seem to be supported yet in WebKit browsers, which is why their text is not scaled. In Firefox, the text height is kept and the font horizontally scaled, while Opera chooses a smaller font.

6.5 Transformations

The usual transformations supported by CSS and SVG are also supported by Canvas: translating, rotating, scaling, and transformation matrices. We can apply them to the frames extracted from the video to give the video some special effects.

Reflections

A simple effect web designers particularly like to use is reflections. Reflections are simple to implement and have a huge effect, particularly when used on a dark website theme. All you need to do is make a copy of the content into a second Canvas underneath, flip it and reduce opacity along a gradient.

We weren't able to perform video reflections either in SVG or CSS in a cross-browser consistent way. Only Opera supports synchronized reflections in SVG because it supports the <video> element inside SVG, and only WebKit has a -webkit-box-reflect property in CSS. So only by using the Canvas can we create reflections in a cross-browser consistent manner, while keeping the copied video and the source video in sync.

Listing 6–14 shows an example implementation. This works in all browsers.

Listing 6–14. Video reflection using a Canvas

```
<div style="padding: 50px; background-color: #090909;">
  <video style="vertical-align: bottom;" width="320">
    <source src="video1.mp4"  type="video/mp4">
    <source src="video1.webm" type="video/webm">
    <source src="video1.ogv"  type="video/ogg">
  </video>
  <br/>
  <canvas id="reflection" width="320" height="55"
          style="vertical-align: top;"></canvas>
</div>
<script>
  window.onload = function() {
    initCanvas();
  }
  var context, rctxt, video;
  function initCanvas() {
    video = document.getElementsByTagName("video")[0];
    reflection = document.getElementById("reflection");
    rctxt = reflection.getContext("2d");
    // flip canvas
    rctxt.translate(0,160);
    rctxt.scale(1,-1);
    // create gradient
    gradient = rctxt.createLinearGradient(0, 105, 0, 160);
    gradient.addColorStop(1, "rgba(255, 255, 255, 0.3)");
    gradient.addColorStop(0, "rgba(255, 255, 255, 1.0)");
    rctxt.fillStyle = gradient;
```

```
            rctxt.rect(0, 105, 320, 160);
            video.addEventListener("play", paintFrame, false);
            if (video.readyState >= video.HAVE_METADATA) {
              startPlay();
            } else {
              video.addEventListener("loadedmetadata", startPlay, false);
            }
          }
          function startPlay() {
            video.play();
          }
          function paintFrame() {
            // draw frame, and fill with the opacity gradient mask
            rctxt.drawImage(video, 0, 0, 320, 160);
            rctxt.globalCompositeOperation = "destination-out";
            rctxt.fill();
            // restore composition operation for next frame draw
            rctxt.globalCompositeOperation = "source-over";
            if (video.paused || video.ended) {
              return;
            }
            setTimeout(function () {
              paintFrame();
            }, 0);
          }
        </script>
```

The example uses the <video> element to display the video, though a second Canvas could be used for this, too. Make sure to remove the @controls attribute as it breaks the reflection perception. We've placed the video and the aligned Canvas underneath into a dark <div> element to make it look nicer. Make sure to give the <video> and the <canvas> element the same width. We've given the reflection one-third the height of the original video.

As we set up the Canvas, we already prepare it as a mirrored drawing area with the scale() and translate() functions. The translation moves it down the height of the video, the scaling mirrors the pixels along the x axis. We then set up the gradient on the bottom 55 pixels of the video frames.

The paintFrame() function applies the reflection effect after the video starts playback and while it is playing back at the maximum speed possible. Because we have decided to have the <video> element display the video, it is possible that the <canvas> cannot catch up with the display, and there is a disconnect between the <video> and its reflection. If that bothers you, you should also paint the video frames in a Canvas. You just need to set up a second <canvas> element and add a drawImage() function on that Canvas at the top of the paintFrame() function.

For the reflection, we now paint the video frames onto the mirrored Canvas. When using two <canvas> elements, you may be tempted to use the getImageData() and putImageData() to apply the Canvas transformations; however, Canvas transformations are not applied to these functions. So you have to use a Canvas into which you have pulled the video data through drawImage() to apply the transformations.

Now we just need a gradient on the mirrored images. To apply the gradient, we use a composition function of the gradient with the video images. We have used the composition before to replace the current image in the Canvas with the next one. Creating a new composition property changes that. We therefore need to reset the compositing property after applying the gradient. Another solution would be to use save() and restore() functions before changing the compositing property and after applying the gradient. If you change more than one Canvas property or you don't want to keep track of what previous value you have to reset the property to, using save() and restore() is indeed the better approach.

Figure 6–14 shows the resulting renderings.

Figure 6–14. Rendering of video with a reflection in Firefox, Safari (top row), Opera, Chrome (middle row), and IE (bottom)

Note that in Firefox there is a stray one-pixel line at the end of the gradient. It's a small glitch in the Firefox implementation. You can make the <canvas> element smaller by one pixel to get rid of it.

Also note that IE's mirror image is not quite correct. The gradient is not properly composed with the imagery. It's just a white overlay onto the mirrored imagery.

You could next consider putting a slight ripple effect on the reflection. This is left to the reader for exercise.

Spiraling Video

Canvas transformations can make the pixel-based operations that we saw at the beginning of this chapter a lot easier, in particular when you want to apply them to the whole Canvas. The example shown in Listing 6–2 and Figure 6–2 can also be achieved with a translate() function, except you will still need to calculate when you hit the boundaries of the canvas to change your translate() function. So you would add a translate(xpos,ypos) function and always draw the image at position (0,0), which doesn't win you very much.

We want to look here at a more sophisticated example for using transformation. We want to use both a translate() and a rotate() to make the frames of the video spiral through the Canvas. Listing 6–15 shows how we achieve this.

Listing 6–15. Video spiral using Canvas

```
<script>
  window.onload = function() {
    initCanvas();
  }
  var context, video;
  var i = 0;
  var repeater;
  function initCanvas() {
    video = document.getElementsByTagName("video")[0];
    canvas = document.getElementsByTagName("canvas")[0];
    context = canvas.getContext("2d");
    // provide a shadow
    context.shadowOffsetX = 5;
    context.shadowOffsetY = 5;
    context.shadowBlur = 4;
    context.shadowColor = "rgba(0, 0, 0, 0.5)";
    video.addEventListener("play", repeat, false);
  }
  function repeat() {
    // try to get each browser at the same frequency
    repeater = setInterval("paintFrame()", 30);
  }
  function paintFrame() {
    context.drawImage(video, 0, 0, 160, 80);
    // reset to identity transform
    context.setTransform(1, 0,
                         0, 1,
                         0, 0);
    // increasingly move to the right and down & rotate
    i += 1;
    context.translate(3 * i , 1.5 * i);
```

```
        context.rotate(0.1 * i);
        if (video.paused || video.ended) {
          clearInterval(repeater);
        }
      }
    }
</script>
```

The `<video>` and `<canvas>` element definitions are unchanged from previous examples. We only need to increase the size of our Canvas to fit the full spiral. We also have given the frames being painted into the Canvas a shadow, which offsets them from the previously drawn frames.

Note that we have changed the way in which we perform the callback. Now, we don't run the `paintFrame()` function as fast as we can, but rather every 30ms at most (depending on the processing speed of the browser). For this, we have introduced the `repeat()` function as the callback to the `play` event. The repeater is cancelled when we reach the end of the video or pause it.

The way in which we paint the spiral is such that we paint the new video frame on top of a translated and rotated canvas. In order to apply the translation and rotation to the correct pixels, we need to reset the transformation matrix after painting a frame. This is very important, because the previous transformations are already stored for the Canvas such that another call — to `translate()`, for example — will go along the tilted axis set by the rotation rather than straight down as you might expect. Thus, the transformation matrix has to be reset; otherwise, the operations are cumulative.

Figure 6–15 shows the resulting renderings in all the browsers.

Note that they all achieve roughly the 130 frames for the four-second long video at 30ms difference between the frames. When we take that difference down to 4s, Firefox and Safari will achieve 153 frames, IE 237, Opera 624, and Chrome 634 out of the possible 1000 frames. This is for browsers downloaded and installed on Mac OS X without setting up extra hardware acceleration for graphics operations.

Note that the WebKit-based browsers don't do the black mirror and consequently the images show much less naturalism.

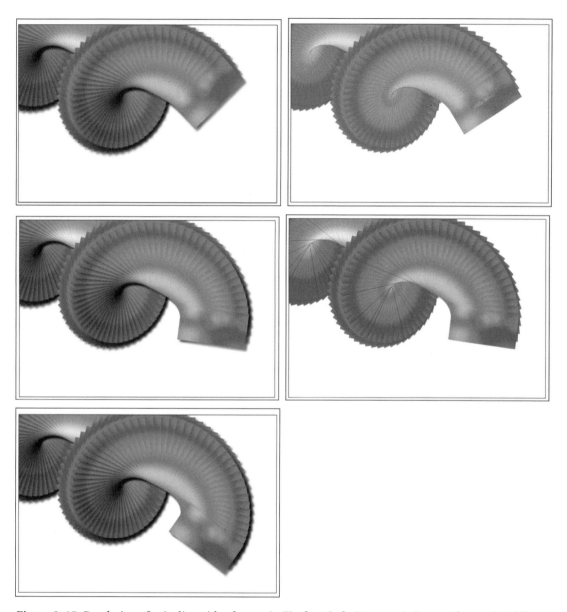

Figure 6–15. Rendering of spiraling video frames in Firefox , Safari(top row), Opera, Chrome (middle row), and IE (bottom)

6.6 Animations and Interactivity

We've already used setInterval() and setTimeout() with video in the Canvas to allow creating animated graphics with the video frames in the Canvas in sync with the timeline of the video. In this section we want to look at another way to animate the Canvas: through user interaction.

In comparison to SVG, which allows detailed attachment of events to individual objects in the graphic, Canvas only knows pixels and has no concept of objects. It thus cannot associate events to a particular shape in the drawing. The Canvas as a whole, however, accepts events, so you can attach the click event on the <canvas> element, and then compare the x/y coordinates of the click event with the coordinates of your Canvas to identify which object it might relate to.

In this section we will look at an example that is a bit like a simple game. After you start playback of the video, you can click at any time again to retrieve a quote from a collection of quotes. Think of it as a fortune cookie gamble. Listing 6–16 shows how we've done it.

Listing 6–16. Fortune cookie video with user interactivity in Canvas

```
<script>
  var quotes =  ["Of those who say nothing,/ few are silent.",
                 "Man is born to live,/ not to prepare for life.",
                 "Time sneaks up on you/ like a windshield on a bug.",
                 "Simplicity is the/ peak of civilization.",
                 "Only I can change my life./ No one can do it for me."];
  window.onload = function() {
    initCanvas();
  }
  var context, video;
  var w = 640, h = 320;
  function initCanvas() {
    video = document.getElementsByTagName("video")[0];
    canvas = document.getElementsByTagName("canvas")[0];
    context = canvas.getContext("2d");
    context.lineWidth = 5;
    context.font = 'bold 25px sans-serif';
    context.fillText('Click me!', w/4+20, h/2, w/2);
    context.strokeRect(w/4,h/4,w/2,h/2);
    canvas.addEventListener("click", doClick, false);
    video.addEventListener("play", paintFrame, false);
    video.addEventListener("pause", showRect, false);
  }
  function paintFrame() {
    if (video.paused || video.ended) {
      return;
    }
    context.drawImage(video, 0, 0, w, h);
    context.strokeRect(w/4,h/4,w/2,h/2);
    setTimeout(function () {
        paintFrame();
    }, 0);
  }
  function isPlaying(video) {
    return (!video.paused && !video.ended);
  }
```

```
    function doClick(e) {
      var pos = clickPos(e);
      if ((pos[0] < w/4) || (pos[0] > 3*w/4)) return;
      if ((pos[1] < h/4) || (pos[1] > 3*h/4)) return;
      !isPlaying(video) ? video.play() : video.pause();
    }
    function showRect(e) {
      context.clearRect(w/4,h/4,w/2,h/2);
      quote = quotes[Math.floor(Math.random()*quotes.length)].split("/");
      context.fillText(quote[0], w/4+5, h/2-10, w/2-10);
      context.fillText(quote[1], w/4+5, h/2+30, w/2-10);
      context.fillText("click again",w/10,h/8);
    }
</script>
```

In this example, we use an array of quotes as the source for the displayed "fortune cookies." Note how the strings have a "/" marker in them to deal with breaking it up into multiple lines. It is done this way because there is no multiline text support for the Canvas.

We proceed to set up an empty canvas with a rectangle in it that has the text "Click me!" Callbacks are registered for the click event on the Canvas, and also for "pause" and "play" events on the video. The trick is to use the "click" callback to pause and un-pause the video, which will then trigger the effects. We restrict the clickable region to the rectangular region to show how regions can be made interactive in the Canvas, even without knowing what shapes there are.

The "pause" event triggers display of the fortune cookie within the rectangular region in the middle of the video. The "play" event triggers continuation of the display of the video's frames thus wiping out the fortune cookie. Note that we do not do anything in paintFrame() if the video is paused. This will deal with any potentially queued calls to paintFrame() from the setTimeout() function.

You would have noticed that we are missing a function from the above example, namely the clickPos() function. This function is a helper to gain the x and y coordinates of the click within the Canvas. It has been extracted into Listing 6–17 because it will be a constant companion for anyone doing interactive work with Canvas.

Listing 6–17. *Typical function to gain the x and y coordinates of the click in a canvas*[10]

```
    function clickPos(e) {
      if (e.pageX || e.pageY) {
        x = e.pageX;
        y = e.pageY;
      } else {
        x = e.clientX + document.body.scrollLeft +
            document.documentElement.scrollLeft;
        y = e.clientY + document.body.scrollTop +
            document.documentElement.scrollTop;
      }
      x -= canvas.offsetLeft;
      y -= canvas.offsetTop;
      return [x,y];
    }
```

---

[10] See http://diveintohtml5.org/canvas.html

Figure 6–16 shows the rendering of this example with screenshots from different browsers.

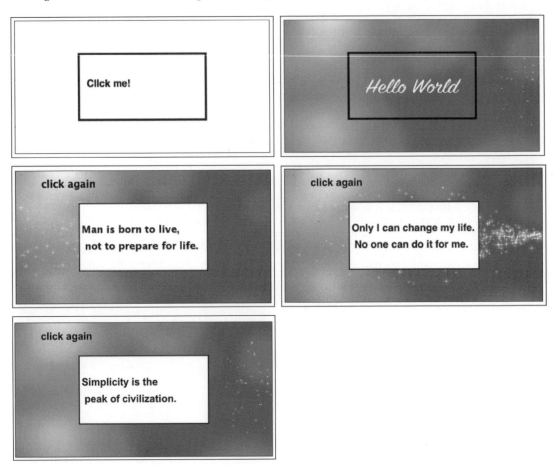

Figure 6–16. Rendering of the fortune cookies example through an interactive Canvas with video in Firefox, Safari (top row), Opera, Chrome (middle row), and IE (bottom).

Note that the fonts are rendered differently between the browsers, but other than that, they all support the same functionality.

6.7 Summary

In this chapter we made use of some of the functionalities of Canvas for manipulating video imagery.

We first learned that the drawImage() function allows us to pull images out of a <video> element and into a Canvas as pixel data. We then determined the most efficient way of dealing with video frames in the Canvas and found the "scratch Canvas" as a useful preparation space for video frames that need to be manipulated once and reused multiple times as a pattern.

We identified the getImageData() and putImageData() functions as powerful helpers to manipulate parts of a video's frame data. However, their full set of parameters aren't implemented across browsers in a compatible manner, so we can use only their simple versions for the time being.

We then made use of pixel manipulation functions such as changing the transparency of certain pixels to achieve a blue screen effect, scaling pixel slices to achieve a 3D effect, or calculating average colors on video frames to create an ambient surrounding. We also made use of the createPattern() function to replicate a video frame across a given rectangle.

Then we moved on to the compositing functionality of the Canvas to put several of the individual functions together. We used a gradient to fade over from the video to an ambient background, a clip path, and text as a template to cut out certain areas from the video.

With the Canvas transformation functionality we were finally able to create a video reflection that works across browsers. We also used it to rotate video frames and thus have them spiral around the Canvas.

We concluded our look at Canvas by connecting user interaction through clicks on the Canvas to video activity. Because there are no addressable objects, but only addressable pixel positions on a Canvas, it is not as well suited as SVG to catching events on objects.

■■■

CHAPTER 7

HTML5 Media and Web Workers

We have learned a lot of ways in which the HTML5 media elements can be manipulated and modified using JavaScript. Some of the video manipulations—in particular when used in Canvas—can be very CPU intensive and slow. Web Workers are a means to deal with this situation.

Web Workers[1] are a new functionality in HTML5. They provide a JavaScript API for running scripts in the background independently of any user interface scripts, i.e. in parallel to the main page and without disrupting the progress of the main page. Any JavaScript program can be turned into a Web Worker. For interaction with the main page you need to use message passing, since Web Workers do not have access to the DOM of the web page. Essentially, Web Workers introduce threading functionality into the Web.

We will not provide an in-depth introduction to Web Workers here. You will find other HTML5 books or articles that do so. A good introduction is provided by Mozilla[2] at https://developer.mozilla.org/En/Using_web_workers or the introduction by John Resig[3]. Instead, we focus here specifically on how to use Web Workers with HTML5 media. As with every HTML5 technology, Web Workers are still novel and improvements of both their specifications and implementations can be expected. Here are the functions and events that Web Workers currently introduce:

- The `Worker()` constructor, which defines a JavaScript file as a Web Worker,

- The `message` and `error` events for the worker,

- The `postMessage()` method used by a worker that activates the `message` event handler of the main page,

- The `postMessage()` method used by the main page that activates the `message` event handler of the worker to talk back,

- JSON, used for message passing,

- The `terminate()` method used by the main page to terminate the worker immediately,

- The error event consisting of a human readable `message` field, the `filename` of the worker, and the `lineno` where the error occurred,

- The `importScripts()` method used by a worker to load shared JavaScript files,

---

[1] See http://www.whatwg.org/specs/web-workers/current-work/

[2] See https://developer.mozilla.org/En/Using_web_workers

[3] See http://ejohn.org/blog/web-workers/

- The ability of Web Workers to call XMLHttpRequest.

Note that Web Workers will work only when used on a web server, because the external script needs to be loaded with the same scheme as the original page. This means you cannot load a script from a "data:", "javascript:", or "file:" URL. Further, a "https:" page can only start Web Workers that are also on "https:" and not on "http:".

Also note that the IE version used for this book does not support Web Workers yet. With the `getImageData()` and `putImageData()` bug in IE mentioned in the previous chapter, none of the non-worker examples in this chapter work either in IE, so we can't show any screen shots from IE.

7.1 Using Web Workers on Video

In this section we look at a simple example that explains how to turn an HTML5 video page with JavaScript operations on the video data into one where the operations on the video data are being executed in a Worker thread and then fed back to the main web page.

As an example, we use a sepia color replica of the video in the Canvas. Listing 7–1 shows how this is achieved without a Web Worker.

Listing 7–1. Sepia coloring of video pixels in the Canvas

```
<video controls height="270px" width="480px" >
  <source src="HelloWorld.mp4"  type="video/mp4">
  <source src="HelloWorld.webm" type="video/webm">
  <source src="HelloWorld.ogv"  type="video/ogg">
</video>
<canvas width="400" height="300" style="border: 1px solid black;">
</canvas>
<canvas id="scratch" width="400" height="300" style="display: none;">
</canvas>
<script>
  window.onload = function() {
    initCanvas();
  }
  var context, video, sctxt;
  function initCanvas() {
    video = document.getElementsByTagName("video")[0];
    canvas = document.getElementsByTagName("canvas")[0];
    context = canvas.getContext("2d");
    scratch = document.getElementById("scratch");
    sctxt = scratch.getContext("2d");
    video.addEventListener("play", playFrame, false);
  }
  function playFrame() {
    w = 320; h = 160;
    sctxt.drawImage(video, 0, 0, w, h);
    frame = sctxt.getImageData(0, 0, w, h);
    // Loop over each pixel of frame
    for (x = 0; x < w; x ++) {
      for (y = 0; y < h; y ++) {
        // index in image data array
        i = x + w*y;
        // grab colors
```

```
      r = frame.data[4*i+0];
      g = frame.data[4*i+1];
      b = frame.data[4*i+2];
      // replace with sepia colors
      frame.data[4*i+0] = Math.min(0.393*r + 0.769*g + 0.180*b,255);
      frame.data[4*i+1] = Math.min(0.349*r + 0.686*g + 0.168*b,255);
      frame.data[4*i+2] = Math.min(0.272*r + 0.534*g + 0.131*b,255);
    }
  }
  context.putImageData(frame, 0, 0);
  if (video.paused || video.ended) { return; }
  setTimeout(function () {
    playFrame();
  }, 0);
}
</script>
```

Each pixel in the frame that is grabbed into the scratch Canvas is replaced by a new RGB value calculated as a sepia mix from the existing colors.[4] The modified frame is then written out into a visible Canvas.

Note that we have to make sure the new color values do not exceed 255, because there are only 8 bits used to store the colors; i.e. any value larger than 255 may lead to an overflow value and thus a wrong color. This, in fact, happens in Opera, while the other browsers limit the value before assigning. In any case, using a `Math.min` function on the color values is the safe thing to do.

Figure 7–1 shows the result. If you look at the example in color, you will see that the video on top is in full color and the Canvas below is sepia-colored.

Figure 7–1. Painting a sepia colored video replica into a Canvas in Firefox, Safari, Opera, and Chrome (left to right).

Now, we can try and speed up the sepia color calculation—which loops over every single pixel and color component of the captured video frames—by delegating the calculation-heavy JavaScript actions to a Web Worker. We'll perform a comparison of speed further down. Listing 7–2 shows the web page code and 7–3 the JavaScript that is the Web Worker for Listing 7–2. The Web Worker code is located in a different JavaScript resource called "worker.js". It has to be delivered from the same domain as the main

---

[4] According to a mix published at http://www.builderau.com.au/program/csharp/soa/How-do-I-convert-images-to-grayscale-and-sepia-tone-using-C-/0,339028385,339291920,00.htm

web page. This is currently the only way in which you can call a Web Worker. Discussions are under way to extend this to allow inline defined Web Workers.[5]

Listing 7–2. Sepia coloring of video pixels using a Web Worker

```
<video controls height="270px" width="480px" >
  <source src="HelloWorld.mp4"  type="video/mp4">
  <source src="HelloWorld.webm" type="video/webm">
  <source src="HelloWorld.ogv"  type="video/ogg">
</video>
<canvas width="400" height="300" style="border: 1px solid black;">
</canvas>
<canvas id="scratch" width="400" height="300" style="display: none;">
</canvas>
<script>
window.onload = function() {
  initCanvas();
}
var worker = new Worker("worker.js");
var context, video, sctxt;
function initCanvas() {
  video = document.getElementsByTagName("video")[0];
  canvas = document.getElementsByTagName("canvas")[0];
  context = canvas.getContext("2d");
  scratch = document.getElementById("scratch");
  sctxt = scratch.getContext("2d");
  video.addEventListener("play", postFrame, false);
  worker.addEventListener("message", drawFrame, false);
}

function postFrame() {
  w = 320; h = 160;
  sctxt.drawImage(video, 0, 0, w, h);
  frame = sctxt.getImageData(0, 0, w, h);
  arg = {
    frame: frame,
    height: h,
    width: w
  }
  worker.postMessage(arg);
}
function drawFrame (event) {
  outframe = event.data;
  if (video.paused || video.ended) {
    return;
  }
  context.putImageData(outframe, 0, 0);
  setTimeout(function () {
    postFrame();
  }, 0);
```

---

[5] See http://lists.whatwg.org/pipermail/whatwg-whatwg.org/2010-October/028844.html

```
        }
    </script>
```

In Listing 7–2 we have marked the new commands in bold. You will notice how the Web Worker is created, a message prepared and then sent, and a function prepared that will take the sepia colored frame as a message from the Web Worker when it finishes and sends it on. The key here is that we have separated the preparation of the data for the calculations in postFrame and the drawing of the results in drawFrame.

The Web Worker that does the calculations is stored in a different file, here called worker.js. It contains only the callback for the onmessage event of the web page; it has no other data or functions to initialize. It receives the original frame from the web page, calculates the new pixel values, replaces them in the picture, and passes this redrawn picture back to the web page.

Listing 7–3. JavaScript Web Worker for Listing 7–2

```
onmessage = function (event) {
    // receive the image data
    var data = event.data;
    var frame = data.frame;
    var h = data.height;
    var w = data.width;
    var x,y;

    // Loop over each pixel of frame
    for (x = 0; x < w; x ++) {
      for (y = 0; y < h; y ++) {
        // index in image
        i = x + w*y;
        // grab colors
        r = frame.data[4*i+0];
        g = frame.data[4*i+1];
        b = frame.data[4*i+2];
        // replace with sepia colors
        frame.data[4*i+0] = Math.min(0.393*r + 0.769*g + 0.189*b, 255);
        frame.data[4*i+1] = Math.min(0.349*r + 0.686*g + 0.168*b, 255);
        frame.data[4*i+2] = Math.min(0.272*r + 0.534*g + 0.131*b, 255);
      }
    }
    // send the image data back to main thread
    postMessage(frame);
}
```

This example provides a good handle on how to hook up video with a Web Worker. You cannot pass a Canvas directly into a Web Worker as a parameter to the postMessage function, because it is a DOM element and the Web Worker doesn't know about DOM elements. But you can pass ImageData to the worker. Thus, the way to manipulate video is to grab a video frame with getImageData(), put it into a message, and send it to the Web Worker with postMessage(), where the message event triggers the execution of the video manipulation algorithm. The result of the calculations is returned to the main thread through a postMessage() call by the Web Worker with manipulated image data as a parameter. This hands control over to the onmessage event handler of the main thread to display the manipulated image using putImageData() into the Canvas.

Because Web Workers are supported in all browsers except for IE, the results of the Web Workers implementation of the sepia toning is no different to the non-worker implementation and its results looks the same as in Figure 7–1.

207

Note that if you are developing in Opera and you expect your Web Worker to be reloaded on a SHIFT-reload of the web page, you will be disappointed. So make sure to keep an extra tab open with a link to the JavaScript file of the Web Worker and make sure to reload that one separately.

The sepia example is a simple one, so a question arises whether the overhead incurred by packaging the message (i.e. copying the message data, including the frame), unpacking it, and doing the same for the result, plus the delay in calling the events, actually outweighs the gain achieved by delegating the video manipulation to a thread.

We compare the number of frames manipulated when run in the main thread with the number of frames that a Web Worker crunches through to discover the limits of the approach. Note that this approach is based on the self-imposed requirement to keep the Web Worker display and video playback roughly in sync rather than allowing the Web Worker to be slower. Table 7–1 shows the results as the number of frames processed during all of the four-second-long "Hello World" example video.

Table 7–1. *Performance of the browsers without (left) and with (right) Web Workers on the sepia example*

Firefox		Safari		Chrome		Opera	
89	53 (WW)	87	96 (WW)	77	54 (WW)	93	95 (WW)

The results in Table 7–1 were achieved on a machine with the same load by reloading the example multiple times and taking the maximum achieved number of recolored frames. Note that the algorithm with Web Workers on Firefox and Chrome churns through fewer frames than when the code is run on the main web page. For Safari there is a speed increase running it in the worker, while Opera basically achieves the same performance with or without a Web Worker.

These results seem to be influenced by the way in which the browsers implement Web Worker support. Note that we are not comparing the performance between the different browsers, which is clearly influenced by the speed of their JavaScript engines. But we see the effects of both the way in which each browser implements Web Workers and the speed of the JavaScript engine.

Opera is built as a single-threaded browser, so its current implementation of Web Workers interleaves code execution in the single thread. This is in contrast to Mozilla's implementation in Firefox, where the Web Worker is actually a real operating system thread and the spawning of multiple workers can take advantage of multiple processor cores. The overhead introduced by spawning a full OS-level thread in our simple example here seems to incur a penalty on the number of frames that can be decoded or handed over from the main thread during the time of playback.

The primary advantage of using a Web Worker is that the main thread's workload is reduced such that it can continue executing at top speed. In particular, it can keep rendering the browsers UI, keep checking your mail, etc. In our example this refers particularly to the playback speed of the video. In the sepia example, our main thread wasn't particularly overloaded with the calculation, so introducing Web Workers didn't actually achieve much. So let's look at something a bit more challenging.

7.2 Motion Detection with Web Workers

The general idea behind motion detection is to take the difference between two successive frames in a video and determine whether there was a large enough change to qualify as motion. Good motion detectors can cope with the change of lighting conditions, moving cameras, and camera and encoding artifacts. For our purposes, we will simply determine whether a pixel has changed to determine if there was motion. It's a simplistic but fairly effective approach and will do for demonstration purposes.

Gray-Scaling

The practical approach to motion detection includes preprocessing of the frames by turning them into a gray-scale image. Because color doesn't influence motion, this is a reasonable abstraction and it reduces the number of calculations necessary, since differences don't have to be calculated on all channels, but only on a single dimension.

Gray-scaling is achieved by calculating the luminance—i.e. the light intensity—of each pixel and replacing the red, green, and blue channel values with the luminance value. Since they then all have identical values, the frame won't have any colors any more and will therefore appear gray.

It is possible to calculate the luminance from an average of the original red, green, and blue channel values, but that does not represent human perception of luminance well. As it turns out, the best way to calculate luminance is by taking 30% of red, 59% of green, and 11% of blue.[6] Blue is perceived as a very dark color and green a very bright one, contributing differently to the human perception of luminance.

Listing 7–4 shows the JavaScript Web Worker that creates a gray-scaled version of the video using this algorithm. The main thread that goes with this Web Worker is identical to Listing 7–2. Figure 7–2 shows the resulting screenshots in different browsers. Note that if you can't see it in color, the video on top is in full color and the Canvas below is in black and white.

Listing 7–4. Gray-scaling of video pixels using a Web Worker

```
onmessage = function (event) {
    // receive the image data
    var data = event.data;
    var frame = data.frame;
    var h = data.height;
    var w = data.width;
    var x,y;

    // Loop over each pixel of frame
    for (x = 0; x < w; x ++) {
        for (y = 0; y < h; y ++) {
            // index in image data array
            i = x + w*y;
            // grab colors
            r = frame.data[4*i+0];
            g = frame.data[4*i+1];
            b = frame.data[4*i+2];
            col = Math.min(0.3*r + 0.59*g + 0.11*b, 255);
            // replace with black/white
            frame.data[4*i+0] = col;
            frame.data[4*i+1] = col;
            frame.data[4*i+2] = col;
        }
    }

    // send the image data back to main thread
    postMessage(frame);
}
```

---

[6] See many more details about luminance at http://www.scantips.com/lumin.html

Figure 7–2. Painting a gray-scaled video replica into a Canvas in Firefox, Safari, Opera, and Chrome (left to right)

Now that we have seen that this algorithm creates a gray-scaled image, we can appreciate that we don't actually need the full gray-scaled image to calculate the motion difference between two such images. There is a lot of repetition that we can avoid in the three color channels, and we are also not interested in the value of the alpha channel. Thus, we can reduce the frames to an array of the luminance values.

Motion Detection

We now move to implementation of the motion detection. To visualize which pixels have been identified as motion pixels, we will paint them in a rare color. We chose a mix of green=100 and blue=255. Listing 7–5 shows the Web Worker that implements the motion detection. The main thread is still the same as in Listing 7–2.

Listing 7–5. Motion detection of video pixels using a Web Worker

```
var prev_frame = null;
var threshold = 25;

function toGray(frame) {
  grayFrame = new Array (frame.data.length / 4);
  for (i = 0; i < grayFrame.length; i++) {
    r = frame.data[4*i+0];
    g = frame.data[4*i+1];
    b = frame.data[4*i+2];
    grayFrame[i] = Math.min(0.3*r + 0.59*g + 0.11*b, 255);
  }
  return grayFrame;
}

onmessage = function (event) {
  // receive the image data
  var data = event.data;
  var frame = data.frame;

  // convert current frame to gray
  cur_frame = toGray(frame);
```

```
    // avoid calling this the first time
    if (prev_frame != null) {
      // calculate difference
      for (i = 0; i < cur_frame.length; i++) {
        if (Math.abs(prev_frame[i] - cur_frame[i]) > threshold) {
          // color in pixels with high difference
          frame.data[4*i+0] = 0;
          frame.data[4*i+1] = 100;
          frame.data[4*i+2] = 255;
        }
      }
    }

    // remember current frame as previous one
    prev_frame = cur_frame;

    // send the image data back to main thread
    postMessage(frame);
}
```

You will have noticed that this Web Worker actually has some global data because we have to remember the previous frame's data across different calls to this Web Worker. We initialize this array with null such that we can avoid performing the difference calculation on the first call to this Web Worker. The other global variable is the threshold, which we've chosen to set to 25, which gives a reasonable tolerance to noise.

You will recognize the toGray() function from the previous algorithm, except we store only the shortened array of gray values per image frame.

In the callback function for the onmessage event, we first calculate the gray-scaled version of the current image frame, then use this to compare it with the previous frame and color in the pixels with a luminance difference larger than the threshold. We then remember the current frame's luminance values as the prev_frame for the next iteration and post the adjusted image frame back to the main thread for display.

Figure 7–3 shows the results of this algorithm applied to the "Hello World" video in all browsers except IE.

Figure 7–3. Motion detection results on a video using Web Workers in Firefox, Safari, Opera, and Chrome (left to right).

Because the "Hello World" video is not very exciting to showcase motion detection, Figure 7–4 shows the effects of the algorithm on some scenes of the "Elephants Dream" video.

Figure 7–4. Motion detection results on a second video using Web Workers in Firefox, Safari, Opera, and Chrome (left to right)

As you are watching this algorithm work on your videos, you will immediately notice its drawbacks and certainly you can come up with ideas on how to improve the performance or apply it to your needs, such as alerting for intruders. There are many better algorithms for motion detection, but this is not the place to go into them.

Let's again look at the performance of this algorithm in the different browsers. Table 7–2 shows the comparison as before between an implementation without Web Workers and one with. The number signifies the number of frames displayed in the Canvas when the algorithm is run without or with Web Workers for the four second "Hello World" video.

Table 7–2. Performance of browsers without (left) and with (right) Web Workers on the motion detection

Firefox		Safari		Chrome		Opera	
82	48 (WW)	64	62 (WW)	105	75 (WW)	140	129 (WW)

In this case, there are basically two loops involved in every iteration of the Web Worker and there is global data to store. The implementation on the main web page achieves more manipulated frames for all of the browsers. The difference for Safari and Opera is not substantial, but the differences for Firefox and Chrome are surprisingly high. This means the Web Worker code is actually fairly slow and cannot keep up with the video playback speed. The Web Workers thus take a lot of load off the main thread to allow the video to playback with less strain. The differences still are not visible when running the algorithm with or without Web Workers, since the video plays back smoothly in both situations. So let's take another step in complexity and introduce some further video processing.

7.3 Region Segmentation

In image processing, and therefore video processing, the segmentation of the displayed image into regions of interest is typically very CPU intensive. Image segmentation is used to locate objects and boundaries (lines, curves, etc.) in images aiming to give regions that belong together the same label.

We will implement a simple region segmentation approach in this section and demonstrate how we can use Web Workers to do the processing-intensive tasks in a parallel thread and relieve the main thread to provide smooth video playback.

Our region segmentation is based on the pixels identified by motion detection using the algorithm of the previous section. In a kind of region-growing approach[7], we will then cluster those motion pixels together that are not too far apart from each other. In our particular example, the distance threshold is set to 2; i.e. we limit the clustering to a 5x5 area around the motion pixel. This clustering can result in many motion pixels being merged into a region. We will display a rectangle around all the pixels in the largest region found per frame.

We will start this by developing a version without Web Workers. Generally, this probably is the best approach, because it makes it easier to debug. Right now, there are no means to easily debug a Web Worker in a web browser. As long as you keep in mind how you are going to split out the JavaScript code into a Web Worker, starting with a single thread is easier.

Listing 7–6 shows the playFrame() function in use by the web page for the segmentation. The remainder of the page in Listing 7–1 stays the same. Also, it uses the toGray() function of Listing 7–5. It looks long and scary, but actually consists of nice blocks provided through comments, so we will walk through these blocks next.

Listing 7–6. Segmentation of video pixels using a Web Worker

```
// initialisation for segmentation
var prev_frame = null;
var cur_frame = null;
var threshold = 25;
var width = 320;
var height = 160;
region = new Array (width*height);
index = 0;
region[0] = {};
region[0]['weight'] = 0;
region[0]['x1'] = 0;
region[0]['x2'] = 0;
region[0]['y1'] = 0;
region[0]['y2'] = 0;

function playFrame() {
  sctxt.drawImage(video, 0, 0, width, height);
  frame = sctxt.getImageData(0, 0, width, height);
  cur_frame = toGray(frame);

  // avoid calculating on the first frame
  if (prev_frame != null) {

    // initialize region fields
    for (x = 0; x < width; x++) {
      for (y = 0; y < height; y++) {
        i = x + width*y;
        // initialize region fields
        if (i != 0) region[i] = {};
        region[i]['weight'] = 0;
        if (Math.abs(prev_frame[i] - cur_frame[i]) > threshold) {
          // initialize the regions
          region[i]['weight'] = 1;
```

_____

[7] See http://en.wikipedia.org/wiki/Segmentation_%28image_processing%29#Clustering_methods

```
            region[i]['x1'] = x;
            region[i]['x2'] = x;
            region[i]['y1'] = y;
            region[i]['y2'] = y;
          }
        }
      }

    // segmentation: grow regions around each motion pixels
    for (x = 0; x < width; x++) {
      for (y = 0; y < height; y++) {
        i = x + width*y;
        if (region[i]['weight'] > 0) {
          // check the neighbors in 5x5 grid
          for (xn = Math.max(x-2,0); xn <= Math.min(x+2,width-1); xn++) {
            for (yn = Math.max((y-2),0);
                 yn <= Math.min((y+2),(height-1)); yn++) {
              j = xn + width*yn;
              if (j != i) {
                if (region[j]['weight'] > 0) {
                  region[i]['weight'] += region[j]['weight'];
                  region[i]['x1'] = Math.min(region[i]['x1'],
                                             region[j]['x1']);
                  region[i]['y1'] = Math.min(region[i]['y1'],
                                             region[j]['y1']);
                  region[i]['x2'] = Math.max(region[i]['x2'],
                                             region[j]['x2']);
                  region[i]['y2'] = Math.max(region[i]['y2'],
                                             region[j]['y2']);
                }
              }
            }
          }
        }
      }
    }

    // find one of the heaviest pixels, i.e. one of the largest clusters
    max = 0;
    index = 0; // reset
    for (x = 0; x < width; x++) {
      for (y = 0; y < height; y++) {
        i = x + width*y;
        if (region[i]['weight'] > max) {
          max = region[i]['weight'];
          index = i;
        }
      }
    }

    // remember current frame as previous one and get rectangle coordinates
    prev_frame = cur_frame;
    x = region[index]['x1'];
```

```
y = region[index]['y1'];
w = (region[index]['x2'] - region[index]['x1']);
h = (region[index]['y2'] - region[index]['y1']);

// draw frame and rectangle
context.putImageData(frame, 0, 0);
context.strokeRect(x, y, w, h);
calls += 1;
if (video.paused || video.ended) {
  return;
}
setTimeout(function () {
  playFrame();
}, 0);
}
```

The code starts with an initialization of the memory constructs required to do the segmentation. The prev_frame and cur_frame are the gray-scale representations of the previous and current frames being compared. The threshold like before, is one that identifies pixels with motion. Width and height identify the dimensions of the video display in the Canvas. The region array is an array of hashes that contain information about each currently regarded image pixel: its weight is initially 1, but will grow larger as more pixels are close to it; the (x1,y1) and (x2,y2) coordinates signify the region from which pixel weights have been added. The index is eventually the index of the region array with the largest cluster.

In playFrame()we start by extracting the current frame from the video and calculating its gray-scale representation. We perform the segmentation only if this is not the very first frame. If it is indeed the first frame, a region of (0,0) to (0,0) will result and be painted on the Canvas.

To perform the segmentation, we first initialize the region fields. Only those that qualify as motion pixels are set to a weight of 1 and an initial region consisting of just their own pixel.

Then, we execute the region growing on the 5x5 grid around these motion pixels. We add the weight of all the motion pixels found in that region around the currently regarded motion pixel to the current pixel and set the extent of the region to the larger rectangle that includes those other motion pixels.

Because we want to mark only a single region, we then identify the last one of the largest clusters, which is the cluster found around one of the heaviest pixels (the one with the largest weight). It is this cluster that we will paint as a rectangle, so we set the index variable to the index of this pixel in the region array.

Finally, we can determine the rectangular coordinates and paint the frame and rectangle into the Canvas. We then set a timeout on another call to the playFrame() function, which makes it possible for the main thread to undertake some video playback before performing the image analysis again for the next frame.

Note that in some circumstances the extent of the region is incorrectly calculated with this simple approach. Whenever a vertical or horizontal shape traces back in rather than continuing to grow, the last motion pixel checked will be the heaviest, but it will not have received the full extent of the region. A second run through this region would be necessary to determine the actual size of the region. This is left to the reader as an exercise.

Figure 7–5 shows the results of this algorithm applied to the "Hello World" video.

Figure 7–5. Image segmentation results on a motion detected video in Firefox, Safari, Opera, and Chrome (left to right)

Note that the video playback in all browsers except Safari now is seriously degraded. The videos are all becoming jerky and it is obvious that the browser is having a hard time finding enough cycles to put into video decoding rather than spending it on the JavaScript. This is a clear case for taking advantage of the help of Web Workers. Turning down the frequency with which the analysis is done will work, too, but it does not scale with the capabilities of the browser.

We have designed the code base such that it is easy to move the video manipulation code into a Web Worker. We will hand over the current video frame and its dimensions into the Web Worker and receive back from it the coordinates of the rectangle to draw. You may want to also manipulate the frame colors in the Web Worker as before and display them in a different color to verify the segmentation result.

The code for the postFrame() and drawFrame() functions of the main web page is given in Listing 7–7. The remainder of the main web page is identical to Listing 7–2. The code for the Web Worker contains much of Listing 7–6, including the initialization and the toGray() function and a function to deal with the onmessage event, receive the message arguments from the main web page, and post the frame and the four coordinates back to the main page. The full implementation is left to the reader or can be downloaded from the locations mentioned in the Preface of the book.

Listing 7–7. Segmentation of video pixels using a Web Worker

```
function postFrame() {
  w = 320; h = 160;
  sctxt.drawImage(video, 0, 0, w, h);
  frame = sctxt.getImageData(0, 0, w, h);
  arg = {
    frame: frame,
    height: h,
    width: w
  }
  worker.postMessage(arg);
}

function drawFrame (event) {
  msg = event.data;
  outframe = msg.frame;
  if (video.paused || video.ended) {
    return;
  }
```

```
context.putImageData(outframe, 0, 0);
// draw rectangle on canvas
context.strokeRect(msg.x, msg.y, msg.w, msg.h);
calls += 1;
setTimeout(function () {
  postFrame();
}, 0);
}
```

Let's look at the performance of this algorithm in the different browsers. Table 7–3 shows the comparison between an implementation without Web Workers and one with. As before, the numbers represent the number of frames the Canvas has painted for the four-second-long example video. The program will always try to paint as many video frames into the Canvas as possible. Without Web Workers, this ends up being on the main thread and the machine is working as hard as it can. With Web Workers, the main thread can delay the postMessage() function without an effect on the performance of the main thread. It can thus hand over fewer frames to the Web Worker to deal with.

Table 7–3. Performance of browsers without (left) and with (right) Web Workers for motion segmentation

Firefox		Safari		Chrome		Opera	
36	22 (WW)	35	29 (WW)	62	50 (WW)	76	70 (WW)

The smallest difference in the number of frames that the Web Worker is given to the amount that is processed when there is only one thread is in Safari and Opera. In Firefox, the Web Worker runs rather slowly, processing only a small number of frames.

Using Web Workers relieves all of the stress from the main threads of Firefox and Chrome and makes the video run smoothly again. The only browser left struggling with a jerky video playback is Opera, which doesn't use proper threading on Web Workers, so this was to be expected.

Note that the video runs on the main thread, while the Canvas is fed from the Web Worker, and we are only measuring the performance of the Web Worker. Unfortunately, we cannot measure the performance of the video element in terms of number of frames played back. However, a statistics API is in preparation for the media elements in the WHATWG that will provide us with this functionality once implemented in browsers.

7.4 Face Detection

Determining whether a face exists in an image is often based on the detection of skin color and the analysis of the shape that this skin color creates.[8] We will take the first step here toward such a simple face detection approach, namely the identification of skin color regions. For this, we will be combining many of the algorithms previously discussed in this chapter.

The direct use of RGB colors is not very helpful in detecting skin color, since there is a vast shade of skin tones. However, as it turns out, the relative presence of RGB colors can help overcome this to a large degree. Thus, skin color detection is normally based on the use of normalized RGB colors. A possible condition to use is the following:

---

[8] See http://en.wikipedia.org/wiki/Face_detection

```
base = R + G + B
r = R / base
g = G / base
b = B / base
```

with

$(0.35 < r < 0.5)$ AND $(0.2 < g < 0.5)$ AND $(0.2 < b < 0.35)$ AND $(base > 200)$

This equation identifies most of the pixels typically perceived as "skin color", but also creates false positives. It works more reliably on lighter than on darker skin, but in actual fact it is more sensitive to lighting differences than skin tone. You may want to check out the literature to find improved approaches.[9] We will use this naïve approach here for demonstration purposes.

The false positive pixels can be filtered out by performing a shape analysis of the detected regions and identify distinct areas such as eyes and mouth positions. We will not take these extra processing steps here, but only apply the above equation and the previously implemented segmentation to find candidate regions of potential faces.

Listing 7–8 shows the code of the main web page and Listing 7–9 shows the Web Worker.

Listing 7–8. Main thread of the face detection approach using a Web Worker

```
<video controls height="270px" width="480px" >
  <source src="video5.mp4"  type="video/mp4">
  <source src="video5.ogv"  type="video/ogg">
  <source src="video5.webm" type="video/webm">
</video>
<canvas width="400" height="300" style="border: 1px solid black;">
</canvas>
<canvas id="scratch" width="400" height="300" style="display: none;">
</canvas>
<script>
  window.onload = function() {
    initCanvas();
  }
  var worker = new Worker("worker.js");
  var context, video, sctxt, canvas;
  function initCanvas() {
    video = document.getElementsByTagName("video")[0];
    canvas = document.getElementsByTagName("canvas")[0];
    context = canvas.getContext("2d");
    scratch = document.getElementById("scratch");
    sctxt = scratch.getContext("2d");
    video.addEventListener("play", postFrame, false);
    worker.addEventListener("message", drawFrame, false);
  }

  function postFrame() {
    w = 320; h = 160;
    sctxt.drawImage(video, 0, 0, w, h);
    frame = sctxt.getImageData(0, 0, w, h);
```

---

[9] See for example `http://www.icgst.com/GVIP05/papers/P1150535201.pdf` for an improved approach.

```
      arg = {
        frame: frame,
        height: h,
        width: w
      }
      worker.postMessage(arg);
    }

    function drawFrame (event) {
      msg = event.data;
      outframe = msg.frame;
      context.putImageData(outframe, 0, 0);
      // draw rectangle on canvas
      context.strokeRect(msg.x, msg.y, msg.w, msg.h);
      if (video.paused || video.ended) {
        return;
      }
      setTimeout(function () {
        postFrame();
      }, 0);
    }
</script>
```

Listing 7–9. *Web Worker for the face detection approach of Listing 7–8*

```
// initialisation for segmentation
var width = 320;
var height = 160;
var region = new Array (width*height);
var index = 0;
region[0] = {};
region[0]['weight'] = 0;
region[0]['x1'] = 0;
region[0]['x2'] = 0;
region[0]['y1'] = 0;
region[0]['y2'] = 0;

function isSkin(r,g,b) {
  base = r + g + b;
  rn = r / base;
  gn = g / base;
  bn = b / base;
  if (rn > 0.35 && rn < 0.5 && gn > 0.2 && gn < 0.5 &&
      bn > 0.2 && bn < 0.35 && base > 250) {
    return true;
  } else {
    return false;
  }
}

onmessage = function (event) {
  // receive the image data
  var data = event.data;
```

```
var frame  = data.frame;
var height = data.height;
var width  = data.width;

// initialize region fields and color in motion pixels
for (x = 0; x < width; x++) {
  for (y = 0; y < height; y++) {
    i = x + width*y;
    if (i != 0) region[i] = {};
    region[i]['weight'] = 0;
    // calculate skin color?
    if (isSkin(frame.data[4*i],frame.data[4*i+1],frame.data[4*i+2])) {
      // color in pixels with high difference
      frame.data[4*i+0] = 0;
      frame.data[4*i+1] = 100;
      frame.data[4*i+2] = 255;
      // initialize the regions
      region[i]['weight'] = 1;
      region[i]['x1'] = x;
      region[i]['x2'] = x;
      region[i]['y1'] = y;
      region[i]['y2'] = y;
    }
  }
}

// segmentation
for (x = 0; x < width; x++) {
  for (y = 0; y < height; y++) {
    i = x + width*y;
    if (region[i]['weight'] > 0) {
      // check the neighbors
      for (xn = Math.max(x-2,0); xn <= Math.min(x+2,width-1); xn++) {
        for (yn = Math.max((y-2),0);
             yn <= Math.min((y+2),(height-1)); yn++) {
          j = xn + width*yn;
          if (j != i) {
            if (region[j]['weight'] > 0) {
              region[i]['weight'] += region[j]['weight'];
              region[i]['x1'] = Math.min(region[i]['x1'],
                                         region[j]['x1']);
              region[i]['y1'] = Math.min(region[i]['y1'],
                                         region[j]['y1']);
              region[i]['x2'] = Math.max(region[i]['x2'],
                                         region[j]['x2']);
              region[i]['y2'] = Math.max(region[i]['y2'],
                                         region[j]['y2']);
            }
          }
        }
      }
    }
  }
}
```

```
// find one of the heaviest pixels, which is one of the largest clusters
max = 0;
index = 0; // reset
for (x = 0; x < width; x++) {
  for (y = 0; y < height; y++) {
    i = x + width*y;
    if (region[i]['weight'] > max) {
      max = region[i]['weight'];
      index = i;
    }
  }
}

// send the image data + rectangle back to main thread
arg = {
  frame: frame,
  x: region[index]['x1'],
  y: region[index]['y1'],
  w: (region[index]['x2'] - region[index]['x1']),
  h: (region[index]['y2'] - region[index]['y1'])
}
postMessage(arg);
}
```

You will notice that the code is essentially the same as for motion region detection, except we can remove some of the administrative work required to keep the difference frames, and the toGray() function has been replaced with an isSkin() function.

For our example we have chosen a Creative Commons licensed video about "Science Commons"[10]. Some of the resulting analyzed frames are shown in Figure 7–6. These are all displayed in real time while the video plays back.

Figure 7–6. Face detection results on a skin color detected video in Firefox, Safari, Opera, and Chrome (left to right)

_____

[10] See http://sciencecommons.org/

221

These examples show where the skin color algorithm works well: the two screenshots from Opera and Chrome show that the region segmentation didn't get the faces, but the hands, which take up larger regions.

Examples of false positives on skin color are shown in Figure 7–7.

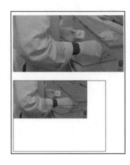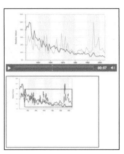

Figure 7–7. False positives on face detection using skin color in Firefox, Safari, Opera, and Chrome (left to right).

The display of the analysis results in the Canvas underneath the video quickly degrades with increasingly complex computational tasks like the ones discussed in this chapter. If you wanted to continue displaying good quality video to your audience, but do the analysis in the background, it is probably best to drop the pixel coloring in the Canvas and to only paint the rectangular overlays for the detected regions onto the original video. This will provide you with a better performance from the Web Worker thread.

7.5 Summary

In this chapter we looked at using Web Workers to take over some of the heavy lifting involved in video processing when run inside web browsers in real-time. We analyzed their use for simple video processing approaches, such as sepia toning, and found that for such simple tasks the overhead created by spawning a thread and passing the data through messages back and forth is not worth off-loading the processing.

We also analyzed their use for larger challenges, such as motion detection, region segmentation, and face detection. Here, the advantage of using a Web Worker is that the incurred processing load can be offloaded from the main thread, freeing it to continue staying responsive with the user. The downside is that the browser does not work as hard at the video processing part and the Web Worker can become starved of video frames. Thus, the increased responsiveness of the browsers overall is paid for by a smaller framerate in video processing.

Web Workers are most productive for tasks that do not need a lot of frequent reporting back and forth between the Web Worker thread and the main thread. The introduction of a simpler means for a Web Worker to get access to the frames in a video outside the message passing path would also be helpful to make Web Workers more productive for video processing.

Most of the algorithms used in this chapter were very crude, but this book does not intend to show you how to do image analysis well. Find yourself a good video analysis book and the latest research results in these fields and go wild. The big news is: you can now do it in your web browser in real time, and Web Workers can help you do it such that it won't disrupt the speed of the display of your main web page.

CHAPTER 8

■■■

HTML5 Audio API

With this chapter, we explore a set of features that are less stable and less firmly defined than the features discussed in previous chapters. This and all following chapters present features that are at the time of writing still work in progress. But they introduce amazing possibilities and we therefore cannot ignore them. Some of the features have implementations in browsers, but no specification text in the HTML5 and related standards. Others have draft specification text in the WHATWG or W3C documents, but no implementations have confirmed the suitability of the specifications yet.

In this chapter we look at some of the work being done for a Web audio API. In the last few chapters we have investigated many features that allow us to manipulate the image data that is provided by videos. The audio API complements this by providing features to manipulate the sound data that is provided by the audio track of videos or by audio resources.

This will enable the development of sophisticated Web-based games or audio production applications where the audio is dynamically created and modified in JavaScript. It also enables the visualization of audio data and the analysis of the data, for example to determine a beat or identify which instruments are playing or whether a voice you are hearing is female or male.

A W3C Audio Incubator Group has been formed to focus on creating an extended audio API. Currently, a draft specification exists[1] which is under discussion. At the same time, the released Firefox 4 includes an implementation of a more basic audio data API[2].

The Incubator Group draft specification is based on the idea of building a graph of AudioNode objects that are connected together to define the overall audio rendering. This is very similar to the filter graph idea that is the basis of many media frameworks, including DirectShow, GStreamer, and also JACK the Audio Connection Kit. The idea behind a filter graph is that one or more input signals are connected to a destination renderer by sending the input signals through a sequence of filters that each modifies the input data in a specific way. The term *audio filter* can mean anything that changes the timbre, harmonic content, pitch, or waveform of an audio signal. The Incubator Group draft specifies filters for various audio uses: spatialized audio, a convolution engine, real-time frequency analysis, biquad filters, and sample-accurate scheduled sound playback.

In contrast to this filter-graph based design, the more basic audio data API of Mozilla provides only two functionalities: reading audio and writing audio. It does so by providing access to the raw audio samples of the currently playing video or audio element, and it enables the writing of samples into an HTML5 audio element. It leaves all the audio filter functionality to the JavaScript implementer.

Currently, Mozilla's audio data API is available for use in Firefox versions greater than 4. The more complex filter graph API has an experimental implementation[3] for Safari[4]. In addition, development of a

---

[1] See http://chromium.googlecode.com/svn/trunk/samples/audio/specification/specification.html

[2] See https://wiki.mozilla.org/Audio_Data_API

[3] See http://chromium.googlecode.com/svn/trunk/samples/audio/index.html

[4] See http://chromium.googlecode.com/svn/trunk/samples/audio/bin/

JavaScript library is in progress that builds on top of Firefox's basic audio data API[5]. No other browsers have any implementations of an audio API.

In this chapter, we will first cover the Mozilla audio data API as supported in Firefox 4 and implement some examples that use it. Then we will gain an overview of the Web audio API and also implement some basic examples that explain how to use it. At this stage, it is unclear what will eventually become of the specification that is the basis for cross-browser compatible implementations of an advanced audio API. This chapter provides you with information on the currently available options.

8.1 Reading Audio Data

The Mozilla audio data API is centered on the existing audio and video elements of HTML5. Extensions have very carefully been made such as not to disrupt the existing functionality of these elements.

8.1.1 Extracting Audio Samples

The way in which Firefox extracts the audio samples from a media resource is by way of an event on the audio or video element which fires for every frame of audio data that has been decoded. The event is accordingly called `MozAudioAvailable`. The event data provides an array called `framebuffer` containing 32bit floating point audio samples from the left and right channels for the given audio frame. An audio sample is the representation of the pressure that an audio wave held (its amplitude) at a certain time point at which it was sampled or measured[6]. A waveform is made up of a series of audio samples over time.

Listing 8–1 shows an example of how to retrieve the audio samples. In order not to distract the playback of the resource by rendering all the samples, only the very first sample in the event `framebuffer` is printed.

Note that you cannot run the examples in this chapter from local file systems, because of security constraints. You have to serve the files from a web server.

Listing 8–1. Reading audio samples from an audio element

```
<audio src="HelloWorld.ogg" controls>
</audio>
<div id="display"></div>
<script type="text/javascript">
  var audio = document.getElementsByTagName("audio")[0];
  var display = document.getElementById("display");
  audio.addEventListener("MozAudioAvailable", writeSamples, false);

  function writeSamples (event) {
    display.innerHTML += event.frameBuffer[0] + ', ';
  }
</script>
```

The registered callback on the `MozAudioAvailable` event writes the sample values simply to a div element. Figure 8–1 shows the result.

---

[5] See https://github.com/corbanbrook/dsp.js

[6] See http://en.wikipedia.org/wiki/Sampling_%28signal_processing%29 for an explanation of audio sampling

0, 0, 0, 0, 0, 0, 0, 0, 0, 0, 0, 0, 0, 0, 0, 0, 0, 0, 0, 0, 0, 0, 0, 8.200877914532612e-7, 0.0000024547766770410817, 0.000009416246030014008, -0.00017358563491143286,
-0.00002415167546132579, -0.00004440120028448291, -0.00013277849939186126, 0.0000479518312204163, 0.00001328754296991974, -0.0001565693382872268,
-0.00004141209501540288, -0.00011892179463757202, -0.00002870900789275764, -0.00017301268235314637, -0.00004017174796899780, 0.00002102681537508033,
-0.0002317451871931553, -0.00001745832560118287, 0.02241772785782814, -0.01237218081951141, -0.03297566995024681, 0.06169551610946655, -0.04620504751801491,
-0.07566284388303757, -0.2708803117275238, -0.303053617477417, -0.3850057125091553, -0.3563714921474457, -0.25862544775009155, -0.17990314960479736,
0.00820576399564743, 0.05022256713807582, 0.04555017128586769, -0.00878502521663904, -0.05851697549223, -0.04038891941308975, -0.00801353715360164,
0.0367877371609211, 0.05060055479407310, 0.19430005550384521, -0.19831213355064392, -0.14221352338790894, -0.1782798171043396, -0.1175363659858703,
-0.10445278882980347, -0.07052537053823471, 0.23368960618972778, 0.00369170494377613, -0.19564889371395, 0.05437732115387916, 0.17425599694252014,
-0.05479446798563003, -0.20555785298347473, 0.12064224481582642, 0.14493806660175323, -0.11360822618007, -0.13728249073028564, 0.17141959071159363,
0.07475831359624863, -0.19335201382637024, -0.33816468715667725, -0.24783185124397278, -0.23165835440158844, -0.15033362805843353, -0.010125380009412766,
0.13539570569992065, 0.23928405344486237, 0.30720275640487670, 0.13502587378025055, -0.08395884931087494, -0.08739902824163437, 0.03480972722172737,
0.04021479189399450, 0.03046543896198272, -0.01493751723319292, -0.08615221083164215, -0.09533686190843582, -0.18019098043441772, -0.0639491528272628,
-0.19574220478534698, 0.02625285080901596, -0.1704399734735489, 0.095767080783844, -0.16621369123458862, 0.10959699004888535, -0.15763114392757416,
0.14071889221668243, -0.07655970007181168, 0.25228139758110046, 0.03339058905839902, 0.30911150574684143, 0.03734088689088214, 0.23630695044994354,
-0.0582362562417984, 0.13113750517368317, -0.18011747300624847, -0.21309402585029602, -0.1265296041965486, 0.05963042750954628, 0.03502504527568817,
0.2499883621931076, 0.17787663638591766, 0.17902864515781403, 0.0965181440114975, 0.07151054590940475, -0.05116149038076401, -0.008266177959740162,

Figure 8–1. Reading audio sample values from an <audio> element using the Mozilla audio data API

The same can be achieved with a <video> element. Listing 8–2 shows the HTML and Figure 8–2 shows the results.

Listing 8–2. Reading audio samples from a video element

```
<video src="video1.ogv" controls>
</video>
<div id="display"></div>
<script type="text/javascript">
  var video = document.getElementsByTagName("video")[0];
  var display = document.getElementById("display");
  video.addEventListener("MozAudioAvailable", writeSamples, false);

  function writeSamples (event) {
    display.innerHTML += event.frameBuffer[0] + ', ';
  }
</script>
```

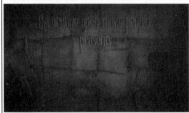

0, 0, 0, 0, 0, 0, 0, 0, 0, 0, 0, 0, 0, 0, 0, 0, 0, 0, 0, 0, 0, 0, 0.00000640576035948470, 0.00001491494640504242, -0.00001030268322210759, -0.00001508785862824879,
-0.00000649761568638496, -0.00001279843581869499, 0.00000732066291675437, -0.00000537511550646740, -0.00000256346356763970, 0.0000020113711798330,
0.0000489744124934077, -0.00003205487882951274, -0.00000969830398389604, -0.00000358404668077128, -0.00011612697562668473, -0.00009585116640664637,
0.0000806987009127624, 0.0000591473508393392, -0.00006706865679007024, 0.00015084548795130104, 0.00014360746718011796, -0.00007631696644239128,
-0.00006364988803397864, -0.0002085742598865181, -0.00007909084524726495, 0.0001464176457375288, -0.0001403212227160111, 0.00009858544217422605,
-0.0003254980256315321, -0.0005056693335063756, -0.0004062810621690005, -0.0004446233025258346, -0.0001988723815884441, -0.0001921148359542712,
0.0000656192423775792, -0.0000114214753865392, -0.0001799220917746424, -0.0001820373145164247, 0.0002793262246996164, -0.0001944810646189508,
-0.00003831232606898993, -0.00011407741840230301, -0.00000934705167310312, -0.0000937406788580119, 0.000196542721823789, 0.00055128725944086,
-0.0000443508033640682, -0.0000172400345392525, -0.0011343021178618073, 0.0001984291709959507, 0.0000938209530431777, 0.0002582181147791922,
-0.0006952622788958251, -0.000264727190369740, 0.00010456317104399204, 0.0005943033029325306, -0.0007700804271735251, 0.0013534667668864,
-0.0029164187144488096, -0.0012253979220986366, -0.0019853885751217604, -0.00040529126999899745, 0.0024112004321068525, 0.004850739147514105,
-0.0023048880879819393, 0.0007467567338608205, 0.0012954256962984, 0.0028379261493682860, 0.0009502613102085888, -0.0004150577879045158, -0.0020527294836938

Figure 8–2. Reading audio sample values from a <video> element using the Mozilla audio data API

8.1.2 Information about the Framebuffer

The audio data API always returns a fixed number of audio samples with every MozAudioAvailable event in the *frameBuffer*. The interpretation of this data depends on two encoding settings of the resource: the number of present audio channels and the sampling rate of the recording. These two key pieces of information about the audio samples are metadata information about the audio resource. They are thus made available as part of the media resource once the loadedmetadata event has fired.

Listing 8–3 shows how to retrieve this information and Figure 8–3 shows the result for our audio and video examples from Listings 8–1 and 8–2.

Listing 8–3. *Reading audio metadata for the audio framebuffer*

```
<audio src="HelloWorld.ogg" controls>
</audio>
<div id="display"></div>
<script type="text/javascript">
  var audio = document.getElementsByTagName("audio")[0];
  var display = document.getElementById("display");
  audio.addEventListener("loadedmetadata", getMetadata, false);

  var channels, rate, fbLength;
  function getMetadata() {
    channels = audio.mozChannels;
    rate     = audio.mozSampleRate;
    fbLength = audio.mozFrameBufferLength;
    duration = fbLength / (channels * rate);
    display.innerHTML = "Channels: " + channels +
                        "<br/>Rate: " + rate +
                        "<br/>Framebuffer length: " + fbLength +
                        "<br/>Framebuffer seconds: " + duration;
  }
</script>
```

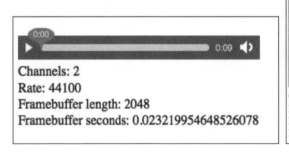

Figure 8–3. *Getting information about the audio sample values in the framebuffer*

To determine the playback time of the audio resource that a framebuffer relates to, you could keep track of the number of framebuffers previously received and their duration. However, the audio data API provides a more robust means of getting this information, which also works across seeking and other discontinuous navigation. As part of the MozAudioAvailable event data there is a field *event.time*, which provides the start time for these samples measured from the start of the resource in seconds. Listing 8–4 and Figure 8–4 show the progress on the time of the samples and how they lag slightly behind the current playback time.

Listing 8–4. Reading the event time for the audio framebuffer

```
<audio src="HelloWorld.ogg" controls>
</audio>
<div id="display"></div>
<script type="text/javascript">
  var audio = document.getElementsByTagName("audio")[0];
  var display = document.getElementById("display");
  audio.addEventListener("MozAudioAvailable", writeSamples, false);
  function writeSamples (event) {
    display.innerHTML += event.time + ', ' + audio.currentTime +'<br/>';
  }
</script>
```

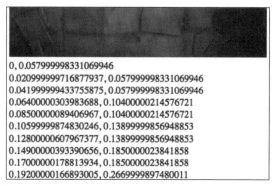

Figure 8–4. Displaying ongoing event times of the audio framebuffer data

The event time is printed first and the current playback position is printed last in every row of numbers in Figure 8–4.

8.1.3 Rendering an Audio Waveform

Now that we have the values of the audio samples, we can display the waveform by painting the samples successively into a Canvas. For this, we set up a Canvas sized preferably the length of the framebuffer, or some integer fraction thereof. Then we paint a path vertically centered with the sample values. Listing 8–5 shows one such implementation.

Listing 8–5. Rendering the audio samples in a waveform

```
<audio src="HelloWorld.ogg" controls></audio>
<canvas width="512" height="200"></canvas>
<script type="text/javascript">
  var audio = document.getElementsByTagName("audio")[0];
  var canvas = document.getElementsByTagName("canvas")[0];
  var context = canvas.getContext('2d');
  audio.addEventListener("MozAudioAvailable", writeSamples, false);
  audio.addEventListener("loadedmetadata", getMetadata, false);
  var fbLength, channels;
  function getMetadata() {
    channels = audio.mozChannels;
    fbLength = audio.mozFrameBufferLength;
  }
  function writeSamples (event){
    var data = event.frameBuffer;
    var samples = 512;
    var step = (fbLength / channels) / samples;
    context.fillRect(0, 0, 500, 200);
    context.strokeStyle = "#FFF";
    context.lineWidth = 2;
    context.beginPath();
    context.moveTo(0, 100-data[0]*100);
    for(var i=1; i< samples; i++){
      context.lineTo(i, 100-data[i*step]*100);
    }
    context.stroke();
  }
</script>
```

Here we have chosen a Canvas width of 512px, which is exactly half the length of the framebuffer on one channel for this particular audio resource. Note that channel values are typically provided in an interleaved fashion and drawing only the samples of one channel is the norm. Figure 8–5 shows the output.

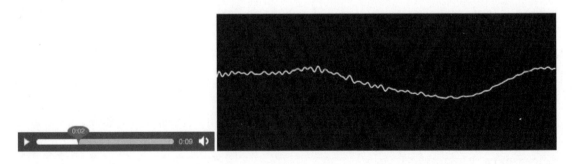

Figure 8–5. Display of the audio waveform

This waveform display is quite interesting to watch, but the window into the waveform that we are provided with is rather small. An improvement is to keep the past waveforms around for a bit longer, but made increasingly transparent, thus keeping a decaying copy of past sample values around. This has been implemented in Listing 8–6.

Listing 8–6. Rendering the audio samples in a waveform with history

```
<audio src="HelloWorld.ogg" controls></audio>
<canvas width="512" height="200"></canvas>
<canvas id="scratch" width="512" height="200"
        style="display: none;"></canvas>
<script type="text/javascript">
  var audio = document.getElementsByTagName("audio")[0];
  var canvas = document.getElementsByTagName("canvas")[0];
  var scratch = document.getElementById("scratch");
  var context = canvas.getContext('2d');
  var sctxt = scratch.getContext("2d");
  context.fillRect(0, 0, 512, 200);
  context.strokeStyle = "#FFFFFF";
  context.lineWidth = 2;
  audio.addEventListener("MozAudioAvailable", writeSamples, false);
  audio.addEventListener("loadedmetadata", getMetadata, false);
  var fbLength, channels;
  function getMetadata() {
    channels = audio.mozChannels;
    fbLength = audio.mozFrameBufferLength;
  }
  function writeSamples (event){
    var data = event.frameBuffer;
    var samples = 512;
    var step = (fbLength / channels) / samples;
    img = context.getImageData(0, 0, 512, 200);
    sctxt.putImageData(img, 0, 0, 512, 200);
    context.globalAlpha = 0.5;
    context.fillRect(0, 0, 512, 200);
    context.drawImage(scratch, 0, 0, 512, 200);
    context.globalAlpha = 1;
    context.beginPath();
    context.moveTo(0, 100-data[0]*100);
    for(var i=1; i< samples; i++) {
      context.lineTo(i, 100-data[i*step]*100);
    }
    context.stroke();
  }
</script>
```

To redraw the lighter version of the waveform, we introduce a second canvas into which we copy the image data. It is then written back into the main Canvas with 50% transparency and thus increasingly fades out as historic data. Figure 8–6 shows the display.

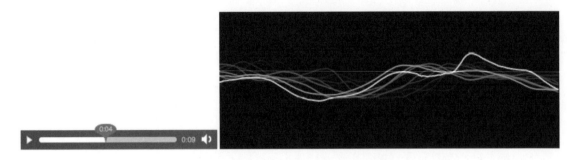

Figure 8–6. *Display of the audio waveform with history*

8.1.4 Rendering an audio spectrum

There are many more visualizations that can be performed using the audio sample data. We will finish off the audio data reading section with a spectral display. For the calculation of the spectrum, we use the Fast Fourier Transform (FFT)[7] as described in https://wiki.mozilla.org/Audio_Data_API[8]. The example is shown in Listing 8–7 with the FFT class omitted with its functions being rendered bold.

Listing 8–7. *Rendering the audio samples in a spectrum*

```
<audio src="HelloWorld.ogg" controls></audio>
<canvas width="512" height="200"></canvas>
<script type="text/javascript">
  var audio = document.getElementsByTagName("audio")[0];
  var canvas = document.getElementsByTagName("canvas")[0];
  var context = canvas.getContext('2d');
  context.strokeStyle = "#FFFFFF";
  context.lineWidth = 2;
  audio.addEventListener("MozAudioAvailable", writeSamples, false);
  audio.addEventListener("loadedmetadata", getMetadata, false);
  var fbLength, channels, rate;
  function getMetadata() {
    channels = audio.mozChannels;
    fbLength = audio.mozFrameBufferLength;
    rate     = audio.mozSampleRate;
    fft      = new FFT(fbLength / channels, rate);
  }
  function writeSamples (event) {
    var data = event.frameBuffer;
    var length = data.length / channels;
    var signal = new Float32Array(length);
    for (var i = 0; i < length; i++ ) {
      if (channels == 2) {
        // merge channels into a stereo-mix mono signal
```

---

[7] See http://en.wikipedia.org/wiki/FFT

[8] See https://wiki.mozilla.org/Audio_Data_API#Complete_Example:_Visualizing_Audio_Spectrum

```
      signal[i] = (data[2*i] + data[2*i+1]) / 2;
    } else {
      signal[i] = data[i];
    }
  }
  fft.forward(signal);
  context.clearRect(0,0, 512, 200);
  for (var i = 0; i < fft.spectrum.length; i++ ) {
    // multiply spectrum by a zoom value
    magnitude = fft.spectrum[i] * 4000;
    // Draw rectangle bars for each frequency bin
    context.fillRect(i * 4, canvas.height, 3, -magnitude);
  }
 }
</script>
```

Note that we are preparing the audio samples for the Fourier transform by averaging the sample values of the left and right channel if there are two channels. The code currently doesn't deal with more than two channels. The result is shown in Figure 8–7.

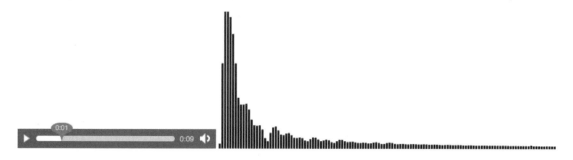

Figure 8–7. Display of an audio spectrum

Note that the authors of the Mozilla audio data API are also working on a JavaScript library for further digital signal processing functions at http://github.com/corbanbrook/dsp.js.

Further reading:

- Description of the full Mozilla audio data API:
  https://wiki.mozilla.org/Audio_Data_API

- Tutorial for reading HTML5 audio data with Firefox 4:
  http://weblog.bocoup.com/read-html5-audio-data-with-firefox-4

- Main author of audio data API David Humphrey:
  Blog: http://vocamus.net/dave/?p=1148
  Demo: http://www.youtube.com/watch?v=1Uw0CrQdYYg

- Diverse HTML5 audio visualizations:
  http://blog.nihilogic.dk/2010/04/html5-audio-visualizations.html with demos at
  http://www.nihilogic.dk/labs/pocket_full_of_html5/
  http://www.storiesinflight.com/jsfft/visualizer/index.html

- Beat detection:
  http://sourceforge.net/projects/beatdetektor/
  http://vimeo.com/11345685
  http://cubicvr.org/CubicVR.js/bd3/BeatDetektor1HD.html

8.2 Generating Audio Data

The other part of the Mozilla audio data API enables JavaScript programmers to create sound from JavaScript. The following methods are added to the media elements:

- `mozSetup(channels, sampleRate)`: Sets the characteristics of a new audio element.

- `mozWriteAudio(buffer)`: Writes an array of 32-bit floats to the audio element.

- `mozCurrentSampleOffset()`: Provides the current position of the audio element in samples rather than time, which the `currentTime` attribute covers.

8.2.1 Creating a Single-Frequency Sound

The simplest example of creating a sound is to write a sine-wave — a single-frequency sound — to a new audio element. Listing 8–8 shows how it's done.

Listing 8–8. *Creating a new audio element with a sine wave*

```
<script type="text/javascript">
  var audio = new Audio();
  audio.mozSetup(1, 44100);
  var samples = new Float32Array(22050);
  for(var i=0, l=samples.length; i< l; i++) {
    samples[i] = Math.sin( i / 40 );
  }
</script>
<button onclick="audio.mozWriteAudio(samples);">Play</button>
```

After creating the audio element and setting it up for single channel and 44.1kHz sampling rate playback, the example creates an array of audio samples for exactly 1 second duration. This array is written once to the audio element upon clicking the button. For displaying what we are writing to the audio element Figure 8–8 includes the canvas waveform code shown earlier.

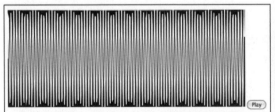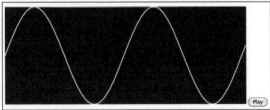

Figure 8–8. *Playback of a sine wave created by a script, displayed at two different resolutions*

Note that in the left image of Figure 8–8 the full sine wave is shown, but only every 43rd sample; this makes for a dense display of the wave. In contrast, the right image of Figure 8–8 shows only the first 512 samples of the sine wave.

8.2.2 Creating Sound from Another Audio Source

Since the `mozWriteAudio()` method accepts a 32-bit float array as input and the `MozAudioAvailable` event returns a `framebuffer` of 32-bit floats, it is possible to take the output of one audio element and play it back through another one, including intermediate processing if required. Listing 8–9 shows the core code to achieve such reading and writing.

Listing 8–9. Creating a new audio element with a sine wave

```
<audio src="HelloWorld.ogg" controls></audio>
<script type="text/javascript">
var input = document.getElementsByTagName("audio")[0];
input.volume = 0;
var audio = new Audio();
input.addEventListener("loadedmetadata", getMetadata, false);
function getMetadata() {
  audio.mozSetup(input.mozChannels, input.mozSampleRate);
}
input.addEventListener("MozAudioAvailable", writeSamples, false);
// Render the waveform
function writeSamples (event){
  audio.mozWriteAudio(event.frameBuffer);
}
</script>
```

We first grab the given audio element and set its volume to 0 so as not to get funny effects with both the input audio element and the scripted audio element playing at the same time. Then we create the scripted audio element and use the metadata of the input audio element to initialize the scripted audio element's metadata. In the callback for the `MozAudioAvailable` event we only need to grab the `framebuffer` data from the event and write it to the scripted audio element.

There is no callback on the scripted audio element for retrieving samples, but since we already have them in the `writeSamples` method, this is not necessary. To draw the samples to a canvas, we can simply add the canvas rendering code of Listing 8–6 straight into the writeSamples function. We can see the results in Figure 8–9.

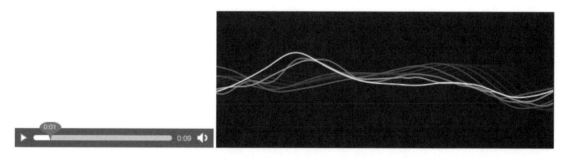

Figure 8–9. Playback of extracted audio data into a new audio element

8.2.3 Continuous Playback

Audio devices have a sample buffer that feeds the playback. No audio is played back before this sample buffer is full. If this buffer runs low on data, you get unwanted pauses in the playback of the sound. If the sample buffer is full and you try to write data to it, only some of your data may be accepted, and the rest may be dropped and ignored; this also results in perceptible breaks in the playback. The simple preceding implementations, where we just feed an array of audio samples straight to the audio element, create such problems because we do not note the state of the sample buffer.

The Mozilla audio data API provides two means that allow us to better feed the sample buffer:

- A return value on the mozWriteAudio method, which tells us how many of the audio samples that we tried to hand on to the sample buffer were actually handed on.

- The mozCurrentSampleOffset method, which tells us how much the audio device has actually played.

Using the mozCurrentSampleOffset() method, we can, for example, calculate the initial delay (or latency) that your audio element is experiencing in comparison to the input audio element's playback time. Listing 8–10 provides the key callback function on the MozAudioAvailable event—the remainder of the page is essentially identical to Listing 8–9 with an extra paragraph.

Listing 8–10. Displaying latency between playback on original audio element and scripted audio

```
var par = document.getElementsByTagname("p")[0];
var showOffset = true;
var started = new Date().valueOf();
function writeSamples(event) {
  prebufferSize = Math.floor(input.mozSampleRate / 1000 *
                 (new Date().valueOf() - started));
  audio.mozWriteAudio(event.frameBuffer);
  offset = audio.mozCurrentSampleOffset();
  if (offset && showOffset) { // Play position moved?
      par.innerHTML += offset + " first output sample position<br/>";
      offset /= (input.mozChannels * input.mozSampleRate);
      par.innerHTML += "Initial Delay: " + offset;
      showOffset = false;
  }
}
```

We set the started time of the input audio playback element first (this should be done in an onplay callback). Then, as the samples come in, we record the first time that mozCurrentSampleOffset() returns a value larger than 0 and print the respective sample offset and the time it maps to. Figure 8–10 shows the result.

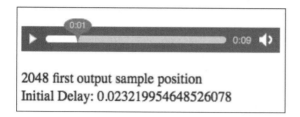

Figure 8–10. Latency between playback of original audio element and scripted audio

This means that our example had a latency of 23ms between the original audio element's sound and the playback on the audio device from the scripted audio element. We now just need to feed the sample buffer regularly with all the output data and not lose any samples from the mozWriteAudio() call. Listing 8–11 shows the loop that should be used for playback. The remainder of the code is as shown in Listing 8–9.

Listing 8–11. Playing back all the samples from an input source

```
var buffers = [];
function writeSamples(event) {
  buffers.push(event.frameBuffer);
  // If there's buffered data, write that
  while (buffers.length > 0) {
    var buffer = buffers.shift();
    var written = audio.mozWriteAudio(buffer);
    // If all data wasn't written, keep it in the buffers:
    if (written < buffer.length) {
      buffers.unshift(buffer.slice(written));
      break;
    }
  }
}
```

Since not always all the audio data is written to the sample buffer of the audio device, it is important to keep track of the samples that were not written for the next writing call. In Listing 8–11, the array *buffers* holds the remaining samples from a previous call to writeSamples(). In *buffer* we then send the data from all elements in *buffers* to the sound device. Figure 8–11 shows a display of this, though nothing apparently changes—only all the sound samples are retained.

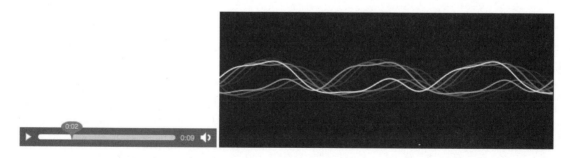

Figure 8–11. Writing all audio samples to the scripted audio element

8.2.4 Manipulating Sound: the Bleep

The aim of grabbing audio samples from one element and writing them to another element is to manipulate the data in between. To demonstrate, we will take the example of replacing short segments of the input data with a sine wave; this is similar to the way swear words are "bleeped" out on TV. Listing 8–12 shows an example for the "Hello World" audio file that bleeps out the word "Hello".

Listing 8–12. *Bleeping out a section of audio with a sine wave*

```
<audio src="HelloWorld.ogg" controls></audio>
<script type="text/javascript">
  var input = document.getElementsByTagName("audio")[0];
  input.volume = 0;
  var audio = new Audio();
  var samples, sampleRate, channels, insertFrom, insertTo;
  input.addEventListener("loadedmetadata", getMetadata, false);
  function getMetadata() {
    sampleRate = input.mozSampleRate;
    channels   = input.mozChannels;
    audio.mozSetup(channels, sampleRate);
    // create enough buffer to play smoothly
    samples = new Float32Array(2*sampleRate);
    var k = 2* Math.PI * 400 / sampleRate;
    for (var i=0, size=samples.length; i < size; i++) {
      samples[i] = 0.1 * Math.sin(k * i);
    }
    insertFrom = 3.0 * sampleRate * channels;
    insertTo   = 4.0 * sampleRate * channels;
  }

  // Render the samples
  var position = 0;
  var insPos = 0;
  input.addEventListener("MozAudioAvailable", writeSamples, false);
  function writeSamples(event) {
    if (position >= insertFrom && position <= insertTo) {
      // replace with sine wave
      for (i=0; i< event.frameBuffer.length; i++) {
        event.frameBuffer[i] = samples[insPos++];
        if (insPos == samples.length) insPos = 0;
      }
    }
    position += audio.mozWriteAudio(event.frameBuffer);
  }
</script>
```

At first we set up the scripted audio element as before with the channels and sampling rate of the input audio element. As we set this up, we also set up a two-second long 400 Hz sine wave buffer (at 10% of the amplitude), which will be used as the bleep. Then, for this simple example, we define the start and end times (in samples) for the bleep. In a real-world program, such information could come from an external cue file and be used to bleep out several sections.

During rendering, as the MozAudioAvailable event is raised, we keep track of the position up to which the audio data has been written and when it reaches the bleep section we replace the samples in the event.frameBuffer with the sine wave samples. We have to be careful with these samples, because the size of the `frameBuffer` is not normally a multiple of the sine wave frequency, which means we will get phase distortion[9] if we just create a sine wave buffer of the frameBuffer length and concatenate these. Instead, we make a long sinewave buffer, longer than the bleep, and take successive samples from that buffer.

The result can be seen in Figure 8–12. We've added the canvas code from Listing 8–7 and we've also added the improved buffer writing that doesn't lose any samples from Listing 8–11.

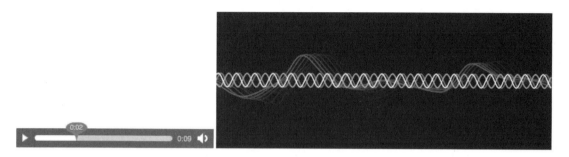

Figure 8–12. *Adding bleeps to an audio source*

8.2.5 A Tone Generator

We conclude this section with an interactive, Web-based tone generator[10]. It is based on the previously shown code for creating single frequency samples, but the user can interactively change the setting. Listing 8–13 shows the code.

Listing 8–13. *A Web-based tone generator*

```
<input type="text" size="4" id="freq" value="880"><label> Hz</label>
<button onclick="start()">play</button>
<button onclick="stop()">stop</button>
<script type="text/javascript">
  var audio = new Audio();
  rate      = 44100;
  audio.mozSetup(1, rate);

  // set up sample array of size 500ms
  var samples = new Float32Array(22050);
  var intervalId;
  function start() {
    // prepare samples
    var currentSoundSample = 0;
    var frequency = 0;
    frequency = parseFloat(document.getElementById("freq").value);
    if (!frequency) {
      return;
```

---

[9] See http://en.wikipedia.org/wiki/Phase_distortion

[10] Motivated by https://wiki.mozilla.org/Audio_Data_API

```
      }
      var k = 2* Math.PI * frequency / rate;
      for (var i=0, size=samples.length; i < size; i++) {
        samples[i] = 0.5 * Math.sin(k * currentSoundSample++);
      }

      // call playback per samples array
      clearInterval(intervalId);
      intervalId = setInterval(playSound,
                              parseInt(samples.length*1000/rate));
    }
    function stop() {
      clearInterval(intervalId);
    }
    function playSound() {
      audio.mozWriteAudio(samples);
    }
  </script>
```

First we set up the Web page with the input element and the buttons. Then we set up the output audio element as a mono 44.1kHz sound and prepare the sample buffer.

As the user hits the "Play" button, the start method is called. Here, we read the user-provided frequency and create a 500ms sample array of sine wave samples at the given frequency. Then we can clear any previously playing sounds and start playing the new sample array. We play it in intervals that are of the exact same duration as a sample array, namely 500ms.

As the user hits the "Stop" button, we remove the playSound method from being called regularly, which stops the playback. Note that the playSound method should be improved with the code from Listing 8–11 in order not to lose any samples during playback.

Figure 8–13 shows the results of Listing 8–13 when extended with the canvas functionality of Listing 8–7.

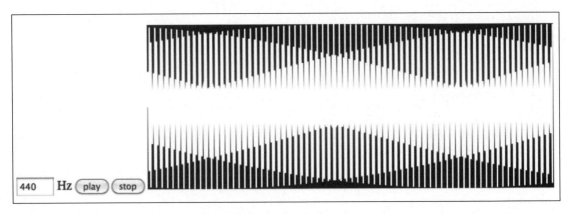

Figure 8–13. An interactive tone generator in Firefox 4+

Further reading:

- Description of the full Mozilla audio data API:
  https://wiki.mozilla.org/Audio_Data_API

- Generating sound with the Mozilla audio data API:
  http://weblog.bocoup.com/generate-sound-with-javascript-in-firefox-4

- Excellent demos:
  http://audioscene.org/?cat=9

- JavaScript audio synthesizer:
  http://acko.net/blog/javascript-audio-synthesis-with-html-5
  http://code.almeros.com/code-examples/sampler-firefox-audio-api/

We've now had a good introduction to the Mozilla audio data API and what is possible with it. We can extract sample values and write sample values to HTML5 audio elements and use libraries of methods in JavaScript to create more sophisticated analysis and synthesis functionality.

8.3 Overview of the Filter Graph API

In this section we want to take a look at the Web audio API[11] as proposed by Google as part of the W3C Audio Incubator Group and understand the differences and commonalities with Mozilla's audio data API. We now have to switch over from running our examples in Firefox 4+ to running an experimental version of Safari or Google Chrome[12] on OS X, since that is the only platform for which an example implementation has been developed.

8.3.1 Basic Reading and Writing

Similar to the way the Canvas introduces a new element into HTML for manipulating image data, the Web audio API proposes the introduction of a new element into HTML for manipulating audio data. It is called AudioContext. As it is currently defined, only one AudioContext can exist per Web page.

The AudioContext provides the environment for the filter graph to be put together and to result eventually in a signal that is being output to the device through an AudioDestinationNode. It is a "terminal" node in the AudioContext's filter graph.

Input to the AudioContext comes from AudioBufferSourceNodes, which can be connected to audio resources. The demo implementation only accepts aif and mp4 audio files.

Listing 8–14 shows how to read an audio resource with the Web audio API and write it back out using the AudioContext element.

Listing 8–14. Reading and writing sound using an AudioContext.

```
<div id="display"></div>
<script type="text/javascript">
  var display = document.getElementById("display");
  var context = new AudioContext();
  display.innerHTML  = context.sampleRate + " sampling rate<br/>";
  display.innerHTML += context.destination.numberOfChannels
                                        + " output channels<br/>";
  display.innerHTML += context.currentTime + " currentTime<br/>";

  // create samples
```

---

[11] See http://chromium.googlecode.com/svn/trunk/samples/audio/specification/specification.html

[12] See http://chromium.googlecode.com/svn/trunk/samples/audio/index.html

```
    source  = context.createBufferSource();
    request = context.createAudioRequest("HelloWorld.aif", false);
    request.onload = function() {
        display.innerHTML += context.currentTime
                          + " currentTime after onload<br/>";
        source.buffer = request.buffer;
        source.connect(context.destination);
        source.noteOn(0);
    }
    request.send();
</script>
```

We first have to instantiate the AudioContext, which by default has a sampling rate of 44.1kHz associated with it and an AudioDestinationNode that has stereo channels. It is unclear why there is a need for an explicit AudioDestinationNode, when the AudioContext already sets up the default environment— or why in fact the number of channels and the sampling rate cannot be different between the AudioContext and the AudioDestinationNode. It is also unclear how an AudioContext can be created with a different sampling rate and a different number of channels, since all of these parameters are read-only. It seems that this part of the writing functionality could be nicely merged with the audio.mozSetup() method of Mozilla's audio data API.

After the setup, we create an audio sample buffer and fill it from an input source aif file with CreateAudioRequest. As we load the resource through request.send(), the onload event is fired, which has the sample buffer. We hand that sample buffer on to the output device through the AudioDestinationNode and tell the source to start playback with noteon(0).

It seems a bit strange to have an extra loading function for audio resources when the audio element already has that functionality. Again, it seems that the MozAudioAvailable event for reading in the Mozilla audio data API could be nicely combined with this functionality.

We will see what specification the W3C Incubator Group will eventually arrive at. For now, you can see the output of Listing 8–14 in Figure 8–14.

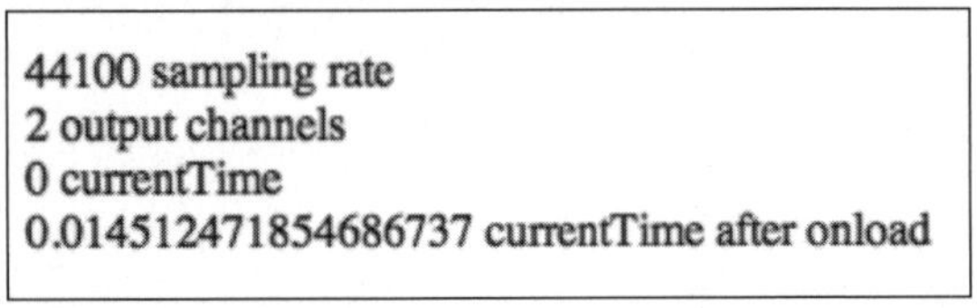

```
44100 sampling rate
2 output channels
0 currentTime
0.014512471854686737 currentTime after onload
```

Figure 8–14. Reading and writing audio data with the Web audio API

8.3.2 Advanced Filters

A set of different AudioNodes with different filter functionalities can be added into an AudioContext to build the filter graph. The following node types are available:

- AudioGainNode: Takes one input, creates one output by changing the gain of the signal smoothly

- DelayNode: Takes one input, creates one output by variably delaying the signal without introducing clicks or glitches.

- LowPass2FilterNode: Takes one input, creates one output by applying a low pass filter, where all the higher frequencies are removed,

- `HighPass2FilterNode`: Takes one input, creates one output by applying a high pass filter, where all the lower frequencies are removed,

- `AudioPannerNode`: Takes one input, creates one output by positioning/spatializing incoming audio samples in three-dimensional space,

- `ConvolverNode`: Takes one input, creates one output by applying a linear convolution given an impulse response[13],

- `AudioChannelSplitter`: Takes one input, creates up to six outputs depending on the number of present input channels,

- `AudioChannelMerger`: Takes up to six inputs and creates one interleaved output sample stream,

- `RealtimeAnalyserNode`: Takes one input and creates one identical output audio sample stream, plus real-time frequency and time-domain analysis information.

These filters are very useful and would make a great addition to the Mozilla audio data API. It is important to add such functions to the core functionality of a Web browser because in this way hardware-acceleration can be applied to functionalities that are otherwise software-only. Even the application of Web Workers, which can relieve the main process from particularly CPU-intensive tasks, cannot make up for reuse of hardware-provided functionality.

In the following, we will explore how these filters are applied to audio signals in a simple example.

8.3.3 Creating a Reverberation Effect

To understand how the Web audio API works, we are using an impulse response sound that creates a spring-like reverberation; we convolve[14] this with our `HelloWorld` audio example file. Listing 8–15 shows how it is done.

Listing 8–15. Creating a reverberation effect using the AudioContext convolution filter

```
<script type="text/javascript">
  var context   = new AudioContext();
  var convolver = context.createConvolver();

  // create filter graph
  source = context.createBufferSource();
  source.connect(convolver);
  convolver.connect(context.destination);

  // load convolution buffer impulse response
  var req1 = context.createAudioRequest("feedback-spring.aif", false);
  req1.onload = function() {
    convolver.buffer = req1.buffer;

    // load samples and play away
    request = context.createAudioRequest("HelloWorld.aif", false);
```

---

[13] See http://en.wikipedia.org/wiki/Impulse_response

[14] See http://en.wikipedia.org/wiki/Convolution

```
        request.onload = function() {
            source.buffer = request.buffer;
            source.noteOn(0);
        }
        request.send();

    }
    req1.send();

</script>
```

First, we set up the audio context and create the convolver in it. Then, we connect the filter graph together—from the source buffer to the convolver to the destination display. Then we load the impulse response of the convolution function. When its onload event returns, everything is ready to start playing. We can load the input audio resource and upon its onload event returning, we call the noteOn(0) function, which starts playback of sound from the pipeline. The resulting effect is that of a reverberation on the original sound—it almost sounds like somebody is inside a cave.

We've now learned about the following interfaces:

AudioContext:

- readonly attribute float sampleRate

- readonly attribute float currentTime

- readonly attribute AudioDestinationNode::numberOfChannels

- AudioBufferSourceNode createBufferSource()

- ConvolverNode createConvolver()

- CachedAudio createAudioRequest(url, asynchronous)

AudioBufferSourceNode:

- attribute AudioBuffer buffer

- void noteOn(timeoffset)

- attribute boolean loop

ConvolverNode:

- attribute AudioBuffer buffer

CachedAudio:

- attribute AudioBuffer buffer

- onload event callback

- onerror event callback

8.3.4 Waveform Display

To visualize the results of Listing 8–15, we need to introduce another filter into the filter graph, called RealtimeAnalyzerNode. This node type allows grabbing time- or frequency-domain data out of the filter graph where it is inserted. We can use this to create a waveform or frequency display.

Listing 8–16 shows how we can grab the sample values off the filter graph and display them in a canvas.

Listing 8–16. Rendering waveform data from an AudioContext filter graph

```
<canvas width="512" height="200"></canvas>
<canvas id="scratch" width="512" height="200" style="display: none;">
</canvas>
<script type="text/javascript">
  var context   = new AudioContext();
  var convolver = context.createConvolver();
  var analyser = context.createAnalyser();
  analyser.fftSize = 2048;
  analyser.smoothingTimeConstant = 0.1;

  // filter graph: source -> convolver -> analyser -> destination
  source = context.createBufferSource();
  source.looping = false;
  source.connect(convolver);
  convolver.connect(analyser);
  analyser.connect(context.destination);
  buffer = new Uint8Array(analyser.frequencyBinCount);

  // prepare for rendering
  var canvas = document.getElementsByTagName("canvas")[0];
  var ctxt = canvas.getContext("2d");
  var scratch = document.getElementById("scratch");
  var sctxt = scratch.getContext("2d");
  ctxt.fillRect(0, 0, 512, 200);
  ctxt.strokeStyle = "#FFFFFF";
  ctxt.lineWidth = 2;

  // load convolution buffer impulse response
  var req1 = context.createAudioRequest("feedback-spring.aif", false);
  req1.onload = function() {
    convolver.buffer = req1.buffer;

    // load samples and play away
    request = context.createAudioRequest("HelloWorld.aif", false);
    request.onload = function() {
        source.buffer = request.buffer;
        source.noteOn(0);
        draw();
    }
    request.send();
  }
  req1.send();
```

```
function draw() {
  analyser.getByteTimeDomainData(buffer);

  // do the canvas painting
  var width = 512;
  var step = parseInt(buffer.length / width);
  img = ctxt.getImageData(0,0,512,200);
  sctxt.putImageData(img, 0, 0, 512, 200);
  ctxt.globalAlpha = 0.5;
  ctxt.fillRect(0, 0, 512, 200);
  ctxt.drawImage(scratch,0,0,512,200);
  ctxt.globalAlpha = 1;
  ctxt.beginPath();
  ctxt.moveTo(0, buffer[0]*200/256);
  for(var i=1; i< width; i++) {
    ctxt.lineTo(i, buffer[i*step]*200/256);
  }
  ctxt.stroke();
  setTimeout(draw, 0);
}
</script>
```

As in previous examples, we have a canvas into which the wave will be rendered. We set up the filter graph by instantiating the AudioContext() and creating the convolver and anlyzer, then hooking them up from the source buffer through the convolver and the analyzer to the destination display. As before, we load the impulse response into the convolver and upon its onload event, we load the input source into the context to hook it up to the filter graph and start playback.

Once we have turned on the filter graph for playback, we go into a draw() function, which grabs from the analyser the waveform bytes. These are exposed through a getByteTimeDomainData() method, which fills a provided Uint8Array. We take this array and draw it into the canvas. Then call the draw() method again in a setTimeout() function call to grab the next unsigned 8–bit byte array for display. This successively paints the waveform into the Canvas.

Figure 8–15 shows the result of running Listing 8–16.

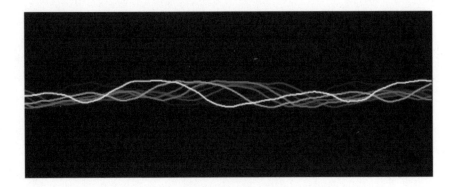

Figure 8–15. Rendering the audio waveform in the Web audio API

The interface of the RealtimeAnalyserNode is as follows:

RealtimeAnalyserNode:

- void getFloatFrequencyData(Float32Array)

- void getByteFrequencyData(Uint8Array)

- void getByteTimeDomainData(Uint8Array)

- attribute unsigned long fftSize

- readonly attribute unsigned long frequencyBinCount

- attribute float minDecibels

- attribute float maxDecibels

- attribute float smoothingTimeConstant

It is thus really easy to grab the frequency values out of this filter node.

The availability of these advanced audio processing methods in the Web audio API makes it very powerful. Since the creation of the filter graph excludes the introduction of random audio processing methods, a special JavaScriptNode had to be introduced which allows the integration of a self-created filter in JavaScript into the filter graph. It has an onaudioprocess event and provides an input and an output buffer for filters to work with.

The difference, therefore, between the audio data API and the Web audio API approach is that the first one provides access directly to the audio samples in an HTML5 audio element and allows the programmer to do anything with these samples—including having them drive other parts of the interface, while the latter provides advanced audio functionalities in a structured filter graph approach, the likes of which have been used successfully for many years to create advanced audio content. The latter also provides hardware-acceleration on functions that would otherwise not be able to run in real time.

Further reading:

- Specification of the Web audio API:
  http://chromium.googlecode.com/svn/trunk/samples/audio/specification/speci
  fication.html

- Use cases under consideration for the audio API specification:
  http://www.w3.org/2005/Incubator/audio/wiki/Audio_API_Use_Cases

- Example uses of the Web audio API by its main author Chris Rogers:
  http://chromium.googlecode.com/svn/trunk/samples/audio/index.html

-

8.4 Summary

In this chapter we learned about the existing proposals for an audio API that gives access to an <audio> element's audio samples, provides manipulation and visualization approaches for such audio data, and explains how samples can be read out to the Web browser through another <audio> element.

There are currently two proposals for an audio API—one is amazingly simple and yet powerful and the other is a complementary collection of manipulation functions.

■ ■ ■

CHAPTER 9

Media Accessibility and Internationalization

Accessibility and internationalization are two aspects of usability: the first one is for those users who have some form of sensory impairment, the second for those who don't speak the language used by the main audio-visual resource.

For web pages, we have developed a vast set of functionalities to cope with the extra requirements introduced by these users: Web sites present themselves in multiple languages, and screen readers or Braille devices provide vision-impaired users with the ability to consume web page content.

With the introduction of audio and video into HTML, we face some very tough additional challenges. For the first time, we are publishing audio content that needs to be made accessible to hearing-impaired users or users who do not speak the language used in the audio data. We are also publishing for the first time HTML imaging content that changes over time and needs to be made accessible to vision-impaired users.

The main means of addressing such needs has been the development of so-called "alternative content technologies", in which users who request it are provided with other content that gives an alternative representation of the original content in a format they can consume. Examples are captions, which are alternative content for the audio track for hearing-impaired users, subtitles, which are alternative content for the audio track for foreign language users, and audio descriptions of video content for vision-impaired users. Sometimes alternative content is also useful as additional content, for example, in the case of subtitles or chapter markers. But we'll still use this terminology.

In this chapter we discuss the features that HTML5 currently offers, introduces, or will need to introduce to satisfy accessibility and internationalization needs for media users. The development of these features is still active for HTML5, and not every user need is currently satisfied by an existing feature proposal. At the time of writing, no browser supports any of the new features natively yet. However, the development of these features, in the form of both specification text in the HTML5 standard and implementations in browsers, is very active and we can already foresee some of the functionality that will be available. Therefore, it would be a big oversight not to address this topic here.

We will start this chapter by providing an overview of the kinds of alternative content technologies that have been developed for addressing the needs of accessibility and internationalization users. Then we will introduce the features that are under discussion for HTML5 at varying stages of maturity.

Note that the creation of alternative content for videos has large implications for all users on the Web, not just those with special needs or non-native users. The biggest advantage is that text is made available that represents exactly what is happening in the video, and this text is the best means for searches to take place. Because search technology is very advanced when it comes to text, but very poor when it comes to audio or video content, alternative text provides the only reliable means of indexing audio-visual content for high quality search.

9.1 Alternative Content Technologies

This section will not contain the typical "feature—example—demo" approach used elsewhere in this book. The reason for this section is, however, to explain the breadth of alternative content technologies that have been developed to make media content usable for people in varying situations and thus to provide a background for the set of features that are being introduced into HTML5 to satisfy these diverse needs.

9.1.1 Vision-impaired Users

For users with poor or no vision, there are two main dimensions that pose a challenge: how to perceive the visual dimension of the video imaging, and how to interact with media elements.

(1) Perceiving Video Content

The method developed to consume the imagery content of video as a vision-impaired user is called *Described Video*. In this approach, a description of what is happening in the video is made available as the video's time passes and the audio continues to play back. The following solutions are possible and need to be supported by HTML5:

- **Audio descriptions**: a speaker explains what is visible in the video as the video progresses.

- **Text descriptions**: time-synchronized blocks of text are provided in time with what is happening on screen and a screen reader synthesizes this to speech for the vision-impaired user.

The spoken description needs to fit into the times of the video when no other important information is being expressed in the main audio. Text descriptions are synthesized at an average reading speed and thus also calculated with a certain duration to fit into the gaps.

This approach doesn't change the timeline of the original content. It can be applied to a lot of content, in particular movies, cartoons and similar TV content that typically have numerous audio gaps. It is very hard to apply to content with continuous speech, such as lectures or presentations. For such situations, it is necessary to introduce gaps into the original content during which the vision-impaired user can consume the extra information. Such content is called "extended" because it extends the timeline of consumption:

- **Extended audio descriptions**: Recordings of spoken descriptions are inserted into the video while the video is paused.

- **Extended text descriptions**: The video is paused until the speech synthesizer finishes reading out a text description.

Note that in a shared viewing experience—where a vision-impaired user and a nonimpaired user are viewing the content together—the use of extensions may be limited depending on the flexibility and needs of the nonimpaired users who will need to wait for the consumption of the video descriptions. There will be situations where the additional information is very welcome to the nonimpaired users and others where the delay would not be acceptable.

From a technical viewpoint, there are three ways of realizing described video:

- **Mixed-in**: audio descriptions are mixed into the main audio track of the video; that is, they are recorded into the main audio track and cannot be extracted again, thus becoming part of the main resource. Such audio descriptions are sometimes also called **open audio descriptions** because they are always active and open for everyone. On the Web, the mixed-in approach can only work if the described video is presented as an alternative to the non-described video, thus keeping multiple copies of the same video around. This also creates the perception that the "normal" content is the one without descriptions, and that described content is something that needs to be specially activated. It thus discourages cross-content browsing and cross-population interaction—something not desirable in a social medium like the Web. In addition, the implied duplication of content is undesirable, so this approach should only be used if no alternative means of providing described video can be found.

- **In-band**: audio or text descriptions are provided as a separate track in the media resource. This allows independent activation and deactivation of the extra information similar to the way descriptive audio has been provided through secondary audio programming (SAP)[1]. It requires web browsers to support handling of multitrack video, something not yet supported by web browsers but commonly found in content material such as QuickTime, MPEG, or Ogg.

- **External**: audio or text descriptions are provided as a separate resource and linked to the media resource through HTML markup. This is sometimes also called "out-of-band" by contrast with "in-band". Similar to using separate tracks, this allows independent activation and deactivation of the extra information. It requires browsers to download, interpret, and synchronize the extra resource to the main resource during playback.

(2) Interacting with Content

Vision-impaired users need to interact with described video in several ways:

- to activate / deactivate descriptions

- to navigate within and into the content

- to navigate between alternative content

- to navigate out of content

Other necessary interactions relate to keyboard-driven video controls (see Chapter 2 for how these are supported), the speech synthesizer (choice of voice, reading speed, shortcuts), the styling of captions (font, font size), and the quality of the content (adapting contrast, brightness, color mix, playback rate, pitch, spatial location).

Activate/Deactivate Descriptions

Where described video is provided through separate in-band tracks or external resources, it is possible to activate or deactivate the descriptions. This can be achieved through **user preference settings**, which for a specific user will always activate descriptions if they are available. It can also be achieved through the creation of **interactive controls** such as a menu of all available tracks and their activation status.

Navigate Within and into Media

Since audio-visual content is a major source of information for vision-impaired users, navigation within and into that content is very important. Sighted users often navigate through video by clicking on time offsets on a playback progress bar. This **direct access** functionality also needs to be available to vision-impaired users. Jumping straight into temporal offsets or into semantically meaningful sections of content helps the consumption of the content enormously. In addition, a more semantic means of **navigating the content along structures** such as chapters, scenes, or acts must also be available.

Navigate Between Alternative Content Tracks

When multiple dependent and hierarchically structured markups of tracks exist such as chapters, scenes, or acts, it is also necessary to be able to **navigate between these related tracks** in a simple and usable manner. Preferably a simple up/down arrow key navigation moves the vision-impaired user to the same time in a different alternative content track.

Navigate out of Content

Finally, an important navigation means for vision-impaired users is the use of **hyperlinks**—the underlying semantic pattern of the Web. Often, on-screen text provides a hyperlink that should not just be read out to a vision-impaired user, but rather be made usable by providing actual hyperlinks in the text description that vision-impaired users can activate. In web pages, vision-impaired users are able to have a screenreader read out paragraphs in one reading, or switch to reading single words only, so they can pause at a hyperlink and follow it. They can also navigate from hyperlink to hyperlink. Such functionality should also be available for described video.

9.1.2 Hard-of-hearing Users

For users who have trouble hearing, the content of the audio track needs to be made available in an alternative way. Captions, transcripts, and sign translations have traditionally been used as alternative representations for audio. In addition, improvements to the played audio can also help hard-of-hearing people who are not completely deaf to grasp the content of the audio.

(1) Captions

Captions are the main method used as alternative content for audio in videos. Captions are blocks of text that transcribe what is being said in the audio track, but they also transcribe significant sound effects or indicate the kind of music being played. Captions can be used both on video and audio resources. For audio resources they are particularly useful in a shared viewing environment with hearing users—otherwise, transcripts are probably preferable because they allow an independent reading speed of what is being said in the audio file. On videos, transcripts cannot replace but only supplement captions. Video with captions is rendered highly usable to hard-of-hearing users, so much that even users who have no hearing-impairment but find themselves in adverse hearing situations, such as at airports or at a noisy work environment, benefit from captions.

For captions, we distinguish between:

- **Traditional captions**: Blocks of text are provided in time with what is happening on screen and displayed time-synchronously with the video. Often they are overlaid at the bottom of the video viewport, sometimes placed elsewhere in the viewport to avoid overlapping other on-screen text, and sometimes placed underneath the viewport to avoid any overlap at all. Mostly, very little if any styling is applied to captions, just making sure the text is well readable with appropriate fonts, colors, and a means to separate it from the video colors through, for example, text outlines or a text background. Some captioned videos introduce color coding for speakers, speaker labeling, and/or positioning of the text close to the speakers on screen to further improve cognition and reading speed.

- **Enhanced captions**: In the modern Web environment, captions can be so much more than just text. *Animated and formatted text* can be displayed in captions. *Icons* can be used to convey meaning—for example, separate icons for different speakers or sound effects. *Hyperlinks* can be used to link on-screen URLs to actual web sites or to provide links to further information making it easier to use the audio-visual content as a starting point for navigation. *Image overlays* can be used in captions to allow displaying timed images with the audio-visual content. To enable this use, general HTML markup is desirable in captions.

From a technical view-point, there are three ways of realizing captions:

- **Mixed-in**: Captions that are mixed into the main video track of the video are also called **burnt-in** captions or **open captions** because they are always active and open for everyone to see. Traditionally, this approach has been used to deliver captions on TV and in cinemas because it doesn't require any additional technology to be reproduced. This approach is, however, very inflexible since it forces all users to consume the captions without possibilities for personal choice, in particular without allowing the choice of using another language for the captions.

  On the Web, this approach is discouraged, since it is easy to provide captions as text. Only legacy content where video without the burnt-in captions is not available should be published in this way.

- **In-band**: captions are provided as a separate track in the media resource. This allows independent activation and deactivation of the extra information. It requires web browsers to support handling of multitrack video.

- **External**: captions are provided as a separate resource and linked to the media resource through HTML markup. Similar to separate tracks, this allows independent activation and deactivation of the extra information. It requires browsers to download, interpret, and synchronize the extra resource to the main resource during playback.

(2) Transcript

Full-text transcripts of the audio track of audio-visual resources are another means of making audio-visual content accessible to hard-of-hearing users and in fact to anyone. It can be more efficient to read—or cross-read—a transcript of a audio or video resource rather than having to sit through its full extent. One particularly good example is a site called Metavid, which has full transcripts of US senate proceedings and is fully searchable[2].

Two types of transcripts are typically used:

- **Plain transcripts**: These are the equivalent of captions but brought together in a single block of text. This block of text can be presented simply as text on the web page somewhere around the video or as a separate resource provided through a link near the video.

- **Interactive transcripts**: These are also equivalent to captions, but brought together in a single block of text with a tighter relationship between the text and video. The transcript continues to have time-synchronized blocks such that a click on a specific text cue will navigate the audio-visual resource to that time offset. Also, as the video reaches the next text cue, the transcript will automatically move the new text cue center stage, for example by making sure it scrolls to a certain on-screen location and/or is highlighted.

Incidentally, the latter type of interactive transcript is also useful for vision-impaired users for navigation when used in conjunction with a screen reader. It is, however, necessary then to mute the audio-visual content while foraging through the interactive transcript, because otherwise it will compete with the sound from the screen reader and make both unintelligible.

(3) Sign Translation

To hard-of-hearing users—in particular to deaf users—sign language is often the most proficient language that they speak, followed by the written language of the country that they live in. They often communicate much quicker and more comprehensively in sign language, which—much like Mandarin and similar Asian languages—communicates typically through having a single symbol for semantic entities. Signs exist for letters, too, but sign speaking in letters is very slow and only used in exceptional circumstances. The use of sign language is the fastest and also most expressive means of communicating between hard-of-hearing users.

From a technical view-point, there are three ways of realizing sign translation:

- **Mixed-in**: Sign translation that is mixed into the main video track of the video can also be called **burnt-in** sign translation or **open sign translation** because it is always active and open for everyone to see. Typically, open sign translation is provided as a picture-in-picture (pip) display, where a small part of the video viewport is used to burn in the sign translation. Traditionally, this approach has been used to deliver sign translation on TV and in cinemas because it doesn't require any additional technology to be reproduced. This approach is, however, very inflexible since it forces all users to consume the sign translation without possibilities for personal choice, in particular without allowing the choice of using a different sign language (from a different country) for the sign translation.

  On the Web, this approach is discouraged. Sign translation that is provided as a small pip video is particularly hard to see in the small embedded videos that are typical for Web video. Therefore only legacy content where video without the burnt-in sign translation is not available should be published in this way. Where possible, the sign translation should exist as separate content.

---

[2] See http://en.wikipedia.org/wiki/Metavid

- **In-band**: sign translation is provided as a separate track in the media resource. This allows independent activation and deactivation of the extra information. It requires web browsers to support handling of multitrack video.

- **External**: sign translation is provided as a separate resource and linked to the media resource through HTML markup. Similar to separate tracks, this allows independent activation and deactivation of the extra information. It requires browsers to synchronize the playback of two video resources.

(4) Clear Audio

This is a feature that is not alternative content for the hearing-impaired, but a more generally applicable feature that improves the usability of audio content. It is generally accepted that speech is the most important part of an audio track, since it conveys the most information. In modern multitrack content, speech is sometimes provided as a separate track to the remainder of the sound environment. This is particularly true for Karaoke music content, but can also easily be provided for professionally developed video content, such as movies, animations, or TV series.

Many users have problems understanding the speech in a mixed audio track. But when the speech is provided in a separate track, it is possible to allow **increasing the volume of the speech track** independently of the rest of the audio tracks, thus rendering "clearer audio"—that is, more comprehensible speech.

Technically, this can only be realized if there is a separate speech track available, either as a separate in-band track or as a separate external resource. Just increasing the volume of typical speech frequency bands may work for some types of content, but not typically for those where the background noise makes the speech incomprehensible.

9.1.3 Deaf-blind users

It is very hard to provide alternative content for users who can neither see nor hear. The only means of consumption for them is basically Braille, which requires text-based alternative content.

(1) Individual Consumption

If deaf-blind users consume the audio-visual content by themselves, it makes sense to only provide a transcript that contains a description of what is happening both on screen and in audio. It's basically a **combination of a text video description and an audio transcript**. The technical realization of this is thus best as a **combined transcript**. Interestingly, Braille devices are very good at navigating hypertext, so some form of enhanced transcript is also useful.

(2) Shared Viewing Environment

In a shared viewing environment, the combination of text and audio description needs to be provided synchronously with the video playback. A typical Braille reading speed is 60 words per minute[3]. Compare that to the average adult reading speed of around 250 to 300 words per minute[4] or even a usual speaking speed of 130-200 words per minute[5] and you realize that it will be hard for a deaf-blind person

---

[3] See http://nfb.org/legacy/bm/bm03/bm0305/bm030508.htm

[4] See http://en.wikipedia.org/wiki/Words_per_minute

[5] See http://www.write-out-loud.com/quick-and-easy-effective-tips-for-speaking-rate.html

to follow along with any usual audio-visual presentation. A **summarized version** may be necessary, which can still be **provided in sync** just as text descriptions are provided in sync and can be handed through to a Braille device. The technical realization of this is thus either as an **interactive transcript** or through a special **text description**.

9.1.4 Learning Support

Some users are not as fast as others in perceiving and understanding audio-visual content; for others, the normal playback speed is too slow. In particular vision-impaired users have learnt to digest audio at phenomenal rates. For such users, it is very helpful to be **able to slow down or speed up** a video or audio resource's playback rate. Such speed changes require keeping the pitch of the audio so as to maintain its usability.

A feature that can be very helpful to people with learning disabilities is the ability to **provide explanations**. For example, whenever a word is used that is not a very commonly used term, it can be very helpful to pop up an explanation of the term, e.g. through a link to Wikipedia or a dictionary. This is somewhat analogous to the aims of enhanced captions and can be provided in the same manner through allowing *hyperlinks* and/or *overlays*.

With learning material, we can also provide **grammatical markup** of the content in time-synchronicity. This is often used for linguistic research, but can also help people with learning disabilities to understand the content better. Grammatical markup can be augmented onto captions or subtitles to provide a transcription of the grammatical role of the words in the given context. Alternatively, the grammatical roles can be provided just as markers for time segments, relying on the audio to provide the actual words.

Under the *learning* category we can also subsume the use case of **music lyrics** or **karaoke**. These provide, like captions, a time-synchronized display of the spoken (or sung) text for users to follow along. Here, they help users learn and understand the lyrics. Similar to captions, they can be technically realized through burning-in, in-band multitrack, or external tracks.

9.1.5 Foreign Users

Users who do not speak the language that is used in the audio track of audio-visual content are regarded as *foreign users*. Such users also require alternative content to allow them to comprehend.

(1) Scene Text Translations

The video track typically poses only a small challenge to foreign users. Most scene text is not important enough to be translated or can be comprehended from context. However, sometimes there is on-screen text such as titles that explain the location, for which a translation would be useful. It is recommended to include such text into the **subtitles**.

(2) Audio Translations

There are two ways in which an audio track can be made accessible to a foreign user:

Dubbing: Provide a supplementary audio track that can be used as a replacement for the original audio track. This supplementary audio track can be provided **in-band** with a multitrack audio-visual resource, or **external** as a linked resource, where playback needs to be synchronized.

(Enhanced) Subtitles: Provide a text translation of what is being said in the audio track. This supplementary text track can be provided **burnt-in, in-band** or as an **external resource**, just like captions. And just like captions, burnt-in subtitles are discouraged because of their inflexibility.

9.1.6 Technology Summary

When analyzing the different types of technologies that are necessary to provide alternatives to the original content and satisfy special user requirements, we can see that they broadly fall into the following different classes:

- **Burnt-in**: This type of alternative content is actually not provided as an alternative, but as part of the main resource. Since there is no means to turn this off (other than through signal processing), no HTML5 specifications need to be developed to support them.

- **Page text**: This type covers the transcriptions that can be consumed either in relation to the video or completely independent of it.

- **Synchronized text**: This type covers text in-band or external that is displayed in sync with the content and includes text descriptions, captions, and subtitles.

- **Synchronized media**: This type covers audio or video in-band or external that is displayed in sync with the content and includes audio descriptions, sign translation, and dubbing.

- **Navigation**: This is mostly a requirement for vision-impaired users or mobility-impaired users but is generally useful to all users.

In the next subsections we will analyze what alternative content technologies are available or planned to be available in HTML5. We start with transcriptions, which are page text, and then go into alternative synchronized text technologies where most of the current standards work is focused. We will briefly touch on the synchronized media challenges and finish with a view of navigation.

9.2 Transcriptions

We identified in the "Transcripts" subsection above the need for plain transcripts and interactive transcripts, and we described what each type consists of. This section demonstrates how to implement each type in HTML5.

9.2.1 Plain Transcripts

Listing 9–1 shows an example of how to link a **plain transcript** to a media element. Figure 9–1 shows the result.

Listing 9–1. Providing a plain transcript for a video element

```
<video poster="video1.png" controls>
  <source src="video1.mp4"  type="video/mp4">
  <source src="video1.webm" type="video/webm">
  <source src="video1.ogv"  type="video/ogg">
</video>
<p>
  <a id="videoTranscript" href="video1.html">
    Read the transcript for this video.
  </a>
</p>
```

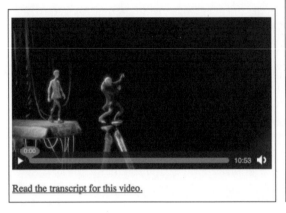

Figure 9–1. Plain external transcript linked to a video element

The plain transcript of Figure 9–1 has a transcription both of the spoken text and of what is happening in the video. This makes sense, since one arrives at a new document that is independent of the video itself, so it must contain everything that happens in the video. It represents both a text description and a transcript, making it suitable for deaf-blind users once rendered into Braille.

9.2.2 Interactive Transcripts

Listing 9–2 shows an example of an **interactive transcript** for a media element.

Listing 9–2. Providing an interactive transcript for a video element

```
<video poster="video1.png" controls>
  <source src="video1.mp4"  type="video/mp4">
  <source src="video1.webm" type="video/webm">
  <source src="video1.ogv"  type="video/ogg">
</video>
<div id="speaking" aria-live="rude" style="display: none;">
</div>
<div id="transcriptBox" style="width:60%; float:right;">
  <div id="transcriptText"
       style="height:300px; overflow-y:scroll;">
    <p id="c1" class="cue" data-time="0.0" aria-live="rude" tabindex="1">
      [Screen text: "The orange open movie project presents"]
    </p>
    <p id="c2" class="cue" data-time="5.0" aria-live="rude" tabindex="1">
      [Introductory titles are showing on the background of a water pool with fishes
swimming and mechanical objects lying on a stone floor.]
    </p>
    <p id="c3" class="cue" data-time="12" aria-live="rude" tabindex="1">
      [Screen text: "Elephant's Dream"]
    </p>
    <p id="c4" class="cue" data-time="15.0" tabindex="1">
```

```
        Proog: At the left we can see...  At the right we can see the... the head-snarlers.
Everything is safe. Perfectly safe. Emo? Emo!
        </p>
…
    </div>
  </div>
  <script type="text/javascript">
window.onload = function() {
  // get video element
  var video = document.getElementsByTagName("video")[0];
  var transcript = document.getElementById("transcriptBox");
  var speaking = document.getElementById("speaking");

  // register events for the clicks on the text
  var cues = document.getElementsByClassName("cue");
  for (i=0; i<cues.length; i++) {
    cues[i].addEventListener("click", function(evt) {
      var start = parseFloat(this.getAttribute("data-time"));
      video.currentTime = start;
      video.play();
    }, false);
  }

  // pause video as you mouse over transcript
  transcript.addEventListener("mouseover", function(evt) {
    video.pause();
  }, false);

  // scroll to text as video time changes
  video.addEventListener("timeupdate", function(evt) {
    if (video.paused || video.ended) {
      return;
    }
    for (i=0; i<cues.length; i++) {
      if (video.currentTime >=
              parseFloat(cues[i].getAttribute("data-time")) &&
          video.currentTime <
              parseFloat(cues[i+1].getAttribute("data-time"))) {
        document.getElementById("transcriptText").scrollTop =
              cues[i].offsetTop -
              document.getElementById("transcriptText").offsetTop;
        if (cues[i].getAttribute("aria-live") == "rude") {
          speaking.innerHTML = cues[i].innerHTML;
        }
      }
    }
  }, false);
}
</script>
```

Next to the <video> element, we position a <div> element, which will be given the text cues that a screenreader should read out. It has an @aria-live attribute, which signifies to the screenreader to read out whatever text has changed inside the element as soon as the change happens. Next to that, we display the transcript in a scrollable <div>. Each cue is provided with a @data-time attribute, which contains its start time, and a @tabindex to allow tabbing through it for vision-impaired users' navigation. A cue implicitly ends with the next cue. The JavaScript handles the following functions:

- we register an onclick event on the cues, such that it is possible to use them to navigate around the video.

- we register an onmouseover event on the transcription box, such that the video is paused as soon as you move the mouse into the transcription box for navigation.

- we register an ontimeupdate event on the video, which checks the scrolling position of the text and scrolls it up as necessary, and it also sets the value of the aria-live <div>, such that the respective content is read out.

Figure 9–2 shows the results.

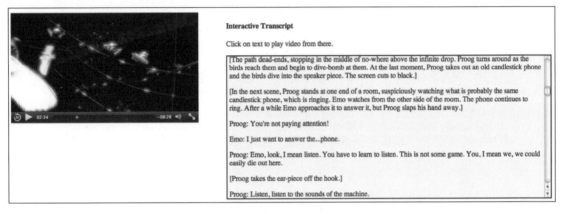

Figure 9–2. Interactive transcript for a video element

The elements as designed here work both for vision-impaired as well as hard-of-hearing users. As you click "play" on the video, the video plays back normally, the caption text that is part of the interactive transcript is displayed in a scrolling display on the right. If you have a screenreader enabled, the markup in the transcript that has been marked with an @aria-live attribute is copied to the screenreader <div> to be read out at the appropriate time.

9.3 Alternative Synchronized Text

While transcriptions provide text alternatives, they are really web page content and not resources that can go with the audio-visual content and be used in desktop applications as well as on the Web. For this purpose we have separate text documents that are synchronized to the audio-visual resources during playback, in particular text descriptions, captions, and subtitles.

We start this subsection by explaining the proposed format for storing such separate text as a baseline format for HTML called WebSRT. Then we explain how such a document format is referenced in HTML markup and synchronized with the media element. Then we move to the in-band representation of this data, and finish with the JavaScript API that is being provided to control such separate text, independent of whether it originated from in-band or an external resource.

9.3.1 WebSRT

WebSRT[6] (Web Subtitle Resource Tracks) is the baseline format under consideration for HTML5 for storing text cues that are supposed to appear in synchronization with an audio or video element.

To be clear, no final decision has been made as to what will be the ultimate baseline format, and other formats could still be adopted. However, right now, the WHATWG version of the HTML5 specification contains the WebSRT specification[7] and most of the browser vendors have indicated that they are willing to undertake test implementations. Nothing, however, has been released at the time of writing of this book.

In this section we introduce WebSRT through examples for the different use cases outlined in Section 9.2.

Note that some of the specification of WebSRT as given in the WHATWG version of HTML5 will almost certainly undergo change, so expect there to be a need to adapt the examples provided here. Some of the changes under discussion at this stage are the introduction of a header and metadata at the beginning of the WebSRT file and a change of the rendering markup. We will stick to the current specification for the purpose of this chapter.

(1) Text Description

An example of a WebSRT file containing a text description is given in Listing 9–3.

Listing 9–3. Example WebSRT file with a text description

```
1
00:00:00,000 --> 00:00:05,000
The orange open movie project presents

2
00:00:05,010 --> 00:00:12,000
Introductory titles are showing on the background of a water pool with fishes swimming and
mechanical objects lying on a stone floor.

3
00:00:12,010 --> 00:00:14,800
Elephants dream

4
00:00:26,100 --> 00:00:28,206
Two people stand on a small bridge.

5
00:00:30,010 --> 00:00:40,000
The old man, Proog, shoves the younger and less experienced Emo on the ground to save him from
being mowed down by a barrage of jack plugs that whir back and forth between the two massive
switch-board-like walls.

6
```

---

[6] See http://www.whatwg.org/specs/web-apps/current-work/websrt.html

[7] See http://www.whatwg.org/specs/web-apps/current-work/multipage/video.html#websrt-0

```
00:00:40,000 --> 00:00:47,000
The plugs are oblivious of the two, endlessly channeling streams of bizarre sounds and data.

7
00:00:48,494 --> 00:00:51,994
Emo sits on the bridge and checks his limbs.

8
00:01:09,150 --> 00:01:16,030
After the squealing plugs move on, Proog makes sure that Emo is unharmed and urges him onwards
through a crack in one of the plug-walls.
```

A WebSRT file contains a sequence of so-called **cues** that have an optional cue identifier, and a start and an end time followed by some text. Cues are separated by two or more newline characters.

If you're familiar with subtitling, you may notice that the above example looks a lot like a typical SRT[8] file as introduced by the SubRip software as a subtitle format. WebSRT as defined at this moment is indeed a compatible extension of SRT with the restriction that WebSRT files have to be provided in the UTF-8 character set, while SRT files can be in any character set. Thus, not all SRT files are legal WebSRT files and most have to be converted to UTF-8 before being usable as a WebSRT file (we recommend use of the open source `iconv` tool for this purpose[9]).

Listing 9–3 has been carefully crafted such that with an average reading speed a screen reader should be able to finish reading the given text cues in the duration given for the cue. But this may not always be the case. In a more general case, it makes a lot more sense for the screen reader to have the ability to pause the video when it reaches the end of its given duration until it has finished speaking every word in the cue. Whether this functionality can be implemented into Web browsers is still an open question.

As a hack to allow for **extended text description** functionality in web browsers, it is possible to specify a pause duration for a description cue, parse this via JavaScript, and pause the video for that duration. This allows specification of heuristic estimates for how long a screen reader will take to read out a cue when there isn't actually time for this cue. Listing 9–4 shows a possible WebSRT file that contains such a duration cue.

Listing 9–4. Example WebSRT file for extended text descriptions

```
1
00:00:00,000 --> 00:00:03,040
<pause>2</pause>
Xiph.org logo

2
00:00:03,040 --> 00:00:05,370
<pause>2</pause>
Redhat logo

3
00:00:05,370 --> 00:00:07,380
<pause>3</pause>
A Digital Media Primer for Geeks
```

---

[8] See http://en.wikipedia.org/wiki/SubRip

[9] See http://en.wikipedia.org/wiki/Iconv

```
4
00:00:07,380 --> 00:00:47,480
<pause>3</pause>
"Monty" Montgomery of Xiph.org

5
00:00:47,480 --> 00:01:03,090
<pause>5</pause>
Monty in front of a whiteboard saying "Consumer—be passive! be happy! look! Kittens!"
```

Note that the <pause> element is something that we made up; it is not part of the WebSRT definition. It is supposed to stop the video element from moving forward along its timelines while the screen reader finishes reading out the cue text. WebSRT allows inclusion of any textual content into the cues. Together with the ability of the <track> element (see next section) to deliver cue content to JavaScript, this flexibility enables Web developers to adapt the functionality of time-synchronized text to their needs. As mentioned above, this particular example is a hack to introduce extended text description functionality while no native solution to this problem is available in the browser yet. It pauses the video for the duration of seconds in the <pause> element at the end of the cue.

(2) Captions

An example of a WebSRT file containing captions is given in Listing 9–5.

Listing 9–5. Example WebSRT file containing captions

```
Proog-1
00:00:15,000 --> 00:00:17,951
At the left we can see...

Proog-2
00:00:18,166 --> 00:00:20,083
At the right we can see the...

Proog-3
00:00:20,119 --> 00:00:21,962
...the head-snarlers

Proog-4
00:00:21,999 --> 00:00:24,368
Everything is safe.
Perfectly safe.

Proog-5
00:00:24,582 --> 00:00:27,000
Emo?
<i>Emo!</i>

Proog-6
00:00:28,206 --> 00:00:29,996
<b>Watch out!</b>
```

Note that in this example we made the cue identifier a string and not a number, which is perfectly valid for a WebSRT file.

Also note that the last two cues in the example extract contain formatting tags, <i></i> for italics and <b></b> for bold. Other allowed markup elements are <ruby></ruby> with <rt></rt> for ruby text inside, and timestamps such as <00:00:29,996> for fine-grained activation of cue text. <ruby> and <rt> are new elements in HTML for short runs of text presented alongside base text, primarily used in East Asian typography as a guide for pronunciation or to include other annotations. Japanese Furigana is an example.

Any further styling can be done using the CSS features 'color', 'text-shadow', 'text-outline', 'background', 'outline', and 'font' through use of CSS pseudo-selectors from within the web page through which a WebSRT file is paired with a media resource.

In Section 9.1.2 we also came across **enhanced captions**. A simple example of captions with enhancement is shown in Listing 9–6.

Listing 9–6. Example WebSRT file containing enhanced captions

```
title-1
00:00:00,000 --> 00:00:02,050
<img src="xifish.png" alt="Xiph logo"/> <a href=http://www.xiph.org/about/ alt="link to
Xiph.org about page">About <i>Xiph.org</i></a>

title-2
00:00:02,050 --> 00:00:05,450
<img src="redhat-logo.jpg" alt="Redhat logo"/> <a href=http://www.redhat.com/ alt="link to
Redhat Website">Sponsored by <b>RedHat</b></a>

title-3
00:00:05,450 --> 00:00:07,450
<a href="http://www.xiph.org/video/vid1.shtml" alt="link to publication web page for
video">Original Publication</a>
<a href="http://webchat.freenode.net/?channels=xiph" alt="link to freenode irc channel for
Xiph">Chat with the creators of the video</a>

1
00:00:08,124 --> 00:00:10,742
<img src="Workstation.jpg" alt="image of workstation"/> Workstations and high end personal
computers have been able to

2
00:00:10,742 --> 00:00:14,749
manipulate <img src="audio_editor.jpg" alt="image of audio editing suite"/> digital audio
pretty easily for about fifteen years now.

3
00:00:14,749 --> 00:00:17,470
It's only been about five years that a decent workstation's been able

4
00:00:17,470 --> 00:00:21,643
to handle <img src="video_editor.jpg" alt="image of video editing suite"/> raw video without a
lot of expensive special purpose hardware.
```

Example 9–6 uses hyperlinks, icon-size images, and text markup to enhance the captions with interactivity and graphics to capture what is going on. Other functionalities, such as more complex CSS, can be included, too. The use of style sheets is again possible through use of CSS pseudo-selectors from within the web page through which a WebSRT file is paired with a media resource. Note that to use this you have to implement the interpretation of the text yourself in JavaScript. Unless the images are really small, some preloading may also be necessary.

(3) Subtitles

Subtitles are not fundamentally different from captions other than the fact that captions contain more transcribed information, in particular about the music used in the video and sound effects, where these make a difference to the perception of the video.

Subtitles transcribe what is being said in a different language to the video's original language. An example of a WebSRT file containing Russian subtitles is given in Listing 9–7.

Listing 9–7. Example WebSRT file containing Russian subtitles

```
1
00:00:08,124 --> 00:00:10,742
Рабочие станции и топовые персональные компьютеры справляются

2
00:00:10,742 --> 00:00:14,749
с обработкой цифрового звука довольно легко последние пятнадцать лет.

3
00:00:14,749 --> 00:00:17,470
Только около пяти лет приличные рабочие станции способны

4
00:00:17,470 --> 00:00:21,643
справляться с несжатым видео без кучи дорогого специализированного оборудования.

5
00:00:21,643 --> 00:00:25,400
Но сегодня даже самый дешевый домашний компьютер имеет процессор и
```

Just as we have extended captions with other markup, we can also extend subtitles with markup. It will look exactly like Listing 9–6, but with the text being in diverse languages. These could include Asian languages that need ruby markup and need to be rendered from top to bottom. All the requirements of internationalization of text are relevant to subtitles, too. Listing 9–8 shows an example of Japanese Furigana markup with the `<ruby>` tag and vertical rendering from top to bottom, top aligned, positioned on the right edge.

Listing 9–8. Example WebSRT file containing Japanese subtitles and rendering instructions

```
00:00:15,042    ‑‑> 00:00:18,042 A:start D:vertical L:98% <ruby>左<rt>ひだり</rt></ruby>に<ruby>
見<rt>み</rt></ruby>えるのは...

00:00:18,750 --> 00:00:20,333 A:start D:vertical L:98% <ruby>右<rt>みぎ</rt></ruby>に<ruby>
見<rt>み</rt></ruby>えるのは.

00:00:20,417 --> 00:00:21,917 A:start D:vertical L:98%
...…首刈り機

00:00:22,000 --> 00:00:24,625 A:start D:vertical L:98%
すべて安全|完璧に安全だ
```

The following rendering instructions, also called "cue settings", are currently specified for WebSRT:

- **vertical text**: D:vertical (growing left) or D:vertical-lr (growing right)—specifies that cue text should be rendered vertically.

- **line position**: L:x% (percent pos) or L:y (+- line pos)—specifies how much above the baseline the cue text should be rendered.

- **text position**: T:x% (percentage of video size)—specifies at what distance from the video's left side the cue text should be rendered.

- **text box size**: S:x% (percentage of video size)—specifies the width of the text box in relation to the video's viewport.

- **alignment**: A:start or A:middle or A:end—specifies whether the text should be start/middle/end aligned.

These are the only rendering instructions available to a WebSRT author. Any further needs for styling and positioning in web browsers can be satisfied through CSS from the web page.

(4) Chapters

Under "Vision-Impaired Users", we discussed that navigation requires a segmentation of the timeline according to semantic concepts. This concept has been captured in WebSRT through so-called *chapter tracks.* Chapter tracks—which could also be called "scenes" or "acts" or anything else that implies a semantic segmentation of the timeline—are larger, semantically relevant intervals of the content. They are typically used for navigation to jump from chapter to chapter or to directly navigate to a semantically meaningful position in the media resource.

An example WebSRT file used for chapter markup appears in Listing 9–9.

Listing 9–9. Example WebSRT file containing chapter markup

```
1
00:00:00,000 --> 00:00:07,298
Opening credits
```

```
2
00:00:07,298 --> 00:03:24,142
Intro

3
00:03:24,142 --> 00:09:00,957
Digital vs. Analog

4
00:09:00,957 --> 00:15:58,248
<group>Digital Audio</group>

5
00:09:00,957 --> 00:09:33,698
Overview

6
00:09:33,698 --> 00:11:18,010
Sample Rate

7
00:11:18,010 --> 00:13:14,376
Aliasing

8
00:13:14,376 --> 00:15:30,387
Sample Format

9
00:15:30,387 --> 00:15:58,248
Channel Count
```

The general format of Listing 9.9 is that of a chapter track as currently defined in the specification. However, the specification does not support hierarchically segmented navigation; that is, navigation at a lower or higher resolution. In Listing 9.9 we experiment with such a hierarchical navigation by introducing a "group" chapter.

Chapter 4 is such a group chapter; that is, it covers multiple chapters which are provided in detail after it. In this case, it covers the time interval of chapters 4-9. This particular use of chapters hasn't yet been standardized. Right now only a linear list of chapters is available.

(5) Lyrics / Karaoke

Under "Learning Support" we mentioned the use of Karaoke or of music lyrics for learning purposes for both foreign-language speakers and people with learning disabilities. In all of these cases we need to present the individual words of a cue successively, such that the reader can follow along better and connect the written words with what is being spoken. This use case can be regarded as a special case of subtitles. WebSRT has a special markup to allow for this functionality.

Listing 9–10 shows an example of a WebSRT file containing Karaoke-style subtitles for a song.

Listing 9–10. Example WebSRT file containing Karaoke-style subtitles for a song

```
1
00:00:10,000 --> 00:00:12,210
<00:00:10,035>Chocolate <00:00:11,000>Rain

2
00:00:12,210 --> 00:00:15,910
<00:00:13,250>Some <00:00:13,500>stay <00:00:13,750>dry <00:00:14,25>and <00:00:14,50>others
<00:00:15,00>feel <00:00:15,25>the <00:00:15,50>pain

3
00:00:15,910 --> 00:00:15,920
<00:00:16,000>Chocolate <00:00:16,500>Rain
<00:00:13,250>Some <00:00:13,500>stay <00:00:13,750>dry <00:00:14,25>and <00:00:14,50>others
<00:00:15,00>feel <00:00:15,25>the <00:00:15,50>pain

4
00:00:15,920 --> 00:00:18,000
<00:00:16,000>Chocolate <00:00:16,500>Rain

5
00:00:18,000 --> 00:00:21,170
<00:00:18,250>A <00:00:18,500>baby <00:00:19,000>born <00:00:19,250>will <00:00:19,500>die
<00:00:19,750>before <00:00:20,500>the <00:00:20,750>sin

6
00:00:21,180 --> 00:00:23,000
<00:00:21,200>Chocolate <00:00:21,500>Rain
```

Note the mid-cue time stamps that allow for a more detailed timing on the words within a cue. There is a CSS pseudo-selector that applies to mid-cue timestamped sections and allows specification of the styling of the text pre- and post-timestamp.

(6) Grammatical Markup

Under "Learning Support" we also mentioned the use of grammatical markup for learning purposes and for people with learning disabilities. An example of a WebSRT file containing a grammatically marked-up transcript is given in Listing 9–11. The <g> tags are made up and do not follow any standard markup provided by WebSRT, but they show how you can go about providing such subtitle- or caption-in-line metadata.

Listing 9–11. Example WebSRT file containing grammatically marked-up subtitles

```
1
00:00:08,124 --> 00:00:10,742
<g noun>Workstations</g> and <g adjective>high end</g> <g adjective>personal</a> <a
noun>computers</g>

2
00:00:10,742 --> 00:00:14,749
```

```
<g verb>have been able to manipulate</g> <g adjective>digital</g> <g noun>audio</g> <g
adverb>pretty easily</g> <g preposition>for</g> <g adjective>about fifteen</g> <g
noun>years</g> <g interjection>now</g>.

3
00:00:14,749 --> 00:00:17,470
<g pronoun>It</g><g verb>'s</g> <g adverb>only</g> <g verb>been</g> <g adjective>about
five</g> <g noun>years</g> <g conjunction>that</g> <g adjective>a decent <g
noun>workstation</g><g verb>'s been able to handle</g>

4
00:00:17,470 --> 00:00:21,643
<g adjective>raw</g> <g noun>video</g> <g preposition>without</g> <g adjective>a lot of</g> <g
adjective>expensive special purpose</g> <g noun>hardware</g>.
```

The rendering of the example in Listing 9–11 is, of course, of paramount importance, since the marked-up text is barely readable. It may be that you choose a different color per grammatical construct, or match it with italics and bold, depending on what you want people to focus on, or just make it such that when you mouse over there is an explanation of the word's grammatical meaning—possibly even matched with a dictionary explanation. This is all up to you to define in your web page—WebSRT simply provides you with the ability to provide this markup in a time-synchronized manner to a video or audio resource.

9.3.2 HTML Markup

In the previous section we learned WebSRT by example. It is still a specification in progress, so we won't go further into detail. WebSRT is one of many existing formats that provide external time-synchronized text for a media resource, and it is likely to become the baseline format with support in many, if not all, browsers because it is so versatile. This is the reason why we discussed it in more depth. Other formats that browsers may support are the Timed Text Markup Language TTML[10] or MPEG-4 Timed Text[11] which is based on an earlier version of TTML and is in use by MPEG-based applications for providing in-band captions. We will look at the handling of in-band time-synchronized text later.

In this section we focus on the markup that has been introduced into HTML to associate such external time-synchronized text resources with a media resource and that triggers download, parsing and potentially rendering of the external resource into a web page.

(1) The <track> element

The HTML specification[12] includes a new element that is to be used inside <audio> and <video> elements. It is called **<track>** and references external time-synchronized text resources that align with the <audio> or <video> element's timeline. Listing 9–12 shows an example for including the WebSRT resource from Listing 9–3 in a web page.

---

[10] See http://www.w3.org/TR/ttaf1-dfxp/

[11] See http://en.wikipedia.org/wiki/MPEG-4_Part_17

[12] See http://dev.w3.org/html5/spec/Overview.html#the-track-element

Listing 9–12. Example of <track> markup with text description WebSRT file

```
<video poster="video1.png" controls>
  <source src="video1.mp4"  type="video/mp4">
  <source src="video1.webm" type="video/webm">
  <source src="video1.ogv"  type="video/ogg">
  <track src="video1_audesc_en.wsrt" kind="descriptions" srclang="en">
</video>
```

Note in particular the **@kind** attribute on the <track> element—it provides the browser with an indication about the type of data that the resource at **@src** should be presented as. The **@srclang** attribute provides an IETF language code according to BCP 47[13]. There are two further attributes available on the <track> element: **@label**, which provides a short label that represents the track in a menu, and **@charset**, which is meant to be used as a hint for track resources where the charset is not clear. This attribute was introduced to allow backward compatibility with plain SRT files, which can use any character set.

The following @kind attribute values are available:

- **subtitles:** Transcription or translation of the dialogue, suitable for when the sound is available but not understood (for example, because the user does not understand the language of the media resource's soundtrack).

- **captions:** Transcription or translation of the dialogue, sound effects, relevant musical cues, and other relevant audio information, suitable for when the soundtrack is unavailable (for example, because it is muted or because the user is deaf).

- **descriptions:** Textual descriptions of the video component of the media resource, useful for audio synthesis when the visual component is unavailable (for example, because the user is interacting with the application without a screen while driving, or because the user is blind).

- **chapters:** Chapter titles, intended to be used for navigating the media resource.

- **metadata:** Tracks intended for use from script.

While we have specified the most useful use cases, we must not forget that there are also use cases for people with cognitive disabilities (dyslexia or color blindness) or for learners of any of these alternative content technologies.

Tracks that are marked as subtitles or as captions will have a default rendering on screen. At the time of writing of this book, the only rendering area under consideration is the video viewport. There are suggestions to also make other CSS boxes available as a rendering target, but these are early days yet. Subtitles and captions can contain simple markup aside from plain text, which includes <i></i> for italics, <b></b> for bold, <ruby><rt></rt><ruby> for ruby markup, and <00:00:00,000> timestamps for word-level timing on cue text.

Tracks marked as descriptions will expose their cues to the screen reader API at the time of their activation. Since screen readers are also the intermediaries to Braille devices, this is sufficient to make the descriptions accessible to vision-impaired users. Descriptions can contain the same kind of simple markup as captions or subtitles. Screen readers can use the italics and bold markup to provide some kind of emphasis, the ruby markup to pick the correct pronunciation, and the timestamps to synchronize their reading speed.

---

[13] See http://www.rfc-editor.org/rfc/bcp/bcp47.txt

Tracks marked as chapters will be exposed by the browser for navigation purposes. It is expected that this will be realized in browsers through a menu or through some kind of navigation markers on the timeline. Past uses of chapters have been analyzed[14].

Finally, tracks marked as metadata will not be exposed by the browser at all, but only exposed in JavaScript in a TimedTrackCueList. The web page developer can do anything they like with this data, and it can consist of any text that the web page scripts want to decode, including JSON, XML, or any special-purpose markup.

Of the WebSRT examples just listed, the following are tracks of type metadata: Listing 9–4 (extended text description), Listing 9–6 (enhanced captions or subtitles), Listing 9–9 (hierarchical chapters), and 9–11 (grammatically marked-up subtitles). The display functionality for these has to be implemented in JavaScript.

For the others, the browsers are expected to provide a default rendering on top of the video viewport: Listing 9–3 (text description—@kind=description), Listing 9–5 (captions—@kind=captions), Listing 9–7 (subtitles—@kind=subtitles, @srclang=ru), Listing 9–8 (subtitles—@kind=subtitles,@srclang=jp) Listing 9–9 for chapters with literal rendering (chapters with literal rendering of cue 4—@kind=chapters), and Listing 9–9 (lyrics—@kind=subtitles).

Listing 9–13 shows a more complete example of a video with multiple types of tracks available.

Listing 9–13. *Example of <track> markup with multiple external WebSRT tracks*

```
<video poster="video6.png" controls>
  <source src="video6.mp4"  type="video/mp4">
  <source src="video6.webm" type="video/webm">
  <source src="video6.ogv"  type="video/ogg">
  <track src="video6_audesc_en.wsrt"  kind="descriptions" srclang="en">
  <track src="video6_chapters_en.wsrt" kind="chapters" srclang="en">
  <track src="video6_en.wsrt"   kind="subtitles" srclang="en">
  <track src="video6_fr.wsrt"    kind="subtitles" srclang="fr">
  <track src="video6_ptbr.wsrt" kind="subtitles" srclang="pt-BR">
  <track src="video6_ru.wsrt"    kind="subtitles" srclang="ru">
  <track src="video6_en_enhanced.wsrt" kind="metadata" srclang="en">
  <track src="video6_en_grammar.wsrt"  kind="metadata" srclang="en">
</video>
```

Language codes in the @srclang attribute are specified according to IETF BCP47[15].

9.3.3 In-band Use

The <track> element allows the association of time-synchronized text tracks with a media resource, and the same effect can be achieved with text tracks that are encoded inside a media resource. Every container format has a different means of "encoding" text tracks. However, the aim of the HTML specification is to provide a uniform interface to the user. This includes the requirement that text tracks that originate from in-band be presented in exactly the same manner to the user as external text tracks. It also means that the same JavaScript API is made available for text tracks no matter whether they originated from in-band or external.

We will look at the JavaScript API in the next section. For now, we want to analyze in some depth what each of the commonly used audio and video container formats have to offer with regards to in-

---

[14] See http://wiki.whatwg.org/wiki/Use_cases_for_API-level_access_to_timed_tracks#Chapter_Markers

[15] See http://www.ietf.org/rfc/bcp/bcp47.txt

band time-synchronized text tracks. We do this at the container level since this is where the choice of time-synchronized text format is being made.

(1) Ogg

The Ogg container offers text tracks in the form of *Kate[16]*, an overlay codec originally designed for Karaoke, but generally used for time-synchronized text encapsulated in Ogg. It is called a "codec" because Kate allows description of much more than just text. There is existing software to encapsulate SRT files in UTF-8 as a *Kate* track and extract it out again without loss. It can take any markup inside a SRT cue. *Kate* supports language tagging (the equivalent of @srclang) and categories (the equivalent of @kind) in the metadata of the text track. In addition, when using Skeleton on Ogg, you can provide a label for the track (the equivalent of @label).

Ogg Kate is a binary encoding of time-synchronized text. There is a textual representation of that binary encoding even though the Kate encoding and decoding tools will also accept other formats, including SRT and LRC (lyrics file format). An example textual Kate file format can be seen in Listing 9–14.

Listing 9–14. Example of the Kate file format as used for Ogg time-synchronized text encapsulation

```
kate {
  defs {
    category "subtitle"
    language "en"
    directionality l2r_t2b
  }
  event {
    id 0
    00:00:15 --> 00:00:17.951
    text "At the left we can see..."
  }
  event {
    id 1
    00:00:18.166 --> 00:00:20.083
    text "At the right we can see the..."
  }
}
```

The textual Kate format starts with a section of defines—header information that helps to determine what is in the file and how it should be displayed. In this example we provide the category, the base language, and the default directionality of display for the text. The cues themselves in Kate in this example have an identifier, a start and end time, and a text.

There are many more parameters in Kate both for the setup section and for cues that can be used to implement support for WebSRT, including markup for cues and positioning information. Kate is very flexible in this respect and a mapping can be provided. Kate is perfectly capable of transporting the cues of WebSRT in an Ogg container, even though the existing software doesn't implement support for WebSRT yet.

---

[16] See http://wiki.xiph.org/OggKate

(2) WebM

The WebM container is a Matroska container. WebM has been specified to only contain VP8 and Vorbis, and no specific choice for a text track format has been made. The idea was to wait until an appropriate text format was chosen as a baseline for HTML5 and use that format to encode text tracks. Interestingly, *Kate* can be encapsulated into Matroska[17], and so can SRT[18]. If WebSRT is picked up as the baseline codec for time-synchronized text, it will be encapsulated into Matroska similarly to the way SRT is currently encapsulated and will then also be added to WebM as a "text codec."

(3) MPEG

The MPEG container has been extended in the 3GPP Forum to carry text tracks[19] as so-called 3GPP Timed Text. This format is similar to QuickTime text tracks[20]. While 3GPP Timed Text is a binary format, several text formats can be used for encoding. QuickTime itself can use the qttext file format[21] (see Listing 9–15 for an example) or the QuickTime TeXML file format[22] (see Listing 9–16 for an example).

Listing 9–15. Example of QTTXT file format as used for QuickTime text tracks

```
{QTtext} {size:16} {font:Lucida Grande} {width:320} {height:42} {language:0}
{textColor:65535,65535,65535} {backColor:0,0,0} {doNotAutoScale:off} {timeScale:100}
{timeStamps:absolute} {justify:center}
[00:00:15.00]
At the left we can see...
[00:00:18.17]
At the right we can see the...
```

Listing 9–16. Example of TeXML file format as used for 3GPP text tracks

```
<?xml version="1.0"?>
<?quicktime type="application/x-quicktime-texml"?>

<text3GTrack
  trackWidth="320.0"
  trackHeight="42.0"
  layer="0"
  language="en"
  transform="translate(0,144)"
  timeScale="600">
  <sample duration="3000">
    <description
      horizontalJustification="Left"
      verticalJustification="Top"
```

---

[17] See http://wiki.xiph.org/OggKate#Matroska_mapping

[18] See http://www.matroska.org/technical/specs/subtitles/srt.html

[19] See http://www.3gpp.org/ftp/specs/html-info/26245.htm

[20] See http://developer.apple.com/library/mac/#samplecode/qttext/Introduction/Intro.html

[21] See http://docs.info.apple.com/article.html?artnum=42643

[22] See http://developer.apple.com/library/mac/#documentation/QuickTime/QT6_3/Chap1/QT6WhatsNew.html

```
      backgroundColor="0%, 0%, 0%, 100%"
      format="tx3g">
      <defaultTextBox width="176" height="36"/>
      <fontTable>
        <font id="1" name="Lucida Grande"/>
      </fontTable>
      <sharedStyles>
        <style id="1">
          {font-table : 1}
          {font-size : 10}
          {font-style : normal}
          {font-weight : normal}
          {text-decoration: normal}
          {color : 100%, 100%, 100%, 100%}
        </style>
      </sharedStyles>
    </description>
    <sampleData targetEncoding="utf8">
      <text styleID="1">
        [00:00:15.00]
        At the left we can see...
        [00:00:18.17]
        At the right we can see the...
      </text>
    </sampleData>
  </sample>
</text3GTrack>
```

A third format used for authoring is GPAC TTXT[23]; see Listing 9–17 for an example. Other formats in use are SRT, SUB, and more recently the W3C Timed Text Markup Language (TTML)[24].

Listing 9–17. Example of TTXT file format as used for 3GPP text tracks

```
<?xml version="1.0" encoding="UTF-8" ?>
<!-- GPAC 3GPP Text Stream -->

<TextStream version="1.0">
  <TextStreamHeader width="320" height="42" layer="0"
                    translation_x="0" translation_y="0">
    <TextSampleDescription horizontalJustification="center"
                           verticalJustification="bottom"
                           backColor="0 0 0 0" verticalText="no"
                           fillTextRegion="no" continuousKaraoke="no"
                           scroll="None">
      <FontTable>
        <FontTableEntry fontName="Lucida Grande" fontID="1"/>
      </FontTable>
```

---

[23] See http://gpac.sourceforge.net/doc_ttxt.php

[24] See http://www.w3.org/TR/ttaf1-dfxp/

```
        <TextBox top="0" left="0" bottom="0" right="0"/>
        <Style styles="Normal" fontID="1" fontSize="36" color="ff ff ff ff"/>
      </TextSampleDescription>
    </TextStreamHeader>

    <TextSample sampleTime="00:00:15.000"
                text="At the left we can see..."/>
    <TextSample sampleTime="00:00:18.166"
                text="At the right we can see the..."/>
</TextStream>
```

Only MP4Box and QuickTime Pro seem to be able to encode 3GPP Timed Text[25], although many hardware and software media players support their decoding.

In the binary encoding there is a configuration section that sets up color, font size, positioning, language, the size of the text box, and so on, similar to the header section of the QTTXT file, the description section of the TeXML file, or the TextStreamHeader of the TTXT file. The data samples are encoded in a different section.

3GPP Timed Text is perfectly capable of transporting the cues of WebSRT in an MP4 container, even though the existing software doesn't implement support for WebSRT yet.

9.3.4 JavaScript API

The JavaScript API for time-synchronized text has been defined to be identical no matter whether the text is sourced from in-band or is externally provided. In addition to these two options there is a means to author and add script-created cues through a MutableTimedTrack interface.

The JavaScript API that is exposed for any of these track types is identical. A media element now has this additional IDL interface:

```
interface HTMLMediaElement : HTMLElement {
...
  readonly attribute TimedTrack[] tracks;
  MutableTimedTrack addTrack(in DOMString kind,
                           in optional DOMString label,
                           in optional DOMString language);
};
```

A media element thus manages a list of TimedTracks and provides for adding TimedTracks dynamically through addTrack().

(1) MutableTimedTrack

The created MutableTimedTrack has the following IDL interface:

```
interface MutableTimedTrack : TimedTrack {
 void addCue(in TimedTrackCue cue);
 void removeCue(in TimedTrackCue cue);
};
```

The constructor for a TimedTrackCue is as follows:

---

[25] See http://en.wikipedia.org/wiki/MPEG-4_Part_17

[Constructor(in *DOMString id*, in *double startTime*, in *double endTime*, in *DOMString text*, in *optional DOMString settings*, in *optional DOMString voice*, in *optional boolean pauseOnExit*)]

The parameters *id*, *startTime*, *endTime*, and *text* represent the core information of a cue—its identifier, time frame of activity and the text to be used during the active time. The *settings* parameter provides positioning and styling information on the cue. The *voice* is a semantic identifier for the speaker or type of content in the cue. The *pauseOnExit* parameter tells the media element to pause playback when the cue *endTime* is reached to allow for something else to happen then.

Listing 9–18 has an example script snippet that uses the core track creation functionality and is expected to work in future implementations of MutableTimedTrack in browsers.

Listing 9–18. Example JavaScript snippet to create a new TimedTrack and some cues in script

```
var video = document.getElementsByTagName("video")[0];
hoh_track = video.addTrack("English HoH", "descriptions", "en");
cue = new TimedTrackCue("1", "00:00:00,000", "00:00:03,040",
                        "<pause>2</pause> Xiph.org logo");
hoh_track.addCue(cue);
cue = new TimedTrackCue("2", "00:00:03,040", "00:00:05,370",
                        "<pause>3</pause> Redhat logo");
hoh_track.addCue(cue);
cue = new TimedTrackCue("3", "00:00:05,370", "00:00:07,380",
                    "<pause>3</pause> A Digital Media Primer for Geeks");
hoh_track.addCue(cue);
```

After creating a new track with English text descriptions, we continue creating new TimedTrackCues and add them to the track. This new track is added to the same list of @tracks for the video to which the resource in-band tracks and the external tracks associated through <track> are also added.

(2) TimedTrack

The timed tracks associated with a media resource in the @tracks attribute are added in the following order:

1. The <track> element children of the media element, in tree order.

2. Tracks created through the addTrack() method, in the order they were added, oldest first.

3. In-band timed text tracks, in the order defined by the media resource's format specification.

The IDL interface on HTMLMediaElement @tracks is a list of TimedTracks. The IDL interface of a TimedTrack is as follows:

```
interface TimedTrack {
  readonly attribute DOMString kind;
  readonly attribute DOMString label;
  readonly attribute DOMString language;
  readonly attribute unsigned short readyState;
           attribute unsigned short mode;
  readonly attribute TimedTrackCueList cues;
  readonly attribute TimedTrackCueList activeCues;
  readonly attribute Function onload;
  readonly attribute Function onerror;
```

```
  readonly attribute Function oncuechange;
};
```

The first three lines capture the value of the @kind, @label, and @srclang attributes of the <track> element, or are provided by the addTrack() function for MutableTimedTracks, or are exposed from metadata in the binary resource for in-band tracks.

The readyState captures whether the data is available and is one of the following: "NONE", "LOADING", "LOADED", or "ERROR". Data is only available in "LOADED" state.

The @mode attribute captures whether the data is activated to be displayed and is either "OFF", "HIDDEN", or "SHOWING". In the "OFF" mode, the UA doesn't have to download the resource, allowing for some bandwidth management with <track> elements.

The @cues and @activeCues attributes provide the list of parsed cues for the given track and the subpart thereof that is currently active, based on the @currentTime of the media element.

The onload, onerror, and oncuechange functions are event handlers for the load, error, and cuechange events of the TimedTrack.

(3) TimedTrackCue

Individual cues expose the following IDL interface:

```
interface TimedTrackCue {
  readonly attribute TimedTrack track;
  readonly attribute DOMString id;
  readonly attribute float startTime;
  readonly attribute float endTime;
  DOMString getCueAsSource();
  DocumentFragment getCueAsHTML();
  readonly attribute boolean pauseOnExit;
  readonly attribute Function onenter;
  readonly attribute Function onexit;
};
```

The @track attribute links the cue to its TimedTrack.

The @id, @startTime, and @endTime attributes expose a cue identifier and its associated time interval. The getCueAsSource() and getCueAsHTML() functions provide either an unparsed cue text content or a text content parsed into a HTML DOM subtree.

The @pauseOnExit attribute can be set to true/false and indicates whether at the end of the cue's time interval the media playback should be paused and wait for user interaction to continue. This is particularly important as we are trying to support extended audio descriptions and extended captions.

The onenter and onexit functions are event handlers for the enter and exit events of the TimedTrackCue.

There are also some positioning and semantic attributes for the TimedTrackCue, but because particularly that part of the specification is still under discussion, we won't elaborate. Please check with the implementations of the browsers as you are trying to implement or use these elements.

9.4 Multitrack Audio/Video

In Section 9.3 we analyzed the use of alternative content technologies that are provided through time-synchronized text. In this section we look at alternative audio and video content and explain some of the challenges that the standardization is currently facing. We have no solutions to offer, since no decisions have been made, but we can explain what kind of solutions will need to be developed.

The following alternative content technologies were mentioned earlier:

- (extended) audio descriptions

- sign language translation

- clear audio

- dubbed audio

Further additional audio-visual tracks may be alternative video angles or alternative microphone positions.

These can be provided either as in-band audio or video tracks, or as separate audio or video resources, which must be synchronized with the main media resource. Sometimes—as is the case for dubbed audio—the respective channel in the main audio resource has to be replaced with this alternative content; sometimes—as is the case for audio descriptions and sign translations—it is additional content.

The extra audio and video tracks or resources create a real or virtual multitrack audio-visual resource for the user. The aim of the browser should therefore be to provide a uniform interface to such multitrack audio-visual resources, both through handling them uniformly in the user interface and in the JavaScript API.

There is indeed a need for development of the following:

- HTML markup to synchronize multiple audio-visual resources together

- a JavaScript API that allows identifying the available types of media tracks, their language, and turning them on and off

The following alternatives are currently under consideration[26]:

- the introduction of a synchronization element for multiple resources, similar to what the <par> element achieves in SMIL[27], together with synchronization control as defined in SMIL 3.0 Timing and Synchronization[28]

- the extension of the <track> mechanism to audio and video tracks

- the introduction of synchronization attributes such as an @mediaSync attribute to declare what element to sync to (instead of <par>) as proposed by Kompozer[29]

What the eventual solution will be is anybody's guess. You should get involved in the standards discussions if you have an opinion and a good proposal.

9.5 Navigation

Thus far in this chapter we have looked at the alternative (or additional) content technologies that can and should be made available for media resources to improve usability of the content for certain audiences. In this section we look at solutions for improving the navigation possibilities within a media

---

[26] See http://lists.w3.org/Archives/Public/public-html-a11y/2010Oct/0520.html

[27] See http://www.w3.org/TR/2005/REC-SMIL2-20050107/smil-timing.html#Timing-ParSyntax

[28] See http://www.w3.org/TR/SMIL3/smil-timing.html#Timing-ControllingRuntimeSync

[29] See http://labs.kompozer.net/timesheets/video.html#syncMaster

resource, into a media resource, and out of a media resource as introduced in the "Navigation" subsection above. This is particularly important for vision-impaired users, but in fact all users will gain improved usability of audio-visual content if it is made more navigable and thus more part of the Web.

9.5.1 Chapters

The first means of introducing navigation possibilities is through chapter markers. These markers provide a means to structure the timeline into semantically meaningful time intervals. The semantic meaning is caught in a short string. A chapter is aligned with a time interval; that is, it has a start and end time. This sounds incredibly familiar and indeed the previously introduced WebSRT format will nicely serve as a means to specify chapter markers. Listing 9–19 has an example.

Listing 9–19. Example WebSRT file created for Chapter markers

```
1
00:00:00,000 --> 00:00:07,298
Opening credits

2
00:00:07,298 --> 00:03:24,142
Intro

3
00:03:24,142 --> 00:09:00,957
Digital vs. Analog
```

Under "HTML Markup" we introduced how chapters provided through such external resources like WebSRT files are combined with media resources using the `<track>` element. Chapters have also been delivered as part of media resources in the past, in particular in QuickTime through QTtext[30], as demonstrated in Listing 9–15. And finally, chapters can also be created using the `MutableTimedTrack` JavaScript API.

When implemented in browsers, a navigation means of some kind is expected to be exposed, for example, a menu or markers along the timeline. The best means still has to be experimented with. In addition to mouse access, there is also a need to make the chapters keyboard accessible.

There may even be a need to allow providing hierarchically structured chapter markers, similar to a table of contents with sections and subsections. These can be specified within the same TimedTrack as overlapping in time. However, right now there is no means to specify the hierarchical level of a chapter marker. An example display of hierarchical chapter markers is provided in Figure 9–3, taken from `http://www.xiph.org/video/vid1.shtml`.

---

[30] See http://developer.apple.com/quicktime/icefloe/dispatch003.html

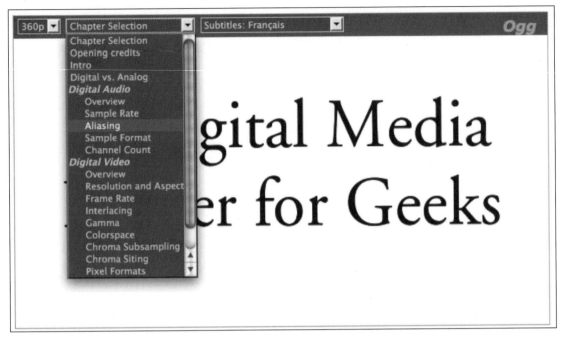

Figure 9–3. Displaying chapter markers

9.5.2 Keyboard Navigation

Another alternative means to the mouse for navigating within media resources is to use the keyboard. This has been discussed in Section 2.4.1. Several browsers are already providing keyboard access to jump around along the timeline of media resources—others are working on it. This functionality allows vision-impaired users a rudimentary form of direct access to time offsets. Further navigation is possible with time-synchronized text through navigation from cue to cue, from word to word, and from voice markup to voice markup. Voice navigation is indeed becoming increasingly important for people with repetitive strain, cognitive, dyslexia, and dexterity issues, or simply for people using a voice input device.

9.5.3 Media Fragment URIs

Means to navigate directly into media content are being standardized through the W3C Media Fragment Working Group. The Media Fragment URI 1.0 spec[31] contains the following syntax options:

---

[31] See http://www.w3.org/TR/media-frags/

1. **Temporal media fragment URIs**:
   For example: `http://example.com/example.ogv#t=10,20`
   These allow direct access to a time offset in a video (with the implicit end being the end of the resource) or to time intervals (with start and end time). The given example specifies the fragment of the media resource from 10 seconds to 20 seconds.

2. **Spatial media fragment URIs**:
   For example: `http://example.com/example.ogv#xywh=160,120,320,240`
   These allow direct access to a region in an image or a video (interval) and will on a video resource probably mostly be used in combination with a temporal dimension. The given example specifies a region that starts at the grid position 160x120 pixels from the top left corner and a 320x240 pixel rectangle.

3. **Track fragment URIs**:
   For example: `http://example.com/example.ogv#track=audio`
   These allow use of only the selected track(s) of a media resource, the audio track in the above example.

4. **Named media fragment URIs**:
   For example: `http://example.com/example.ogv#id=chapter-1`
   These allow direct addressing of the identifier of a marker in one of the other dimensions— typically in the temporal dimension— making it possible to address by semantic rather than syntax. Identifiers of text tracks are a particularly good means of using the named fragment URI specification.

All of these media fragment URIs are expected to be interpreted by the web browser and requests to the server are sent where these fragments can be mapped to a **byte range request**. In an optimal world, no changes to the web server should be necessary since most modern web servers understand how to serve HTTP 1.1 byte ranges. This is particularly true for the **temporal media fragment URIs**—web browsers already need to understand how to map time to byte ranges since they want to allow seeking on the timeline. Therefore, retrieving just a time interval full of media data is simply a matter of having the index of the video available, which tells the browser the mapping between time and byte range.

For the **spatial dimension** byte ranges can typically not be identified because, with typical modern codecs, frame regions are not encoded into separately decodable byte ranges. Therefore, the complete picture dimensions are retrieved and the web browser is expected to apply the fragmentation after receiving the resource. It is expected that web browsers will implement spatial fragmentation as image splicing; that is, they will crop the imagery to the given dimensions. This provides a great focus for the viewer.

Implementation of **track fragmentation** is by only retrieving data that belongs to the requested tracks. This has not been implemented by any web browser, since there is no simple means to get a mapping to byte ranges for tracks. Typically, videos are encoded in such a way that the data of the different tracks is interleaved along the timeline such as to flatten the delivery of the time-parallel tracks and make the track data available to the player at the exact time that it needs it. A media index simplifies identification of byte ranges along the time dimension, but not along the track dimensions. Therefore, the solution to implementing track fragmentation is to retrieve the complete resource and only allow the user access to the requested parts after retrieving the data. Browser vendors will probably only be able to implement this kind of media fragment URI by muting or visually hiding the display of tracks.

Finally, **named media fragment URIs** are basically a means to address temporal or spatial regions by giving them a name. For temporal regions we have already seen means of doing so: providing identifiers on `TimedTrackCues` exactly fulfills that need. For spatial regions it would be necessary to introduce image maps for video with identifiers for regions to allow such named addressing. We cannot see that happen in the near future, so we'll focus on cue identifiers for now as the source of named media fragment URI addresses.

Media fragment URIs will be used basically in three distinct ways for direct access navigation in browsers:

1. As URLs in the @src attribute or <source> elements of the <video> or <audio> elements.

2. As direct URLs into just the media resource presented as the only content

3. As part of web page URLs to identify to the browser that a media resource needs to be displayed with an active fragmentation rather than with the settings given through the @currentSrc using a URL such as http://example.com/page.html#video[0]:t=10.

All three cases are about displaying just the media fragment. In the first two cases it is simply a media fragment URI as specified. If the media controls are shown, they will likely have a highlight on the transport bar for the selected time range or chapter. However, no browser has implemented support for media fragments yet, so this cannot be confirmed as yet.

The third case has not been standardized yet, so it is right now a matter of the web page author to make use of and resolve such a URL. The web page author would reset the @currentSrc of a media element on a page with the given URL fragment information using JavaScript. It is possible that if such use becomes common it will at a later stage be turned into a standard URL scheme for HTML pages. Listing 9–20 shows an example JavaScript extract for dealing with web page URI fragments such as #video[0]:t=10&video[1]:t=40.

Listing 9–20. Example JavaScript for dealing with time offsets on page hash

```
// when the hash on the window changes, do an offset
window.addEventListener("hashchange", function() {
  var url = location.href;
  setVideoTimeFragments(url);
}, false);

// parse the time hash out of the given url
function setVideoTimeFragments(url) {
  var fragment = url.split("#")[1];
  if (fragment == null) return;
  var params = fragment.split("&");
  for (i=0; i<params.length; i++) {
    var name = params[i].split("=")[0];
    var video = name.split("video[")[1].split("]")[0];
    var value = params[i].split("=")[1];
    videos[video].currentTime = value;
  }
}
```

At the time of writing of this book only Opera had experimented with an implementation of temporal media fragment URIs in <video> elements. No released browser supports media fragment URIs yet.

9.5.4 URLs in Cues

Finally, in order to navigate out of media content, one has to introduce hyperlinks inside media resources. The most appropriate means for this is to have them as part of the markup of cues in text tracks. This can be achieved by introducing hyperlinks into WebSRT cues—something that has previously been discussed in the context of enhanced captions or enhanced subtitles. It is also possible to be introduced into text descriptions and would then allow vision-impaired users to jump from hyperlink to hyperlink inside audio or video resources. An example use of URLs in WebSRT cues was shown in Listing 9–6.

9.6 Accessibility Summary

Table 9–1 provides an overview of the identified accessibility functions and their planned or specified possibilities of realization in HTML5.

Table 9–1. Overview of all the media accessibility functions

Function	Possibility 1	Possibility 2	Possibility 3	Possibility 4
(extended) audio description	Mixed into the main audio track	In-band of media resource as extra audio track	External audio resource to sync with main media resource	–
(extended) text description	–	In-band of media resource as extra text track	External text resource (for example, WebSRT) to sync with main media resource	Added dynamically through JavaScript API
(enhanced) captions	Mixed into the main video track	In-band of main resource as extra text track	External text resource (for example, WebSRT) to sync with main media resource	Added dynamically through JavaScript API
Sign language translation	Mixed into the main video track	In-band of main resource as extra video track	External video resource to sync with main media resource	–
Clear audio	–	In-band of main resource as extra audio track	External audio resource to sync with main media resource	–
Subtitles / Lyrics / Karaoke / Metadata	Mixed into the main video track	In-band of main resource as extra text track	External text resource (for example, WebSRT) to sync with main media resource	Added dynamically through JavaScript API

Function	Possibility 1	Possibility 2	Possibility 3	Possibility 4
Dubbed audio	Replacing the main audio track	In-band of main resource as extra audio track	External audio resource to replace main audio track	–
Semantic Navigation: chapters	–	In-band of main resource as extra text/navigation track	External text resource (for example, WebSRT) to sync with main media resource	Added dynamically through JavaScript API
Transcription	Plain on web page next to media resource	Linked web page next to media resource display	Interactive transcript on web page scrolling in sync with media playback	–
More Navigation:	Keyboard controls to navigate within resource	Media fragment URIs to navigate into resource	URLs in text track cues to navigate out of resource	–
Activate / deactivate	User preferences	Interactive selection in user menu	Activate / deactivate through JavaScript API	–

We started this chapter by analyzing alternative content technologies that users with different needs require from accessibility technology. We looked at the needs of vision-impaired users, hard-of-hearing users, deaf-blind users, and of people using the material for learning or internationalization purposes.

We then analyzed content technologies that have been created to provide access to people with these special needs. We covered transcriptions, text descriptions, captions, subtitles, chapters, lyrics/karaoke, and grammatical markup examples. In HTML5 the solutions created for the text-based alternative content technologies are the WebSRT file format, the `<track>` element, and a JavaScript API that does not distinguish between accessibility tracks that were provided through the `<track>` element or came directly from the media resource. Even the navigation requirements can be satisfied using WebSRT.

CHAPTER 10

■ ■ ■

Audio and Video Devices

In this chapter we look at the efforts that are being made to allow HTML5 to access audio and video devices and to use these for live communications such as audio and video conferencing.

The specifications in this domain are still very raw. We will touch upon the components under consideration with no guarantee that any of them will actually persist in the future. Interesting trial implementations exist and will be discussed, since they lead the way. The main trial implementation that we will refer to is one by Ericsson, which is an internal branch of WebKit and not publicly available.

We are concerned in this chapter with the <device> element, the Stream API, and the use of WebSockets in conjunction with the <audio> and <video> elements. But let's start with an overview of different architectural scenarios for which external devices can be used.

10.1 Architectural Scenarios

Device access by a web browser can take on several forms, from simply transporting data from an external device into the browser for display in <audio> or <video>, to recording from an audio/video device to a file on a server, all the way to teleconferencing with another browser.

In these and similar scenarios, the following components are necessary:

1. a means to access and control a device (camera, microphone): the <device> element

2. transcoding the camera/microphone data to another format: the Stream API

3. saving to an audio or video file: the File API

4. transporting the audio/video data to a connected peer: the ConnectionPeer API or the WebSocket API

5. display of the audio/video data: the <audio> and <video> elements

We already know how to perform the last part: how to get data into an <audio> or <video> element. Let's approach the other components one by one.

10.2 The <device> element

The **<device>** element represents a device selector, to give the user the ability to allow the web page access to a device, for example, a video camera or microphone. This is done through a dialog interface that pops up and asks the user to choose which devices to grant access to. See Figure 10–1 for an example as implemented by Ericsson[1].

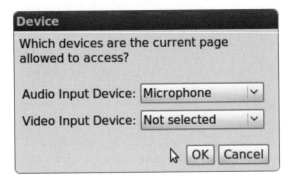

Figure 10–1. Ericsson's implementation of the <device> element in WebKit

@type

The <device> element has a single attribute @type. This is where you specify which kind of device the page wants to access through that <device> element.

   The attribute can take on one of the following values:

- media: for a stream of audio/video data such as a Webcam and Microphone — returns a Stream object

- fs: for a filesystem device such as a DVD player — returns a LocalFS object

- and some others that specify types of ports (usb, rs232) rather than devices, and for which it is unclear if they will continue to be supported in the future

   The example in Figure 10–1 will be created through Listing 10–1. Note that Ericsson used an old type called "video_capture", which was later renamed "media".

Listing 10–1. Creating a device selector for a video stream

```
<device type="media">
</device>
```

@data

The data resulting from the <device> element is available through the @data IDL attribute to JavaScript. It is of dynamic type, being a Stream object for type="media".

---

[1] See https://labs.ericsson.com/developer-community/blog/beyond-html5-conversational-voice-and-video-implemented-WebKit-gtk

10.3 The Stream API

The Stream API consists of a Stream and a StreamRecorder interface as follows:

```
interface Stream {
  readonly attribute DOMString url;
  StreamRecorder record();
};
interface StreamRecorder {
  File stop();
};
```

Self-view video

The <device> element in conjunction with a Stream object can be used to take the video from a webcam, turn it into a video URL, and display it in a <video> element. Ericsson has an example implementation of this in WebKit.[2] Listing 10–2 shows the required JavaScript code as per the current specification.

Listing 10–2. Displaying captured video from a device in a <video> element

```
<device type="media"></device>
<video width="320" height="240"></video>
<script type="text/javascript">
  var video, videoDevice;
  window.onload = function() {
    videoDevice = document.getElementsByTagName("device")[0];
    video = document.getElementsByTagName("video")[0];
    videoDevice.addEventListener("change", play, false);
  }
  function play() {
    var videoStream = this.data;
    video.src = videoStream.url;
    video.play();
  }
</script>
```

The Stream API allows us to turn the data received from a <device> element into a URL that can be used by the <video> element. Data will be received from the <device> element as soon as the user has chosen the device in the <device> element. This event is raised in an onChange event.

Figure 10–2 shows a still from a YouTube video that Ericsson shot of a working implementation of the self-view video, as described here.[3]

---

[2] See https://labs.ericsson.com/developer-community/blog/beyond-html5-implementing-device-and-stream-management-WebKit

[3] See http://www.youtube.com/watch?v=VjJ7EsJSgVk

Figure 10–2. Ericsson's implementation of the self-view example

The picture shows the <device> selector and underneath it the video with the stream as coming from the camera. The device is using a Webcam mounted onto the computer and pointed at the little playmobil guy, which can be seen clearly in the screenshot, but also in the video element on the monitor at the back.

Recording

As the next step we can use the Stream API to record from local devices. Ericsson has also done some experiments with Stream and StreamRecorder objects for this type of application.[4] A StreamRecorder object is created from a Stream by using the Stream's **record**() function. Listing 10–3 shows how this is done from a media source.

---

[4] See https://labs.ericsson.com/developer-community/blog/beyond-html5-audio-capture-web-browsers

Listing 10–3. Recording media from a device

```
<device type="media"></device>
<input type="button" value="Record" disabled></input>
<script type="text/javascript">
  var device = document.getElementsByTagName("device")[0];
  var button = document.getElementsByTagName("input")[0];
  var recording = false;
  window.onload = function() {
    device.addEventListener("change", enableButton, false);
    button.addEventListener("click", recordToggle, false);
  }
  function enableButton() {
    var stream = this.data;
    button.disabled = false;
  }
  function recordToggle() {
    if (!recording) {
      recorder = stream.record();
      recording = true;
      button.value = "Stop";
    } else {
      file = recorder.stop();
      // do something with the file
      upload(file);
      recording = false;
      button.value = "Record";
    }
  }
}
</script>
```

Here we have a button that activates or stops the recording. When the <device> element is ready, the button is enabled through the onChange event. When the button is clicked, recording is started if it wasn't recording, or stopped if it was. When recording is stopped, a media file has been created.

It is unclear how to distinguish between a recorded audio or video file at this time, since only a blob (binary large object) of type File is created. There used to be a distinction between a <device> of type "video_capture" and "audio_capture", but that seems to have been removed. It is possible that this is supposed to be a Blob object[5], which actually has a MIME type and so could distinguish audio and video recording results.

To handle the created file, you may want to check out the File API[6] specification in more detail. You can, for example, turn it into a temporary URL through the createObjectURL() method[7] and show a preview of the recorded file, or do local editing before uploading it to the server through an XMLHttpRequest. That is, once browsers have actually implemented the <device> and Stream API functionalities.

---

[5] See http://www.w3.org/TR/FileAPI/#dfn-Blob

[6] See http://www.w3.org/TR/FileAPI/

[7] See http://www.w3.org/TR/FileAPI/#dfn-createObjectURL

10.3 The WebSocket API

The next application that is enabled with the <device> element is video communication, such as video-conferencing. This is where things become rather underspecified.

One approach to exchanging the video data created from a <device> element with another service bi-directionally is WebSockets. This is the approach used by a further example implementation by Ericsson.[8] WebSockets are supported by all major browsers (Opera currently with a trial release, but included in 10.70). Let's start by understanding how WebSockets work.

WebSockets API

WebSockets provide a JavaScript API for bi-directional communication between a browser and a server natively by using a WebSocketProtocol running directly on TCP instead of using HTTP. WebSockets communicate over a single TCP connection that is kept open between the browser and server. It is even possible to multiplex several WebSockets over a single TCP connection. Every data exchange only contains the data in question and thus WebSockets do not attract the overhead that Ajax attracts, where every XMLHttpRequest creates a new HTTP exchange.

We're not providing much detail here; we encourage the interested reader to check out the W3C specification for WebSockets[9]. An example WebSocket exchange can be seen in Listing 10–4, adapted from websockets.org[10] for a simple text echo service.

Listing 10–4. Simple WebSocket example using the websocket.org echo service

```
<div id="output"></div>
<script type="text/javascript">
  var output = document.getElementById("output");
  var socket = new WebSocket('ws://websockets.org:8787/echo');
  socket.addEventListener("open", onOpen, false);
  socket.addEventListener("close", onClose, false);
  socket.addEventListener("message", onMessage, false);
  function onOpen () {
    output.innerHTML += "CONNECTED<br/>";
    message = "Here comes the data";
    socket.send(message);
    output.innerHTML += "SENT: " + message + "<br/>";
  }
  function onClose() {
    output.innerHTML += "DISCONNECTED<br/>";
  }
  function onMessage(evt) {
    output.innerHTML += '<span style="color: blue;">RESPONSE: '
                        + evt.data+'</span><br/>';
    socket.close();
  }
</script>
```

---

[8] See https://labs.ericsson.com/developer-community/blog/beyond-html5-conversational-voice-and-video-implemented-WebKit-gtk

[9] See http://dev.w3.org/html5/websockets/

[10] See http://www.websockets.org/echo.html

A WebSocket is created that sets up a connection to a web server. Once the connection is established, data frames can be sent back and forth between the client and the server in full-duplex mode. The send() method allows the sending of frames and the onMessage event notifies of the arrival of a message and provides that message. Since WebSockets are implemented in all modern browsers, we can provide a screenshot of the example in Listing 10–4; see Figure 10–3.

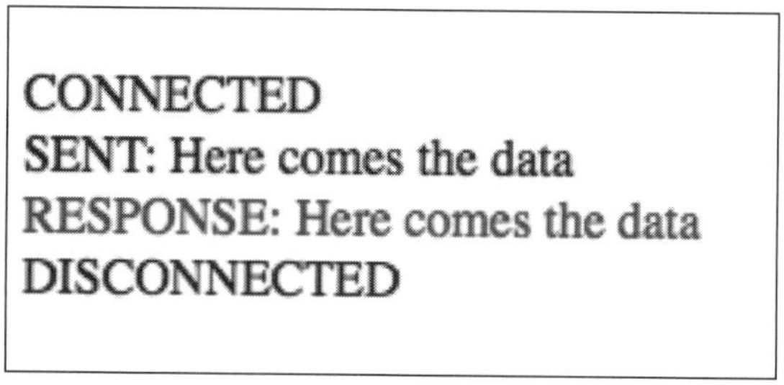

CONNECTED
SENT: Here comes the data
RESPONSE: Here comes the data
DISCONNECTED

Figure 10–3. WebSockets example of an echo server

For security reasons, WebSockets are not the same as raw TCP sockets. Instead, WebSockets extend the HTTP protocol by defining a special handshake between the browser and the server so they can establish a connection. Once both client and server have opted into the protocol, the message exchange can happen without further overhead.

A WebSocket with a server is not sufficient to set up a two-way video exchange, for example a video conference. What is required is a web server that connects two browsers together and hands on data from one to the other. Let's look at an example for this.

Message exchange

In the following example, we will set up a WebSocket server that takes messages from a user and broadcasts them to all connected users. In this way it is possible to share a local action with a remotely connected user.

First we set up the server. For this we use node.js[11] as a light-weight web server that runs applications written in JavaScript. We also install the Node WebSocket Server[12] called websocket-server, which provides WebSocket functionality to JavaScript server applications. Now we are running a WebSocket-enabled evented I/O framework for which we can easily write a WebSocket server.

The WebSocket server that we require will listen on a certain port for incoming WebSocket requests, accept connections, return an identifier to the connection requestor, and broadcast all incoming messages out to all connected WebSocket clients. Listing 10–5 has the details.

Listing 10–5. A WebSocket server written in JavaScript for node.js that broadcasts all incoming messages

```
var ws = require("./websocket-server/lib/ws");
var server = ws.createServer();
server.addListener("connection", function(conn){
  conn.send("** Connected as: "+conn.id);
```

---

[11] See http://nodejs.org/

[12] See https://github.com/miksago/node-websocket-server/

```
    conn.addListener("message", function(msg){
      server.broadcast("<"+conn.id+"> "+msg);
    });
  });
  server.addListener("close", function(conn){
    server.broadcast("<"+conn.id+"> disconnected");
  });
  server.listen(8080);
```

We send the connection acknowledgement back to the connecting client only, so it can identify its connection number, which makes it possible to later separate its own messages from the messages of other browsers.

Now we can write the web page that makes use of the WebSocket server to exchange messages. Listing 10–6 has the details.

Listing 10–6. A client for the WebSocket server in Listing 10–5 that sends which buttons are pressed

```
<input type="button" value="Play"></input>
<input type="button" value="Pause"></input>
<div id="output"></div>
<script type="text/javascript">
  var buttonPlay = document.getElementsByTagName("input")[0];
  var buttonPause = document.getElementsByTagName("input")[1];
  var output = document.getElementById("output");
  var socket = new WebSocket('ws://localhost:8080/');
  socket.addEventListener("open", onOpen, false);
  socket.addEventListener("close", onClose, false);
  socket.addEventListener("message", onMessage, false);
  buttonPlay.addEventListener("click", sendPlay, false);
  buttonPause.addEventListener("click", sendPause, false);
  function onOpen () {
    output.innerHTML += "CONNECTED<br/>";
  }
  function onClose() {
    output.innerHTML += "DISCONNECTED<br/>";
  }
  function onMessage(evt) {
    output.innerHTML += 'RESPONSE: ' + evt.data;
  }
  function sendPlay() {
    message = "Play";
    socket.send(message);
    output.innerHTML += "SENT: " + message + "<br/>";
  }
  function sendPause() {
    message = "Pause";
    socket.send(message);
    output.innerHTML += "SENT: " + message + "<br/>";
  }
</script>
```

This client is a fairly simple extension of the previous example in Listing 10–4. The page has two buttons. It connects to the web server that we created before and is running with `node` through port 8080. When the user clicks on one of the buttons, the button value will be packaged into the text content of the WebSocket data, sent to the WebSocket server, and then the server broadcasts it out to everyone connected. When the web page receives a message, it prints it. Figure 10–4 has examples of two web browsers connected to the same WebSocket server.

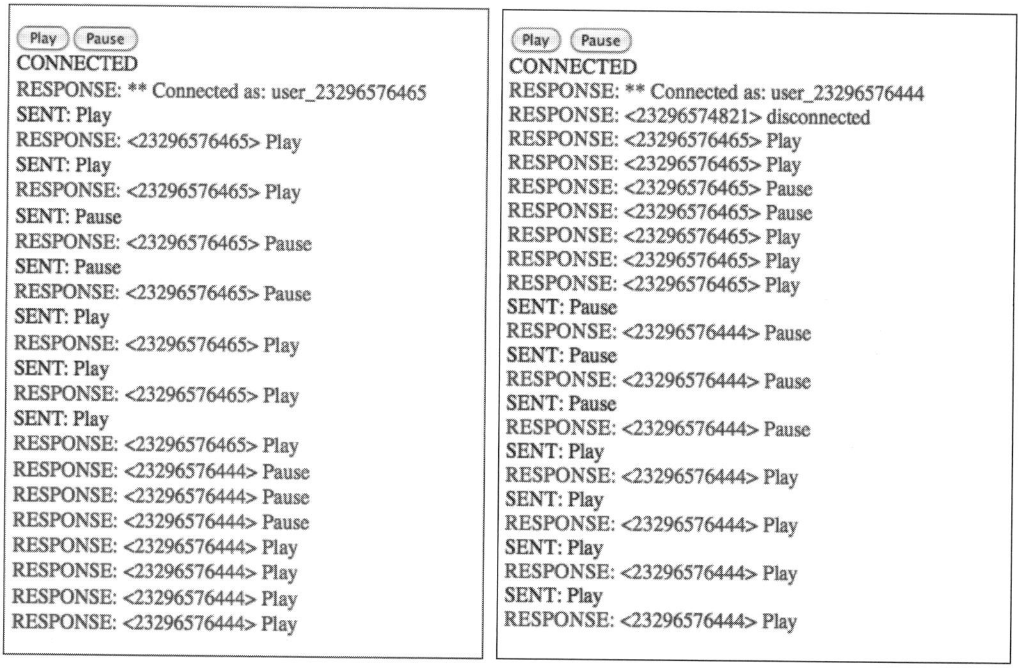

Figure 10–4. WebSocket example of communicating sides, left in Firefox, right in Google Chrome

You will notice that the blue (if you're looking at this in black-and-white: the grey) lines are all responses, whereas the black ones are sent requests. The browser on the left (Firefox) is connected under the id 23296576465, the one on the right (Google Chrome) under 23296576444. We start by clicking "Play", "Play", "Pause", "Pause", "Play", "Play", "Play" in Firefox and can see that the response is received by both Firefox and Google Chrome. Then we do a few clicks in Google Chrome and again the responses are received by both browsers.

Shared video control

To make the WebSocket message-passing example a bit more useful, let's use it to control a video from multiple browsers. You can imagine a use case where you share a web page with your friends for shared remote viewing of a video and you all get to have control over the position and state of the video — if one of you pauses, all players pause — if one seeks, all players seek.

Listing 10–7 shows the code for the web page. It still uses the same server as in Listing 10–5.

Listing 10–7. A client for the WebSocket server in Listing 10–5 that allows shared video viewing

```
<video controls>
    <source src="video1.mp4" type-"video/mp4">
    <source src="video1.webm" type="video/webm">
    <source src="video1.ogv" type="video/ogg">
</video>
<script type="text/javascript">
  window.onload = function() {
    var video = document.getElementsByTagName("video")[0];
    var socket = new WebSocket('ws://localhost:8080/');
    socket.addEventListener("message", onMessage, false);
    video.addEventListener("play", sendPlay, false);
    video.addEventListener("pause", sendPause, false);
    video.addEventListener("seeked", sendSeek, false);
    var me = "";
    var prev_seek = 0;
    function onMessage(evt) {
      pos = evt.data.indexOf("Connected as:");
      if (pos != -1) {
        // identify myself
        me = evt.data.substring(pos+14);
      } else {
        id = evt.data.match(/<(.*?)>/);
        if (id[1] != me) {
          // execute commands if from peer
          pos = evt.data.indexOf(">");
          switch (evt.data.substring(pos+2,pos+7)) {
            case "play ": video.play(); break;
            case "pause": video.pause(); break;
            case "seek ":
              seekTime = evt.data.substring(20);
              if (prev_seek != parseFloat(seekTime)) {
                video.currentTime = parseFloat(seekTime);
              }
              break;
            default:
          }
        }
      }
    }
    function sendPlay() {
      socket.send("play ");
    }
    function sendPause() {
      socket.send("pause");
    }
    function sendSeek() {
      prev_seek = video.currentTime;
      msg = "seek "+prev_seek;
      socket.send(msg);
    }
  }
</script>
```

We set up a WebSocket with the server. All involved clients will connect to the same WebSocket service and thus they all share the same messages. We set up a video element and callbacks for the "play", "pause", and "seeked" events, which send a text message to the WebSocket service and broadcast these messages to all other browsers. As we receive a message from the WebSocket service, and it's not a message that we have sent ourselves, we execute the video.play(), video.pause(), or video.currentTime seek actions to replicate the actions of the video elements in the other clients.

We have to be careful with the seek action, though, because when we seek, others will seek, too, and we will go into an endless loop of seeks as the clients tell each other that they have just seeked and need that replicated. We avoid that by only seeking again if we receive a new seekTime from another client. For a real-world implementation of such a service we recommend a more robust implementation - for example use of more informative messages in JSON - that will signify if a seek was user-originated or just an acknowledgement for executing a remote command.[13]

Figure 10–5 shows the result in three parallel running browsers: Chrome, Safari, and Opera.

Figure 10–5. WebSocket example of communicating videos in Chrome, Safari, and Opera

As a user controls the video in one browser, all the other browsers receive the events and replicate the same actions. You should try it out for yourself with a friend at http://html5videoguide.net/.

Video conferencing

With WebSockets we have seen a means to share data through a web server with other browser instances. This now paves the way for hooking up the <device> element and a local camera and microphone with a remote viewer.

Ericsson has made an implementation of a video chat web application using HTML5[14] based on WebSockets. It builds on the earlier introduced implementation of self-view video in Listing 10–2.

---

[13] Here is an example implementation in Java using Glassfish: http://weblogs.java.net/blog/spericas/archive/2010/09/29/web-sockets-and-html5-glassfish

[14] See https://labs.ericsson.com/developer-community/blog/beyond-html5-conversational-voice-and-video-implemented-WebKit-gtk

To use WebSockets for a video chat application one needs to transport **binary data**. However, right now the WebSocket API is restricted to only deliver text strings. It is possible to encode binary data as text, e.g. through base64 encoding[15], however that will introduce the need to encode the data before transmission and decode afterwards, adding delay to a video pipeline that already has network delay and where real-time is of utmost importance. Work is ongoing to introduce such binary content functionality into the WebSocket standard. Ericsson has a trial implementation.

In addition to the extension of the WebSocket functionality, Ericsson also had to hook up the media data coming out of the Stream API to the WebSockets and make sure the data is handed on to the right peer. As shown in the shared video control example, Listing 10–7, managing the data flow is important so as not to overload the network or the receivers. Ericsson introduced a MediaStreamManager to package audio-visual data from the Stream URIs for WebSocket transport. They also introduced a MediaStreamTransceiver to control the network transport and data flow over WebSockets.

The core of their resulting example web page for video conferencing is replicated in Listing 10–8.

Listing 10–8. A video conferencing web page example using WebSockets and the <device> element

```
<device type="media"></device>
<video width="320" height="240" id="self_view"></video>
<video width="320" height="240" id="remote_video"></video>
<script type="text/javascript">
  var transceiver = new
    MediaStreamTransceiver("ws://150.132.141.60:8880/delayswitch?sid=0");

  var videoDevice = document.getElementsByTagName("device")[0];
  var selfView = document.getElementById("self_view");
  var remoteVideo = document.getElementById("remote_video");
  videoDevice.addEventListener("change", playLocal, false);
  transceiver.addEventListener("connect", playRemote, false);

  function playLocal(evt) {
    var videoStream = this.data;
    // exclude audio from the self view
    selfView.src = videoStream.url + "#video";
    selfView.play();
    // set the stream to share
    transceiver.localStream = videoStream;
  }
  function playRemote() {
    remoteVideo.src = transceiver.remoteStream.url;
    remoteVideo.play();
  }
</script>
```

This page first sets up a device element and a video element each for local and remote playback. In JavaScript it then creates a MediaStreamTransceiver which enables the connection and communication to another browser identified through the stream identifier (sid) provided in the WebSocket URL. As the user chooses a local device to take video input from, the video self-view is activated and the stream handed on to the transceiver for remote sharing. This causes the connected party at the other end to receive a connect event on their MediaStreamTransceiver object. The video element that is set up for display of the remote stream then is handed the URL of the remote stream and set to play.

---

[15] See http://en.wikipedia.org/wiki/Binary-to-text_encoding

Note that for the local self-view video, the audio channel is turned off. Ericsson has created a specific video URI for this with a "#video" fragment. This allows them to single out the video track from the media resource and just play that back. The media fragment URI, as discussed in the previous chapter, would be useful for this example and already provides a specification for addressing specific tracks in a media resource. To extract just the video track out of an audio-visual resource would require a URI fragment of the following form: "#track=video". Neither is implemented by default in any released browser, so do not expect this functionality to be available in <video> elements at this stage.

Ericsson's experiments were undertaken on a patched WebKit version and show the amazing possibilities of this technology. Figure 10–6 shows a screenshot of Ericsson's demo video of the video chat. They even applied CSS3 transformations to the video to show the full potential of the technology when available in HTML5.

Figure 10–6. WebSocket-based video chat demo by Ericsson[16]

10.3 The ConnectionPeer API

The use of WebSockets for many-to-many communication is somewhat limiting. You always have a server in the middle through which the data is replicated to everyone else. This makes sense in an application where many people are working together so you don't have to build an *n*-by-*n* connection

---

[16] See https://labs.ericsson.com/developer-community/blog/beyond-html5-conversational-voice-and-video-implemented-WebKit-gtk

network, but rather just *n* connections to a single server. However, where only two peers are involved, a direct connection without the intermediary web server is a lot more resourceful.

The WHATWG has a `ConnectionPeer` API[17] under development which is expected to provide this functionality. Since the API is still very immature, we will not go into much detail here. The idea is that a third-party server is used to gain information about the other party, which allows setting up a direct connection. During the connection setup, there will be an exchange of their respective configuration to agree on the protocol and share their respective IP addresses and other necessary details. Once connected, there will be functions such as the following:

- sendText() — to send straight text

- sendBitmap() — to send HTMLImageElements

- sendFile() — to send arbitrary files

- addStream() — to send a video or audio stream

Similar to how WebWorkers hand on URLs, an `addStream()` method would also create a message callback (tentatively called *onStream*) which would allow retrieval of the remote video URL to set a `<video>` element's @src attribute to it for playback. The specification has some examples with a code outline, in case you are curious.[18] This part of the specification will still need a substantial amount of work before we will see it rolled out in browsers.

10.4 Summary

In this chapter we took a peek at the possibilities that the `<device>` element introduces into the web browser. This part of the HTML5 specification is still very raw and will likely see many changes before stable implementations in browsers will exist. We were able to use the WebSocket functionality to implement message passing between browser instances about video states and thus demonstrate a shared video viewing application. Once this can be hooked up with the functionality of the `<device>` element, we will see real-time video communication features become common practice in web applications.

---

[17] See http://www.whatwg.org/specs/web-apps/current-work/complete/commands.html#peer-to-peer-connections

[18] See http://www.whatwg.org/specs/web-apps/current-work/complete/commands.html

■■■

Summary and Outlook

It has been a long journey—almost 300 pages about a couple of new elements in HTML. Who would have thought there was this much to learn. However, realistically, we are only at the start of what will be possible with audio and video in the coming years. Right now we are only seeing the most basic functionality of multimedia implemented on the Web. Once the technology stabilizes, publishers and users will follow, and with them businesses, and further requirements and technologies will be developed. However, for now, we have a fairly complete overview of existing functionalities.

Before giving you a final summary of everything that we have analyzed in this book, let us mention two more areas of active development.

A.1 Outlook

Two further topics deserve a brief mention: metadata and quality of service metrics. Both of these topics sound rather ordinary, but they enable functionalities that are quite amazing.

A.1.1 Metadata API

The W3C has a Media Annotations Working Group[1]. This group has been chartered to create "an ontology and API designed to facilitate cross-community data integration of information related to media objects in the Web, such as video, audio, and images". In other words: part of the work of the Media Annotations Working Group is to come up with a standardized API to expose and exchange metadata of audio and video resources. The aim behind this is to facilitate interoperability in search and annotation.

In the Audio API chapter we have already come across something related: a means to extract key information about the encoding parameters from an audio resource through the properties `audio.mozChannels`, `audio.mozSampleRate`, and `audio.mozFrameBufferLength`.

The API that the Media Annotations Working Group is proposing is a bit more generic and higher level. The proposal is to introduce a new Object into HTML which describes a media resource. Without going into too much detail, the Object introduces functions to expose a list of properties. Examples are media resource identifiers, information about the creation of the resource, about the type of content, content rights, distribution channels, and ultimately also the technical properties such as framesize, codec, framerate, sampling-rate, and number of channels.

While the proposal is still a bit rough around the edges and could be simplified, the work certainly identifies a list of interesting properties about a media resource that is often carried by the media

---

[1] See http://www.w3.org/2008/WebVideo/Annotations/

resource itself. In that respect, it aligns with some of the requests from archival organizations and the media industry, including the captioning industry, to make such information available through an API.

Interesting new applications are possible when such information is made available. An example application is the open source Popcorn.js semantic video demo[2]. Popcorn.js is a JavaScript library that connects a video, its metadata, and its captions dynamically with related content from all over the Web. It basically creates a mash-up that changes over time as the video content and its captions change.

Figure A–1 has a screenshot of a piece of content annotated and displayed with popcorn.js.

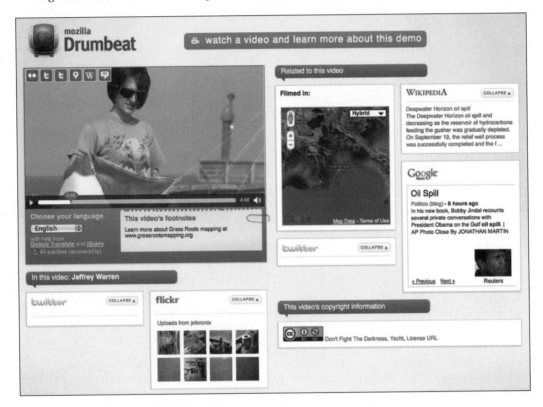

Figure A–1. A screenshot of a video mashup example using popcorn.js

A.1.2 Quality of Service API

A collection of statistics about the playback quality of media elements will be added to the media element in the near future. It is interesting to get concrete metrics to monitor the quality of service (QoS) that a user perceives, for benchmarking and to help sites determine the bitrate at which their streaming should be started. We would have used this functionality in measuring the effectiveness of Web Workers in Chapter 7 had it been available. Even more importantly, if there are continuously statistics available about the QoS, a JavaScript developer can use these to implement adaptive HTTP streaming.

---

[2] See http://webmademovies.etherworks.ca/popcorndemo/

We have come across adaptive HTTP streaming already in Chapter 2 in the context of protocols for media delivery. We mentioned that Apple, Microsoft, and Adobe offer solutions for MPEG-4, but that no solutions yet exist for other formats. Once playback statistics exist in all browsers, it will be possible to implement adaptive HTTP streaming for any format in JavaScript. This is also preferable over an immediate implementation of support for a particular manifest format in browsers—even though Apple has obviously already done that with Safari and m3u8. It is the format to support for delivery to the iPhone and iPad.

So, what are the statistics that are under discussion for a QoS API? Mozilla has an experimental implementation of `mozDownloadRate` and `mozDecodeRate`[3] for the HTMLMediaElement API. These respectively capture the rate at which a resource is being downloaded in bytes per second, and the rate at which it is being decoded in bytes per second. Further, there are additional statistics for video called `mozDecodedFrames`, `mozDroppedFrames`, and `mozDisplayedFrames`, which respectively count the number of decoded, dropped, and displayed frames for a media resource. These allow identification of a bottleneck either as a network or CPU issue.

Note that Adobe has a much more extensive interface for Flash[4]. A slightly different set of QoS metrics for use in adaptive HTTP streaming is suggested in the WHATWG wiki[5]:

- *downloadRate*: The current server-client bandwidth (read-only)

- *videoBitrate*: The current video bitrate (read-only)

- *droppedFrames*: The total number of frames dropped for this playback session (read-only)

- *decodedFrames*: The total number of frames decoded for this playback session (read-only)

- *height*: The current height of the video element (already exists)

- *videoHeight*: The current height of the videofile (already exists)

- *width*: The current width of the video element (already exists)

- *videoWidth*: The current width of the videofile (already exists)

These would also allow identification of the current bitrate that a video has achieved, which can be compared to the requested one and can help make a decision to switch to a higher or lower bitrate stream. We can be sure that we will see adaptive HTTP streaming implementations shortly after, when such an API has entered the specification and is supported in browsers.

This concludes the discussion of HTML5 media technologies under active development.

A.2 Summary of the Book

In this book we have taken a technical tour of HTML5 `<audio>` and `<video>`.

The **Introduction** told the story behind the formats and technologies that we have arrived at today and, in particular, explained why we don't have a single baseline codec for either `<audio>` or `<video>`. This is obviously a poor situation for content providers, but the technology has been developed around it and there are means to deal with this. Ultimately, the availability of browser plugins—such as Adobe

---

[3] See http://www.bluishcoder.co.nz/2010/08/24/experimental-playback-statistics-for-html-video-audio.html

[4] See http://help.adobe.com/en_US/FlashPlatform/reference/actionscript/3/flash/net/NetStreamInfo.html

[5] See http://wiki.whatwg.org/wiki/Adaptive_Streaming#QOS_Metrics

Flash, VLC, and Cortado for Ogg Theora—can help a content provider deliver only a single format without excluding audiences on browsers that do not support that format natively.

The Introductory Chapters

In the **Audio and Video Elements** chapter we had out first contact with creating and publishing audio and video content through the <audio> and <video> elements. We dug deep into the new markup defined for <audio>, <video>, and <source>, including all their content attributes. We took a brief look at open source transcoding tools that are used to get our content into a consistent format for publishing. We briefly explained how to publish the content to a Web server and how it is delivered over HTTP. We concluded the chapter with a comparison of user interfaces to the media elements between browsers, in particular paying attention to the support of accessibility in implemented player controls.

Chapter 3 on **CSS3 Styling** saw us push the boundaries of how to present audio and video content online. Simply by being native elements in HTML, <audio> and <video> are able to make use of the amazing new functionalities of CSS3 including transitions, transforms, and animations. We also identified some short-comings for video in CSS3, in particular that reflections cannot be achieved through CSS alone, that the marquee property is too restricted to create a video scroller, and that video cannot be used as a background to a web page. However, we were able to experiment with some amazing new displays for video collections—one about a pile of smart phones where you can basically pick one up and watch the video on it, and one with video playing on the faces of a 3D spinning cube.

The **JavaScript API** chapter saw us dig deep into the internal workings of the <audio>, <video>, and <source> elements. The interface of these media elements is very rich and provides a web developer with much control. It is possible to set and read the content attribute values through this interface. Particular features of the underlying media resources are exposed, such as their intrinsic width and height. It is also possible to monitor the stats and control the playback functionalities of the resources. We concluded this chapter with an implementation of a video player with our own custom controls that make use of many of the JavaScript API attributes, states, events, and methods.

At this point, we reached quite a sophisticated understanding of the HTML5 media elements and their workings. These first four chapters provided a rather complete introduction. The next three chapters focused on how <audio> and <video> would interact with other elements of HTML5, in particular SVG, Canvas, and Web Workers.

Interacting with other HTML Elements

In **HTML5 Media and SVG** we used SVG to create further advanced styling. We used SVG shapes, patterns, or manipulated text as masks for video, implemented overlay controls for videos in SVG, placed gradients on top of videos, and applied filters to the image content, such as blur, black-and-white, sepia, or line masks. We finished this section by looking at the inclusion of <video> as a native element in SVG or through <foreignObject>. This, together with SVG transformations, enabled the creation of video reflections or the undertaking of edge detection.

For further frame- and pixel-based manipulation and analysis, SVG isn't quite the right tool. In Chapter 6, **HML5 Media and Canvas,** we focused on such challenges by handing video data through to one or more <canvas> elements. We demonstrated video frames bouncing through space, efficient tiling of video frames, color masking of pixels, 3D rendering of frames, ambient color frames for video, and transparency masks on video. These functions allowed us to replicate some of the masking, text drawing, and reflection functionalities we had previously demonstrated in SVG. We finished the chapter with a demonstration how user interactions can also be integrated into Canvas-manipulated video, even though such needs are better satisfied through SVG, which allows attachment of events to individual graphical objects.

In Chapter 7, about **HTML5 Media and Web Workers,** we experimented with means of speeding up CPU-intensive JavaScript processes by using new HTML5 parallelization functionality. A Web Worker is a JavaScript process that runs in parallel to the main process and communicates with it through message passing. Image data can be posted from and to the main process. Thus, Web Workers are a great means to introduce sophisticated Canvas processing of video frames in parallel into a web page, without putting a burden on the main page; it continues to stay responsive to user interaction and can play videos smoothly. We experimented with parallelization of motion detection, region segmentation, and face detection.

A limiting factor is the need to pass every single video frame that needs to be analyzed by a Web Worker through a message. This massively slows down the efficiency of the Web Worker. There are discussions in the WHATWG and W3C about giving Web Workers a more direct access to video and image content to avoid this overhead.

All chapters through Chapter 7 introduced technologies that have been added to the HTML5 specifications and are supported in several browsers. The three subsequent chapters reported on further new developments that have only received trial implementations in browsers, but are rather important. Initial specifications exist, but we will need to see more work on these before there will be interoperable implementations in multiple browsers.

Recent Developments

In Chapter 8, on the **HTML5 Audio API,** we introduced two complementary pieces of work for introducing audio data manipulation functionalities into HTML5. The first proposal is by Mozilla and it creates a JavaScript API to read audio samples directly from an <audio> or <video> element to allow it to be rendered, for example, as a waveform or a spectrum. It also has functionality to write audio data to an <audio> or <video> element. Through the combination of both and through writing processing functions in JavaScript, any kind of audio manipulation is possible. The second proposal is by Google and introduces an audio filter network API into JavaScript with advanced pre-programmed filters such as gain, delay, panning, low-pass, high-pass, channel splitting, and convolution.

The chapter on **Media Accessibility and Internationalization** introduced usability requirements for <audio> and <video> elements with a special regard towards sensory impaired and foreign language users. Transcriptions, video descriptions, captions, sign translations, subtitles, and navigation markers were discussed as formats that create better access to audio-visual content. Support for these alternative content technologies is finding its way into HTML5. We saw the newly defined <track> element, a JavaScript API, and the WebSRT file format as currently proposed specifications to address a large number of the raised requirements.

Finally, Chapter 10, **Audio and Video Devices,** presented early experiments on the <device> element and the Stream API, which together with Web Sockets allow the use of web browsers for video conferencing. We referred to experiments made by Ericsson on an unreleased version of Webkit that demonstrated how such live audio or video communication can be achieved. Many of the components are already specified, so we were able to explain them in example code. We also analyzed how recording from an audio or video device may be possible, and demonstrated how to use Web Sockets to create a shared viewing experience of video presentations across several participating web browser instances.

I hope your journey through HTML5 media was enjoyable, and I wish you many happy hours developing your own unique applications with these amazing new elements.

Index

■ ■ ■

■ T

You Need the Companion eBook

Your purchase of this book entitles you to buy the companion PDF-version eBook for only $10. Take the weightless companion with you anywhere.

We believe this Apress title will prove so indispensable that you'll want to carry it with you everywhere, which is why we are offering the companion eBook (in PDF format) for $10 to customers who purchase this book now. Convenient and fully searchable, the PDF version of any content-rich, page-heavy Apress book makes a valuable addition to your programming library. You can easily find and copy code—or perform examples by quickly toggling between instructions and the application. Even simultaneously tackling a donut, diet soda, and complex code becomes simplified with hands-free eBooks!

Once you purchase your book, getting the $10 companion eBook is simple:

❶ Visit **www.apress.com/promo/tendollars/**.

❷ Complete a basic registration form to receive a randomly generated question about this title.

❸ Answer the question correctly in 60 seconds, and you will receive a promotional code to redeem for the $10.00 eBook.

eBookshop

233 Spring Street, New York, NY 10013

Offer valid through 6/11.